Exploring Art

The cover design incorporates Gabriele Münter's *Staffelsee in Autumn*, painted in 1923. The art work was chosen so that students could see the textural qualities characteristic of rhythmic brush strokes and compare the detail to the complete work (see insert). This work is characterized by broad, flat areas of color; intense and expressive color contrast; and bold and simple compositional designs.

Staffelsee in Autumn represents a view of the Bavarian landscape. Münter often said she felt moved to go beyond "painting from nature" to something more abstract—the painting of essences. Essences, both pictorial and natural, are superbly unified in this small masterpiece of expressionistic painting.

Exploring Art

Gene Mittler, Ph.D.
Professor of Art
Texas Tech University

Rosalind Ragans, Ph.D.
Associate Professor Emerita
Georgia Southern University

GLENCOE

Macmillan/McGraw-Hill

Lake Forest, Illinois   Columbus, Ohio   Mission Hills, California   Peoria, Illinois

Send all inquiries to:
Glencoe Division, Macmillan/McGraw-Hill
15319 Chatsworth Street
P.O.Box 9609
Mission Hills, CA 91346-9609

ISBN 0-02-662281-5 (Student Text)
ISBN 0-02-662282-3 (Teacher's Wraparound Edition)

3   4   5   6   7   97   96   95   94   93   92

Editorial Consultants

Nancy C. Miller
Booker T. Washington High School
for the Performing and Visual Arts
Dallas, Texas

Jean Morman Unsworth
Art Consultant to Chicago
Archdiocese Schools
Chicago, Illinois

Contributors/Reviewers

Josephine Julianna Jones
Booker T. Washington High School
for the Performing and Visual Arts
Dallas, Texas

Rebecca Robertson
W.W. Samuell High School
Dallas, Texas

Carolyn F. Sollman
Eminence School
Eminence, Indiana

Anne Nicholson
Our Lady of Grace Elementary School
Encino, California

Studio Lesson Consultants

Acknowledgments: The authors wish to express their gratitude to the following art coordinators and specialists who participated in the field test of the studio lessons.

Janette Alexander, Denver City Junior High, Denver City, TX; Nan Ball, Camp Creek Middle School, College Park, GA; Wendy Bull, Colonial High School, Memphis, TN; Isabelle Bush, Crabapple Middle School, Roswell, GA; Ann Campoll, Sauk City, WI; Pam Carsillo, Floyd Middle School, Marietta, GA; Kellene Champlin, Fulton County Art Supervisor, Fulton County, GA; Michael Chapman, Treadwell Junior High School, Memphis, TN; Fay Chastain, Hilsman Middle School, Athens, GA; Greg Coats, Havenview Junior High School, Memphis, TN; Rebecca Crim, Holcomb Bridge Middle School, Alpharetta, GA; Jeannie Davis, Hallsville Junior High, Hallsville, TX; Lane Dietrick, Freedom Junior High School, Freedom, WI; Jean Carl Doherty, Sandy Springs Middle School, Atlanta, GA; Joan Elsesser, Beaver Dam, WI; Linda Eshom, Corpus Christi Intermediate School District, Corpus Christi, TX; Eva Fronk, Hales Corners, WI; Kay Godawa, Savannah Country Day School, Savannah, GA; Dr. Nadine Gordon, Scarsdale High School, Scarsdale, NY; Thomas Healy, Canutillo Middle School, El Paso, TX; Garlan Hodgson, Tapp Middle School, Powder Springs, GA; Florence Kork, Harold Wiggs Middle School, El Paso, TX; Nellie Lynch, Duval County Art Supervisor, Jacksonville, FL; Kelly Mann, All Saints Episcopal School, Lubbock, TX; Theresa McDaniel, Towson High School, Towson, MD; Barbara Merritt, Canyon Hills Middle School, El Paso, TX; Bunyan Morris, Marvin Pittman Laboratory School, Statesboro, GA; Jimmy Morris, Clarke County Fine Arts Supervisor, Clarke County, GA; Perri Ann Morris, Jenkins County High School, Millen, GA; Mary Lee Nance, Harris Middle School, Shelbyville, TN; Jackie Norman, East Middle School, Tullahoma, TN; Susan R. Owens, Haynes Bridge Middle School, Atlanta, GA; Robert M. Perry, Jr., Paxon Middle School, Jacksonville, FL; Eunice Plieseis, West Allis, WI; Dr. Marilyn Ragaty, Burney-Harris-Lyons Middle School, Athens, GA; A.P. Register, Bassett Middle School, El Paso, TX; M. Joi Roberts, Stanton High School, Jacksonville, FL; Julia Russell, Art Supervisor, Memphis City Schools, Memphis, TN; Karen Sandborn, Metter High School, Metter, GA; Wandra Sanders, Mandarin Middle School, Jacksonville, FL; Russ Sarasin, Green Bay, WI; Dr. Barbara Shaw, Cobb County Art Supervisor, Marietta, GA; Linda W. Smith, Jenkins County Elementary School, Millen, GA; Ellen Stanley, All Saints Episcopal School, Lubbock, TX; Linda Strong, La Pietra School, Honolulu, HI; Ola Underhill, Chula Vista Academy of Fine Arts, Corpus Christi, TX; A. Villalobos, Guillen School, El Paso, TX; C. Waites, Guillen School, El Paso, TX; Shirley Yokley, Tennessee Visual Arts Consultant, TN; Barbara Zelt, Reistertown, MD.

Photography Credits

Contents

Text

Daniel Alonzo, 302; American Weaving Association, 224L; Ansel Adams, 318; Art Resource, 190; Atari Games Corp., 263T; Craig Aurness/WestLight, 72; Margaret Bourke-White, 250, 267; Mathew Brady, 253B; Robert Brenner/PhotoEdit, 295R; D&R Bretzfelder/PhotoEdit, 194R; California State University, Northridge (materials courtesy of), 34; Jeffrey Clements, 107R; Paul Conklin/PhotoEdit, 294L, 297R; Laima Druskis, 295L; Marcel Eskanazy/PhotoEdit, 242; Tony Freeman/PhotoEdit, 291; Rick Fowler, selected student works; Ann Garvin, 290; Beryl Goldberg, 139L; David Heald, 241; Dr. Jesse Lovano Kerr, 240B; Dorothea Lange, 254; Eric Lessing/PhotoEdit, 236R; Lossen Foto, 161 (courtesy of Heidelberg West, Brisbane, CA); Douglas Mazonowicz, 54; Stephen McBrady/ PhotoEdit, 296R; Guy Motil/WestLight, 73; William Nettles, 181L; John Neubauer/PhotoEdit, 152R; Michael Newman/PhotoEdit, 31T, 293R; Dr. Denny Pett, 238; PhotoEdit, 236, 249; Gene Plaisted OSC, 5; M. Richards, 244R, 294R; Sandak, 240T; Scala/Art Resource, 244L; Rhoda Sidney, 292L; Alfred Stieglitz, 255; William Henry Fox Talbot, 256; Tektronix, 296L; Texas Software, Inc., 262T; The Art Store, Pasadena, CA (materials courtesy of), 32T, 38, 45; Susan Van Etten, 30; Lorin D. Whittaker, 209B; David Young-Wolff, 261, 292R, 297L; Anna E. Zuckerman, 293L.

Illustrations

Michael Rowley

CONTENTS

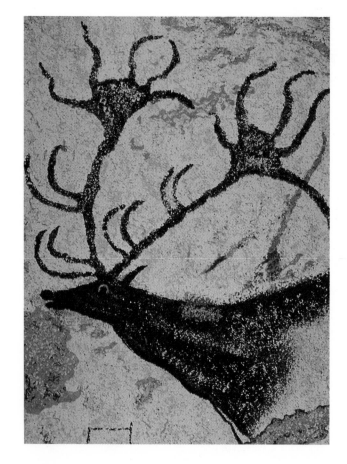

LISTING OF STUDIO LESSONS BY MEDIA

▲ A self-portrait is an artist's painting of himself or herself. Do you know the artists in any of the self-portraits on the upper right of the artist's easel?

Norman Rockwell. *Triple Self-Portrait*. 1960. Oil on canvas. 113 x 87.2 cm (44½ x 34⅓"). Norman Rockwell Museum at Stockbridge, Stockbridge, Massachusetts. Norman Rockwell Art Collection Trust.

Art in Your World

You are about to begin a journey to an interesting and exciting place. This is a place where your curiosity and creativity will be stirred. It is a place where you will be invited to make discoveries and share feelings and ideas. It is the world of art.

Throughout your journey you will see many works of art like the one at the left. This is a painting both *of* and *by* an artist. What makes this picture art? What makes the person who did it an artist? In the pages that follow you will find answers to these and many other questions.

OBJECTIVES

After completing this chapter, you will be able to:
- Explain what can be learned by looking at art made by others.
- Explain what is meant by perceiving.
- Define the term *artist*.
- Name sources of ideas that artists might use.
- Make a collage.

WORDS YOU WILL LEARN

applied art
artists
collage
fine art

patrons of the arts
perceiving
point of view

ARTISTS YOU WILL MEET

Rosa Bonheur
Salvador Dali
Lois Dvorak
Winslow Homer
Allan Houser
Joan Miro

Bartolomé Esteban
  Murillo
Norman Rockwell
William John Wilgus
Mary Ann Willson

The Art Experience

Can you imagine what it would be like to play a new game without first learning the rules, or to read a story in a language that is not familiar to you? Neither of these activities can be carried out automatically. Both, and especially the reading, demand that you have some knowledge beforehand. Both require you to be prepared.

The same is true of art. Understanding art takes more than just looking at an object. It takes looking—and knowing *how* to look—to find meaning. It takes truly seeing, or perceiving the object. **Perceiving** is *looking at and thinking deeply about what you see.*

On your journey through the world of art, you will learn how to "see" art. You will learn how to perceive artistically.

A FIRST LOOK AT ART

You will begin your journey with the painting below (Figure 1–1). Look at this painting. If you were asked to write a description of what you see, what would you write? You might note that this is a skillfully made painting of two ducks. You might add that the ducks are flying above a stormy sea.

▲ Figure 1–1 Notice the artist's use of different shades of gray. What mood does the color gray bring to mind? Why might he have chosen this color for this painting?

Winslow Homer. *Right and Left.* 1909. Canvas. 71.8 x 122.9 cm (28¼ x 48⅜"). National Gallery of Art, Washington, D.C. Gift of the Avalon Foundation.

So far, so good. But this description only begins to scratch the surface. There is much more going on in this painting. Look again, and you will notice something strange about the duck on the right. Namely, it seems to be plunging downward into the sea. Searching for clues to explain this odd behavior, you might notice the boat in the picture. It is partly hidden by the feet and tail feathers of the other duck. Looking more closely still, you might see the red flash and smoke above the boat. There is a hunter in the boat, and he is shooting at the ducks. The duck on the right has been hit. Now, for the first time, you notice the small white feather floating nearby. It was set free when a shotgun blast struck the duck.

Curiosity mounts as you realize the flash you are now seeing is the second shot. (The first has already found its target.) Try to imagine that you can hear the noise of the gun. Will the duck on the left, its wings beating wildly, escape? Will it become the hunter's next victim?

Far from just a picture of ducks, this is an action-packed glimpse of a dramatic event. Notice, by the way, where the artist has placed you, the viewer. What point of view has the artist used? **Point of view** is *the angle from which the viewer sees the scene.* Are you watching this drama unfold through the eyes of the hunter? No, you are staring, like the hunter's targets, down the barrels of the shotgun.

LEARNING FROM ART

Art, as you have just seen, has the power to challenge our minds and stir up our feelings. The ability to see the kinds of things just described can be learned with practice. This book will prepare you to use your eyes and mind to understand many different kinds of art. As each new art experience unfolds, your ability to see or perceive art will increase.

STUDIO EXPERIENCE

Look once more at the painting in Figure 1–1. One of the most interesting things about this painting is its unusual point of view. Using an unexpected point of view can add interest to art.

Using a pencil, make a drawing of an object you know well. One possibility might be one of the shoes you are wearing right now. Draw the object as well as you can. Now draw the same object from the point of view of a bug looking up at it. What details might the bug see? Compare your two drawings. Which one do you consider more interesting?

You will also learn, through looking at art by others, ways of making your own art. Looking at art created by others will develop your powers of creative thinking. It will help you find fresh and exciting ideas and reveal different ways of expressing those ideas. It will highlight the many kinds of tools and techniques you can use. Studio experiences, like the one above, will give you a chance to practice what you have learned.

✔ CHECK YOUR UNDERSTANDING

1. What is meant by the term *perceiving*?
2. What are some of the things to be gained by looking at art made by others?
3. Define *point of view*.

Examining Art Works

When you see a great movie, do you keep the experience to yourself or do you tell friends all about it? This eagerness to share experiences and feelings with others is a typically human trait. It is also a reason why artists like to make art. **Artists** are *people who use imagination and skill to communicate ideas in visual form.* These ideas may represent experiences, feelings, or events in the artist's life.

Artists are creative thinkers. They combine a knowledge of art materials, tools, and methods with a rich imagination and deep sensitivity. They use this combination to present their reactions to the world around them.

ARTISTS AND THEIR WORK

All works created by artists are made to be viewed. Some are created with an added purpose; they are meant to be *used.* People who study art have a separate term for each of these two kinds of art. *Art made to be experienced visually* is called **fine art**. *Art made to be functional as well as visually pleasing* is called **applied art**.

Fine Art

A phrase sometimes used for fine art is "art for art's sake." This means the only use for fine art is to communicate the artist's feelings or ideas.

Fine art can be made from a number of different materials. Figures 1–2 and 1–3 show examples of these types. Figure 1–2 is a drawing. Do you know what kind of fine art is shown in Figure 1–3?

◀ **Figure 1–2   Compare this painting with Figures 1–3 and 1–4. In what ways do the three pieces of art work seem alike? In what ways do they seem different?**

Joan Miro. *Three Women*. 1934. Pen and black ink with pink and brown pastel on laid paper. 63.2 x 46.8 cm (24⅞ x 18⁷⁄₁₆"). National Gallery of Art, Washington, D.C. Gift of Frank and Jeannette Eyerly.

▲ **Figure 1–3   See caption for Figure 1–2.**

Allan Houser. *Waiting for Dancing Partners*. 1980. Tennessee
marble. 76.2 x 53.3 cm (30 x 21). Museum of the
Southwest, Midland, Texas.

Applied Art

Applied arts are usually found in our everyday lives. Objects of applied art may be either made by hand or with machines. What other kinds of applied art can you name?

Sometimes the small differences between applied art and fine art become confused over a period of time. Look, for instance, at the stained glass church windows shown in Figure 1–4. These windows were originally designed at a time in history when few people could read. One of their purposes was to teach stories from the Bible. Today these same windows are also enjoyed as fine art because of their great beauty.

✔CHECK YOUR UNDERSTANDING

1. What is an artist?
2. Name the two basic kinds of art.
3. What is fine art? What are two types of fine art shown in this chapter?
4. What is applied art?

◀**Figure 1–4   See caption for Figure 1–2.**

Stained glass window. *Elijah and Chariot*. House of Hope, Presbyterian, St. Paul, Minnesota.

Artists and Ideas

What do you see when you look at a blank sheet of paper? An artist will look at the blank sheet and see a challenge. That challenge—to come up with an idea—may be one of the toughest an artist faces.

Through the ages artists have answered the challenge of finding ideas, or sources of inspiration, in different ways. In this lesson you will learn about some of these ways.

WHERE ARTISTS GET IDEAS

The ancient Greeks routinely prayed to special goddesses called Muses (**myooz**-uhz)

to send them inspiration for ideas. They even built shrines to honor the Muses.

In more recent times artists in search of ideas have looked elsewhere for sources of inspiration. Here are some of the resources they have explored:

- **The world of myths and legends.** Some artists borrow ideas from famous works of literature. The artist of Figure 1–5 has brought to life characters from one of these literary works. Do you know these characters? Do you know the legend surrounding them?

▲ Figure 1–5   Do you know what is about to happen in this scene? Do you know what the rider of the black horse is holding?

William John Wilgus. *Ichabod Crane and the Headless Horseman.* c. 1855. Canvas. 53.3 x 76.7 cm (21 x 30¼"). National Gallery of Art, Washington, D.C. Gift of Edgar William and Bernice Chrysler Garbisch.

- **The world of imagination.** Everyone has dreams and fantasies. Artists have the creative ability to turn dreams, and even nightmares, into the illusion of reality. Look at Figure 1–6. What message about the world of dreams might the artist be giving us?
- **Their own hearts and minds.** Personal beliefs, or feelings, are often a source of ideas for art. Sometimes artists will express those feelings in their work. Can you think of a good example of this kind of painting?
- **Real-world events and people.** People and events often turn up in art. Figure 1–7 offers a rare glimpse of Wild West hero Buffalo Bill Cody.

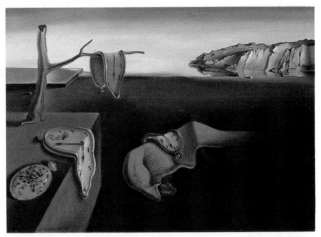

▲ **Figure 1–6** Has the artist painted a happy place or a forlorn, lonely place? What might he be telling us about time in the land of dreams?

Salvador Dali. *Persistence of Memory.* 1931. Oil on canvas. 24.1 x 33 cm (9½ x 13"). Museum of Modern Art, New York, New York. Given anonymously.

◀ **Figure 1–7** The artist did this painting of Buffalo Bill when he came to France to visit her.

Rosa Bonheur. *Buffalo Bill on Horseback.* 1889. Oil on canvas. 47 x 38.7 cm (18½ x 15¼"). Buffalo Bill Historical Center, Cody, Wyoming. Given in memory of Wm. R. Coe and Mai Rogers Coe.

▲ Figure 1–8   Do you know the Biblical story told by these two paintings? Do you notice anything different about the clothing in the painting at the right? During what period of American history was clothing like this worn?

Bartolomé Esteban Murillo. *Return of the Prodigal Son*. 1667/70. Oil on canvas. 236.3 x 261 cm (93 x 102¾"). National Gallery of Art, Washington, D.C. Gift of the Avalon Foundation.

- **Ideas commissioned by employers.** Many artists are hired by individuals or companies to create works of art. In the past such employers of artists were called patrons. **Patrons of the arts** are *sponsors, or supporters, of an artist or art-related places and events*. For example the Catholic Church, as you will see, was at one time a major patron of the arts. It employed artists to create paintings and sculptures illustrating stories from the Bible.

- **Artists of the past.** Art is not made in a vacuum. Artists learn from and build on the work of artists who came before them. Sometimes artists base works directly on earlier pieces. (See Figures 1–8 and 1–9.) The artist of the painting that opened this chapter shows his appreciation to the past in a different way. Look back at that painting (page **xvi**). Do you know any of the artists in the small pictures at the upper right?

▲ **Figure 1–9   See caption for Figure 1–8.**

Mary Ann Willson. *The Prodigal Son Reclaimed*. c. 1815. Pen and black ink and watercolor. National Gallery of Art, Washington, D.C. Gift of Edgar William and Bernice Chrysler Garbisch.

IDEAS FOR YOUR OWN ART

In the coming chapters you will be asked to come up with ideas of your own. Like all other artists, you may at times find yourself stuck. At such moments, an idea bank may be just the answer. It may help boost your powers of creative thinking.

The following studio experience will explain how to make an idea bank for your classroom.

STUDIO EXPERIENCE

Find four envelopes. Label one *Noun*, one *Adjective*, one *Verb*, and one *Adverb*. Think up words for each part of speech. Use a dictionary for help. Avoid proper nouns (those beginning with capital letters). Write each of your words on a separate slip of paper. Place your slips in the correct envelope. Take turns choosing four slips, one from each type of envelope. Share envelopes with other class members to get more variety in the word combinations. These envelopes will be your idea bank for future art projects.

When you have a word combination that you like, arrange the slips on a table in this order: adjective–noun–verb–adverb. Make the words form an interesting idea.

On a sheet of white paper, 9 x 12 inch (23 x 30 cm), sketch your idea. The sketch should show the thing or object (noun) described doing the action (or verb) named.

✔CHECK YOUR UNDERSTANDING

1. What are patrons of the arts?
2. List and describe four sources artists use for inspiration.

LESSON 4

Making a Content Collage

This work of art by Lois Dvorak is made with handmade paper. Called a **collage** (kuh-**lahzh**), this is *art work arranged from cut or torn materials pasted to a surface*. The lizards are native to the New Mexico desert where she lives. (See Figure 1–10.)

WHAT YOU WILL LEARN

You will create a collage using a combination of drawn and found materials. You will combine natural materials that you find in your environment with your own drawings of insects and other small creatures from your local environment. (See Figure 1–11.)

▶ **Figure 1–10** Where did the artist go for ideas in this art work? Can you name the different materials the artist used?

Lois Dvorak. *The Lizards.* Handmade paper assemblage. 81.3 x 101.6 cm (32 x 40″). Private collection.

WHAT YOU WILL NEED

- Pencils and sketch paper
- Small pieces of white paper
- Watercolor markers
- Natural, found materials such as leaves, twigs, pebbles, dirt, bark, wild flowers, and grasses
- White glue
- White paper, 9 x 12 inch (23 x 30 cm)

WHAT YOU WILL DO

1. Brainstorm with your classmates for ideas of what insects, spiders, frogs, and lizards you might find outdoors in your area. Look for pictures of these creatures in the library, and in science books. Notice the difference in body structure between insect and spider.
2. Collect natural materials from your outdoor environment. Look for leaves, twigs, grasses, bark, dirt and sand, wild flowers, and pebbles. If you live in a city, the florist might have old leaves and ferns to give away.
3. Make some rough sketches of the creatures. Then make finished drawings with pencil on white paper of the creatures for your work. Decide whether you want your creatures to contrast with the background or to blend in to the colors. Color them with watercolor markers.
4. Arrange your found objects with the creatures you drew. When you are satisfied with the composition glue everything down.
5. Display your work. Can you find similarities and differences?

EXAMINING YOUR WORK

- **Describe**   Tell about the creatures you selected and explain why you selected them. Describe the found materials you collected. Invent a title for your composition. Are you satisfied with your work? Explain.

SAFETY TIP

Make sure to use only ordinary household glue for your collage. Wallpaper paste and similar glues have poisons in them. These poisons can enter the body through the skin.

▲ **Figure 1–11   Student work. A content collage.**

OTHER STUDIO IDEAS

- Make the collage using construction paper for all the objects.

- ●● Imagine that these little creatures have human characteristics such as expressive faces, and human hands and feet. Draw a scene of these imaginary creatures at home.

CHAPTER 1 REVIEW

BUILDING VOCABULARY

Number a sheet of paper from 1 to 7. After each number, write the term from the box that best matches each description below.

applied art	patrons of the arts
artists	perceiving
collage	point of view
fine art	

1. Looking at and thinking deeply about what you see.
2. The angle from which viewers see the scene in a painting.
3. People who use imagination and skill to share ideas in visual form.
4. Art made purely to be experienced visually.
5. Art made to be both looked at and used.
6. Art made up of cut and torn materials pasted to a surface.
7. A sponsor, or supporter, of an artist or art-related places and events.

REVIEWING ART FACTS

Number a sheet of paper from 8 to 15. Answer each question in a complete sentence.

8. What are some of the things people can learn by looking at art?
9. Name two kinds of fine art.
10. Name a type of applied art.
11. What were Muses? How did the ancient Greeks use the Muses?
12. Name six sources to which artists turn for ideas.
13. What are patrons of the arts? What is the connection between art patrons and artists?
14. How can an idea bank expand your creative thinking?
15. When Dvorak created the collage, *The Lizards*, where did she turn for her idea?

THINKING ABOUT ART

On a sheet of paper, answer each question in a sentence or two.

1. **Extend**. Based on what you learned in this chapter, how would you define *art*?
2. **Analyze**. Write a description of some object in the art room without naming it. Mention as many details as you can. See whether anyone in your class can identify the object.
3. **Summarize**. How could changing the point of view in an art work help make it more interesting?
4. **Analyze**. Name three examples of applied art in your home. Tell how useful you find each of the objects.
5. **Extend**. Do you think makers of applied art and fine art turn to the same sources for ideas? Explain your answer.

MAKING ART CONNECTIONS

1. **Language Arts**. Look at Rockwell's self-portrait on page **xvi**. What does the art work tell about the artist other than how he looks? How has the artist shown other information? An autobiography, a story of one's own life, is a written self-portrait. Write an autobiography. Begin by describing your physical, mental, and social characteristics. Other details to include are: Where and when you were born. Where you have lived and traveled. What your favorite things are.
2. **Science**. Using books and field guides, try to identify the kind of ducks shown in Winslow Homer's painting, *Right and Left*, on page **2**. In what parts of the world can this species be found? Where do you think Homer might have observed these ducks? Can you tell what time of year it is? Reading about migration might help to answer the question.

CHAPTER 1 REVIEW

LOOKING AT THE DETAILS

The detail shown below is from Norman Rockwell's *Triple Self-Portrait*. Study the detail and answer the following questions.

1. What might hint to you that Rockwell was an artist who built on the works of artists who came before him?
2. How do you perceive the artist in this detail? Why?
3. Look at the entire portrait on page **xvi**. Does your perception change? Explain your answer.
4. Certain clothing, furniture, backgrounds, and props the artist chooses to show can also tell us about the subject's character, beliefs, and personality. What do you think Rockwell is trying to tell you if anything about his fellow self-portrait artists? About himself? What things in the painting helped you in forming your answer?
5. Is the entire work a more interesting perspective than if his portrait included only the face you see in the detail? Why? How do you think Rockwell was able to paint the back view of himself?
6. Why do you think Rockwell omitted painting a background or a floor?

Norman Rockwell. *Triple Self-Portrait*. 1960. Oil on canvas. (Detail.) 113 x 87.2 cm (44½ x 34⅓"). Norman Rockwell Museum at Stockbridge, Stockbridge, Massachusetts. Norman Rockwell Art Collection Trust.

▲ It is hard to tell what the subject of this painting is without reading the credit line. What do you think the inspiration for this painting was?

Natalia Goncharova. *Cats*. 1913. Oil on canvas. 84.4 x 83.8 cm (33¼ x 33"). Solomon R. Guggenheim Museum, New York, New York.

CHAPTER ■ **2**

$\mathscr{E}$njoying $\mathscr{A}$rt

Imagine you were in the museum where the painting at the left hangs. You might overhear someone say he or she doesn't like the painting because there is not anything familiar or recognizable in it. That might even sum up your own feelings about the painting.

But is this all there is to say about a painting? Does art succeed as art *only* because of lifelike details? Are there other ways of looking at — and evaluating the success of — an art object? In this chapter you will find out.

OBJECTIVES

After completing this chapter, you will be able to:
- Explain how subject, composition, and content relate to works of art.
- Define the term *aesthetics*.
- Discuss three schools of thought on what is important in art.
- Make a torn paper face.

WORDS YOU WILL LEARN

aesthetics	non-objective
aesthetic views	subject
composition	super-realism
content	work of art
credit line	

ARTISTS YOU WILL MEET

T. C. Cannon	Edward Hopper
Mary Cassatt	Éduoard Manet
Natalia Goncharova	Robert Motherwell
Duane Hanson	Frank Stella
William Harnett	

15

Understanding Art

To praise a job well done, people sometimes borrow a term from art. That term is *work of art*. A well-cooked meal might be described as "a work of art." So might a neatly arranged clothes closet.

In the study of art, the term **work of art** has a specific meaning. It is *any object created or designed by an artist*. Works of art, however, are not all equally successful.

► **Figure 2–1 The opera and the theatre were often subjects of art work. Why do you think this is so?**

Mary Stevenson Cassatt. *At the Opera.* 1879. Oil on canvas. 80 x 64.8 cm (31½ x 25½"). Museum of Fine Arts, Boston, Massachusetts. Hayden Collection.

▲ **Figure 2–2   An elegy is a speech or song of sorrow. How is sorrow expressed in this painting?**

Robert Motherwell. *Elegy to the Spanish Republic 108.* 1966. Oil and acrylic on canvas. 213.4 x 373.4 cm (84 x 147"). Museum of Art, Dallas, Texas.

THE WORK OF ART

Works of art may be defined by three basic properties, or features. These properties are subject, composition, and content.

Subject

The subject answers the question "What do I see when I look at this art work?" The **subject** is *the image viewers can easily identify.* The subject may be a person or persons. It may be a thing, such as a tree. It may be a place. It may even be an event, such as a parade. The subject of the painting in Figure 2–1 is easily recognized. It is a woman seated in a theater box gazing through opera glasses.

In recent years some artists have chosen to create non-objective artwork. **Non-objective** means *there is no recognizable subject matter in the work.* The picture in Figure 2–2 is such a work.

Composition

All art works are made up of parts known as visual elements. These elements, which you will learn more about in Chapter 4, include color, line, shape, form, space, and texture. You will also learn that artists use certain guidelines, called principles of art, to organize these elements in their work. The principles of balance, variety, harmony, emphasis, proportion, movement, and rhythm will be discussed in Chapter 5. The **composition** of an art work is *how the principles are used to organize the elements.*

Look again at the picture in Figure 2–1. With your finger, trace the line of the railing beginning at the lower left edge. Where does this line take you? It carries you upward along the woman's right arm. From there the dark straps of her hat lead you to her lightly colored face. The woman's face is the most important part of the painting. The artist has skillfully used lines to direct your attention to it. Part of the picture's composition is how the artist uses the element of line and the principle of movement.

Content

Often a work of art communicates a message, idea, or feeling. This *message, idea, or feeling* is the art work's **content**. Look once more at Figure 2–1. Notice the man in the distance, leaning out of his theater box. He is using his own opera glasses, not to watch the show, but to stare at the woman. She, too, must be spying on people in other boxes. Notice where her glasses are pointed. Are they aimed downward, toward the stage?

Maybe the artist, Mary Cassatt, is trying to tell us something about human nature. Maybe she is saying that while we are busy looking at—and judging—others, we are being judged ourselves. This message is the painting's content.

Sometimes the content of a work is expressed as a feeling, such as love or hate. Can you identify the feeling expressed by the picture in Figure 2–3? What details of the picture give you a clue to that feeling?

▲ Figure 2–3 What might this young woman be feeling? What clues do you have that she is feeling this way?

Edward Hopper. *New York Movie*. 1939. Oil on canvas. 81.9 x 101.9 cm (32¼ x 40⅛"). Museum of Modern Art, New York, New York. Given anonymously.

Notice that even art works without recognizable subjects can show a feeling. Look again at Figure 2–2. The artist of this work depends on composition alone to express content. He uses scary dark shapes to communicate the terror and destruction of a civil war. These dark shapes overpower the brightly colored shapes behind, which stand for peace and happiness.

THE CREDIT LINE

Look once more at Figure 2–3. Do you see the name of the artist who created this work? Do you know the title of the work? Answers to these and other questions can be found in the credit line appearing alongside the work. A **credit line** is *a listing of important facts about an art work*.

Every art work in this book has a credit line. It is there to help you learn as much as you can about the work.

Reading a Credit Line

Most credit lines are made up of six facts. These facts, in the order in which they appear, are as follows:

- **The artist's name.** This information always comes first. Who is the artist of the work in Figure 2–1? Who is the artist of the work in Figure 2–2?
- **The title of the work.** Many titles give useful information about the subject or content. Some are meant to stimulate viewers' curiosity. Do you remember the title of the painting of the ducks back in Chapter 1 (Figure 1–1, page **2**)? Can you find a work in the present chapter with the title *New York Movie*? Who painted it?

- **The year the work was created.** Sometimes, in the case of older works, *c.* appears before the year. This is an abbreviation for *circa*, which means "around" or "about" in Latin. Which work in this lesson was created in 1966? What is its title?
- **The tools and materials used in creating the work.** Artists, as you will learn, use many different materials to create an art work. Watercolor paint is one of these materials. Pencil is another. How many works in Chapter 1 and in this chapter were made using oil on canvas?
- **The size of the work.** Size helps you imagine how the work would appear if you were standing before it. Height, in centimeters as well as in inches, is always listed first. The width is listed second. A third number refers to depth. What is the height of the painting in Chapter 1 by Bartolomé Esteban Murillo?
- **The location of the work.** Location includes the name of the gallery or museum where the work is housed and its city and state or country. Where would you go to view the painting in this chapter by Mary Cassatt? In what city is the National Gallery of Art located?

✔CHECK YOUR UNDERSTANDING

1. What is a work of art?
2. What are three properties of art works?
3. Name four pieces of information given in a credit line.

LESSON 2

Aesthetics

When you hear a new song on the radio, what do you listen for? Are you mostly interested in the words? Do you tune in, instead, to the beat? Maybe what matters to you most is the skill of the performers.

The question of what counts most in a work is not only a concern of listeners of music. It is a major concern of viewers and creators of every kind of art. This question is one art scholars have been wrestling with since earliest times.

In this lesson you will learn some of the ways they think about works of art.

AESTHETICS IN ART

You have probably heard the saying "beauty is in the eye of the beholder." People see beauty in different ways. Pinpointing the meaning of beauty is only one goal of the branch of learning called **aesthetics,** (ess-**thet**-iks) *the philosophy or study of the nature and the value of art.*

▶ **Figure 2–4 Notice how the objects in the painting seem to project out into space. Which object looks most lifelike to you?**

William Harnett. *My Gems.* 1888. Paint on wood. 45.7 x 35.6 cm (18 x 14"). National Gallery of Art, Washington, D.C. Gift of the Avalon Foundation.

The chief goal of aesthetics is finding an answer to the question "What is art?" In their search for an answer, art scholars have put forth different views on what is important in art. *These ideas, or schools of thought, on what to look for in works of art* are called **aesthetic views**.

AESTHETIC VIEWS

Today, students of art recognize three main aesthetic views. These aesthetic views are based on the properties of an artwork: subject, composition, and content. One aesthetic view has to do with an art work's subject. The second view relates to composition. The third view is tied to content.

View #1: Subject

The first aesthetic view states that art should imitate what we see in the real world. A successful work in this view is one with realistic subject matter. Look at the painting in Figure 2–4. Notice how lifelike the objects in this work look. The image of the light-blue pitcher could pass for a photograph. Art scholars of this first school would praise this painting for being so true to life. Would you agree with them?

Modern artists have found ways of creating works with even more convincingly lifelike subjects than the type found in Figure 2–4. A style of *art devoted to extraordinarily realistic works*, called **super-realism**, has come into being. Without being told, would you ever guess that Figure 2–5 is a photo of an art work and not a real person?

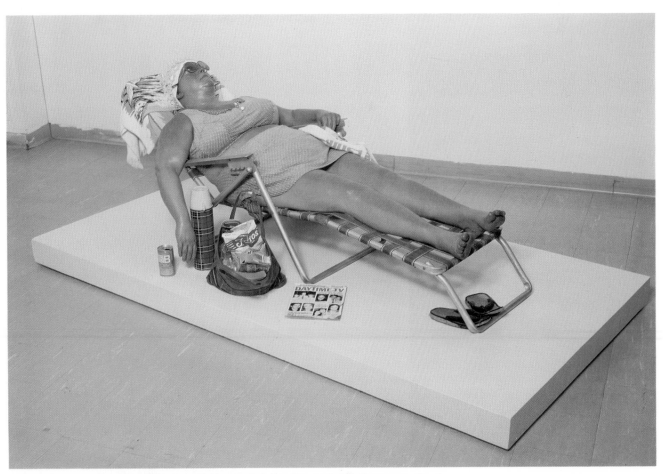

▲ **Figure 2–5**   Notice the details the artist has included in this work. What message about certain American values might he be trying to express?

Duane Hanson. *Sunbather*. 1971. Polyester fiberglass polychromed in oil. Life-size. Wadsworth Atheneum, Hartford. National Endowment for the Arts/Gift of Roscoe Nelson Gray in memory of Roscoe Nelson Dalton Gray and Rene Gabrielle Gray.

View #2: Composition

The second aesthetic view or school of thought argues that what counts in art is composition. In this view a successful art work is one in which the artist has used the principles of art to skillfully combine the art elements. Look again at Figure 2–4. Supporters of this view would find much to admire in the painting. They might note the way the shapes have been arranged to balance the composition. They might explain how the contrast between light and dark emphasizes certain objects.

Some artists have paid more attention to composition than to any other feature. How would art scholars of the second school react to the work in Figure 2–6? What visual elements and principles might they refer to when discussing this work?

View #3: Content

The third aesthetic view holds that what is most important in an art work is its content. In this view a successful art work is one that sends a clear message or feeling. Look once more at Figure 2–4. Notice the work's title, *My Gems*. The artist seems to be giving us a peek at some of his most prized possessions. Note how worn some of these objects are. What feeling about favorite things might the artist be expressing? How would individuals taking this third aesthetic view react to that feeling? How do you react to it?

▲ **Figure 2–6** Many of this artist's works were not rectangular. He worked on a huge scale and painted designs that followed the unusual shapes of his canvases. This art work is called a "hard-edged painting." Why do you think it is called that?

Frank Stella. *Agbatana III*. 1968. Flourescent acrylic on canvas. 305 x 457 cm (120 x 180″). Allen Art Museum, Oberlin College, Ohio. Ruth C. Roush Fund for Contemporary Art and National Foundation for the Arts & Humanities Grant, 1968.

▲ **Figure 2–7** What is the subject of this painting? What is the composition? What is the content?

T. C. Cannon. *Turn of the Century Dandy*. 1976. Acrylic on canvas. 152.4 x 132.1 cm (60 x 52"). Private collection.

AESTHETICS AND THE "BIG PICTURE"

It is important to note that few students of art accept just one aesthetic view. Most believe that to achieve a full understanding of art requires keeping an open mind. How might a person with all three views react to the painting that opened this chapter? (See page **14**.) Do you think the person would describe this work as true to life? Would you describe it that way? How have color, line, and shapes been used to create this work? Do you think they have been used effectively to create an unified and visually interesting design? Do you think the picture communicates a message, idea, or feeling? What might that message be? Look at the painting above. (See Figure 2–7.) Ask yourself the same questions regarding this art work.

✔ CHECK YOUR UNDERSTANDING

1. What is the study of aesthetics? What is the chief goal of aesthetics?
2. Briefly describe the three main aesthetic views described.
3. What is super-realism?
4. Why do few students of art accept just one aesthetic view?

Torn Paper Face

Look closely at the woman in Figure 2–8. She sits in a garden overlooking the tracks of a railroad station. She stares off into space, lost in her own thoughts. What contrast do you notice between her and the young girl?

If you had to describe this woman's mood, what words would you use? If you were going to create a piece of art, how would you show this mood?

WHAT YOU WILL LEARN

This studio lesson will test your skill in creating a face as seen from the front. The face will express a mood. In your work, you will focus totally on content. No effort will be made to create a real-looking face. You will exaggerate the features in your face and select colors that will communicate a mood.

You will "build" your face of torn bits of construction paper. (See Figure 2–9.)

WHAT YOU WILL NEED

- Pencil and notepad
- Scrap pieces of colored construction paper
- Sheet of construction paper, 12 x 18 inch (30 x 46 cm)
- Small brush and slightly thinned white glue

WHAT YOU WILL DO

1. Working with a partner, practice acting out different moods. On your notepad, jot down notes about which facial expressions fit which moods. What happens to

▶ **Figure 2–8** **What are the subjects in this painting? How does content differ from subject in art works?**

Édouard Manet. *Gare Saint-Lazare.* 1873. Canvas 93.3 x 114.5 (36¾ x 45⅛"). National Gallery of Art, Washington, D.C. Gift of Horace Havemeyer in memory of Louisina W. Havemeyer.

your eyes, for instance, when you feel anger? What happens to your mouth when you feel sadness? Decide what mood your work will show and write this on your notepad.

2. Select one sheet of construction paper for the background. Choose colors of construction paper scraps that show up clearly against one another. Keep in mind that certain colors call to mind certain moods. Red is commonly thought of as a color connected with anger. Blue might be thought of in connection with sadness. (See Figure 2–9.)

3. Begin tearing your scraps into a variety of large and small shapes to represent features of a face. Exaggerate these features to capture the mood you have chosen. To show happiness, for example, make the mouth unusually large and smiling. Position your shapes on the sheet of construction paper to form a face seen from the front. Using the brush, apply a small amount of glue to the back of each scrap. (For information on applying glue, see Technique Tip **28**, *Handbook* page **281**.) Lightly press each scrap into place.

4. When the glue has dried, display your torn paper face. Compare your work with that of your classmates. See how many of your friends can tell immediately which mood your face shows. Try to guess the moods their faces show.

- **Describe**   Tell whether your work reveals a front view of a face. Point to the features you exaggerated. Tell what different colors you used for your torn paper face. Explain whether they helped capture the mood of your work. Tell what mood your work shows. Discuss what reactions members of your class had toward your work.

▲ **Figure 2–9   Student work. A torn paper face.**

OTHER STUDIO IDEA

- Create a non-objective picture to express another mood. Use brightly colored markers and draw a non-objective picture. Draw seven triangles, eight circles, and nine rectangles on a page. Have some of the shapes overlap. Color as you wish to create an interesting non-objective picture. If you choose to color the background, color it only one color for contrast.

CHAPTER 2 REVIEW

BUILDING VOCABULARY

Number a sheet of paper from 1 to 9. After each number, write the term from the box that best matches each description below.

aesthetics	non-objective
aesthetic views	subject
composition	super-realism
content	works of art
credit line	

1. Objects created or designed by artists.
2. The image viewers see and can easily identify in an art work.
3. How the principles are used to organize the elements in an art work.
4. The message, idea, or feeling expressed by an art work.
5. A list of facts about an art work.
6. The philosophy or study of the nature and the value of art.
7. Ideas, or schools of thought, about what to look for in art.
8. Type of art devoted to creating works with convincingly lifelike subjects.
9. Art which has no recognizable subject.

REVIEWING ART FACTS

Number a sheet of paper from 10 to 15. Answer each question in a complete sentence.

10. What are three properties, or features, of art works?
11. Which property is concerned with how the principles of a work are used to organize the elements?
12. Name five pieces of information that appear on a credit line.
13. What is the abbreviation for circa? What does this term mean?
14. What is the key question asked by people who work in the field of aesthetics?
15. Why do many students of art accept more than one aesthetic view?

THINKING ABOUT ART

On a sheet of paper, answer each question in a sentence or two.

1. **Analyze**. Pick two works of fine art from Chapter 2 that have subjects. List the subjects found in each.
2. **Analyze**. Pick two works of fine art from Chapter 2 that you believe express a feeling. Identify the feeling of each. Explain how these feelings were shown.
3. **Extend**. Look around the room you are in at the moment. Try to imagine that you are looking at a very lifelike painting. Can you find a message in this scene? What is it?
4. **Compare and contrast**. In what ways is a painting like a short story or poem? In what ways is it different?
5. **Interpret**. Why do you think the final fact in a credit line includes the city and state or country in which a museum is found?

MAKING ART CONNECTIONS

1. **Drama**. Theater and television productions include the same features as works of visual art. The subject is represented by the characters, the content is represented by the script, and the composition determines how the characters and ideas are presented. Choose a play or television production that you have seen. Write a brief report identifying the subject, content, and composition.
2. **Music**. Music also has subject, content, and composition. Music may tell a story through instrumentation or through lyrics. Choose a type of music, such as rock, jazz, country, or classical and analyze the piece for its subject, content, and composition.

LOOKING AT THE DETAILS

The detail shown below is from Natalia Goncharova's *Cats*. Study the detail and answer the following questions.

1. Do the colors and shapes suggest a certain feeling? Explain.
2. Cover up the credit line. What is the subject of this painting? Look at the entire work on page **14**. Does this help? Explain.
3. Which aesthetic view or views would you take in judging this painting? Explain.
4. Do you think this work is successful as art? Why or why not?

Natalia Goncharova. *Cats*. 1913. Oil on canvas. (Detail.) 84.4 x 83.8 cm (33¼ x 33"). Solomon R. Guggenheim Museum, New York, New York.

▲ The artist is famous for his paintings of ordinary people and events. Here you see him showing a drawing technique to children. On the shelf, the sculpture of the ox stands for St. Luke, the saint who watched over artists.

Jan Steen. *The Drawing Lesson.* 1665. Oil on wood. 49.3 x 41 cm (19⅜ x 16¼″). J. Paul Getty Museum.

Exploring Art Media

Every profession has its "tools of the trade." Carpenters use hammers and wood. Plumbers use wrenches and pipes. Baseball players use bats and balls.

Artists, too, have their tools of the trade. One of these, shown in the painting at the left, is a pencil. How many tools of the artist's trade can you find in the painting? Can you think of any others that are not shown here?

In this chapter you will learn more about the materials used by artists.

OBJECTIVES

After completing this chapter, you will be able to:

- Define the term *medium of art*.
- Name the different kinds of media used in drawing, printmaking, painting, and sculpting.
- Experiment with drawing, printmaking, painting, and sculpting media.
- Use mixed media to create a work of art.

WORDS YOU WILL LEARN

binder
edition
freestanding
medium of art
mixed media
pigment
print

relief
reproduction
solvent
style
three-dimensional
two-dimensional

ARTISTS YOU WILL MEET

Mary Cassatt
Ann Chernow
Marisol Escobar
Nancy Graves
Edward Hopper
Wassily Kandinsky
Käthe Kollwitz

Henri-Charles
   Manguin
Georgia O'Keeffe
Jan Steen
Henri de Toulouse-
   Lautrec

Drawing

Do you remember drawing or scribbling with crayons when you were a small child? Although you didn't know it at the time, you were using a medium of art. A **medium of art** is *a material used to create a work of art.* Crayons are one medium of art. Colored markers are another. Modeling clay is a third. When we talk about more than one medium at a time, we use the term media. Colored markers and modeling clay are two media that you have probably used.

Sometimes artists combine several media to create a work of art. This is called mixed media. **Mixed media** is *the use of more than one medium.* Can you find a work of art in this chapter that is created with more than one medium?

In this lesson you will learn about the different kinds of media used in drawing. In later lessons you will learn about media used in other areas of art. You will also get a chance to experiment with some of these art media.

THE IMPORTANCE OF DRAWING

Before a person can run or jump or pedal a bicycle, he or she must be able to stand and walk. Walking is a stepping-stone to all these other activities.

In much the same way, drawing is a stepping-stone to almost all types of art production skills. Fashion designers make drawings of a design before patterns can be made for cutting fabric (Figure 3–1). Architects need to draw sketches and blueprints before the actual building of a house can begin (Figure 3–2). Some painters make sketches, or studies, before they put a brush to canvas. Figure 3–3 shows a sketch made by Edward Hopper for his painting called *Gas.*

▶ **Figure 3–1 Drawing is an important step in many designing professions. How many careers can you think of that might require drawing?**

◄Figure 3–2 Architects have to be careful and precise in their work. Why do you think this is so?

▲ Figure 3–3 Hopper made this sketch at the scene. Then he took the sketch back to his studio where he made a painting based on this drawing. Why do you suppose he didn't just rely on his memory?

Edward Hopper. *Gas (Study for Gas)*. 1940. Charcoal on paper. 38.1 x 56.2 cm (15 x 22⅛″). Whitney Museum of American Art, New York. Josephine N. Hopper Bequest.

THE MEDIA OF DRAWING

The media of drawing are many. You have already looked at some. Some others are shown in Figure 3–4. How many of these can you name? How many of them have you used?

Drawing media are used for planning a work of art and sometimes they are used to create a finished work of art. The drawing in Figure 3–5 is such a work.

Throughout this book you will have the opportunity to practice your drawing skills. Experiment with different drawing media to achieve the results you want. Learning to draw, like other skills, takes practice and concentration.

▲ Figure 3–4   There are many kinds of drawing media. This picture shows a few. Can you name other media?

▲ Figure 3–5   Compare Chernow's drawing to Hopper's sketch (Figure 3–3). You can see that Chernow spent a long time using a pencil and eraser to create this finished work.

Ann Chernow. *Lady of L.A.* 1984. Pencil on paper. 52.7 x 80 cm (20¾ x 31½"). National Museum of Women in the Arts, Washington, D.C. Gift of Mr. & Mrs. Edward P. Levy.

▲ Figure 3–6   Student work. Leaf drawing.

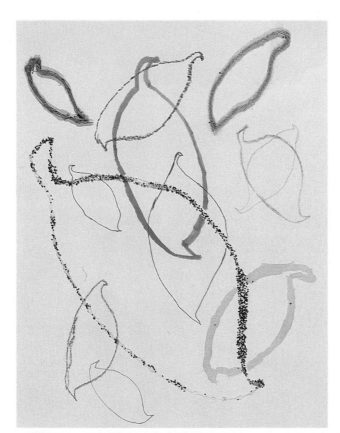

▲ Figure 3–7   Student work. Leaf drawing.

STUDIO EXPERIENCE

Select a leaf that you would like to draw. On a large piece of white paper, draw the leaf with a pencil. Next, draw the same leaf in different places on the paper, using a different drawing medium each time. Turn the paper so that you fill the paper with leaves. Draw some large ones and then draw some smaller ones to fill the smaller spaces. As you work, notice that some media make broad lines, while others make fine lines. Use your imagination to come up with new ways to make a line with each medium. (See Figures 3–6, 3–7.) Experiment with using broad-line media to make larger leaves and fine-line media to make smaller leaves.

Place the finished drawings up for study by the class. Can you tell what media other students used in their works? Does everyone's work look the same? Why or why not?

✔ CHECK YOUR UNDERSTANDING

1. What is a medium of art?
2. Name three media that are used in drawing.
3. How is drawing used by an architect? How is drawing used by a painter?

Printmaking

Have you ever made a fingerprint? A fingertip is pressed on an inked pad, and ink is transferred to the raised ridges of the skin. Then the fingertip with the ink on it is pressed on clean white paper. The print on the paper shows the pattern of lines made by the raised ridges of that finger.

An art print can be made in a similar way. Special printing ink is applied to a prepared surface. Then paper or fabric is pressed against the inked surface. An original art **print** is *an image that is transferred from a prepared surface to paper or fabric.* An artist who makes prints is known as a printmaker.

THE IMPORTANCE OF PRINTMAKING

Like other types of art, printmaking allows artists to produce an image on various surfaces. In printmaking, though, an artist can produce multiple copies of the original work. Each print is signed by the artist.

Notice that a print is not the same as a reproduction of an art work, such as those you see on these pages. A **reproduction** is *a photograph of a print.* Confusing original prints with a reproduction of an art work is a mistake many people make.

The printmaker uses a number of tools and materials in making a print. These are shown in Figure 3–8. How many of these media can you name? How many have you used?

THE STEPS OF PRINTMAKING

In making a print, the printmaker follows three basic steps. The first step is to make a plate. The printmaker creates a printing plate

by altering a surface to create an image. Next, the printmaker applies ink to, or inks, the plate. Finally, the printmaker transfers the ink to the paper or cloth by pressing the paper or cloth against the plate. Then the paper or cloth is pulled off the plate.

▲ **Figure 3–8** This picture shows printmaking media and tools. What are some of the similarities in drawing and printmaking? What are some of the differences?

This set of steps may be repeated many times for a given plate. *A series of prints that are all exactly alike* is called an **edition**. The printmaker signs his or her name, usually in pencil in the bottom margin, and writes the title on each print of an edition. He or she also writes on each print a number that has this form: 10/20. The second number tells how many prints there are in the edition. The first number tells which print you are viewing. A print labeled 10/20 means that you are looking at the tenth of 20 prints that were made from one plate.

THE PRINTMAKER'S MEDIA

Plates in printmaking are usually made of wood, stone, or metal. Sometimes, however, other materials are used. Often prints are done in color. To make a print with more than one color, the printmaker must use a separate plate for each color.

The final appearance of a print will depend on the media, colors, and techniques the printmaker used. Different combinations will give different results. When inked and printed, lines etched in metal will look different from lines drawn with grease crayon. Figures 3–9 and 3–10 show some of these differences.

◀ **Figure 3–9** A "drypoint" is made by scratching lines into a metal plate with a sharp pointed tool. When it is printed, a drypoint looks like a drawing. The difference is that the lines in the drypoint will be raised where the paper has been pressed into the scratches.

Mary Cassatt. *Maternal Caress.* 1891. Drypoint, soft ground etching and aquatint printed in color. 36.5 x 26.8 cm (14⅜ x 10⁹⁄₁₆"). Metropolitan Museum of Art, New York, New York. Gift of Paul J. Sacks, 1916.

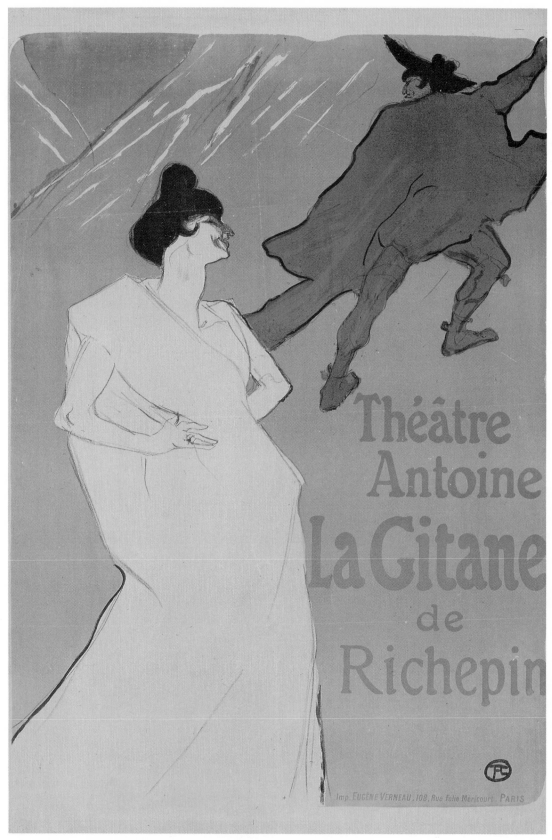

▲ **Figure 3–10   This print is made with four colors. Can you tell which ones?**

Henri de Toulouse-Lautrec. *La Gitane*. 1900. Lithograph. 160 x 65 cm (63 x 25⅝″). Los Angeles
County Museum of Art. Gift of Dr. & Mrs. Kurt Wagner.

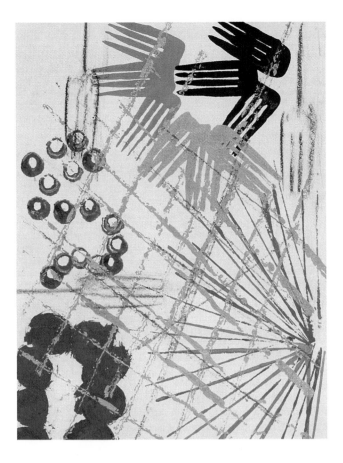

▲ Figure 3–11   Student works. Gadget prints.

STUDIO EXPERIENCE

Gather small items with different shapes that might be dipped into paint to make a gadget print. Some possibilities are paper clips, erasers, clothespins, spools, cork, and buttons. Be as imaginative as you can. Brush tempera paint on each gadget, and press the gadget firmly on a sheet of white paper. Exchange gadgets with your classmates. (See Figure 3–11.)

Once the paint has dried, select one of the gadgets, and place it underneath the paper near a printed image of the same gadget. Make a crayon rubbing of the gadget. (See Technique Tip **25**, *Handbook* **280**.) Discuss your work with your classmates. Do the rubbings look like the prints? Why or why not?

✔ CHECK YOUR UNDERSTANDING

1. How does an original print differ from a reproduction?
2. Summarize the three basic steps in printmaking.
3. What is an edition? What is the meaning of the numbers an artist will write on a print?
4. Name two materials that can be used to make plates in printmaking.

Painting

You have probably worked with paints at one time or another. The paints may have been the kind that you smear on wet paper with your fingers or paints you mix with water. These are just two of the media used in painting. In this lesson you will learn about others.

CHARACTERISTICS OF PAINTS

Painting is the process of covering a surface with color using a brush, a painting knife, a roller, or even fingers. Sometimes paint is made into a mist by being blown onto a surface with an airbrush. Some paints dry fast, some look bright, and some blend easily. Different effects can be achieved by using different types of paints.

THE PAINTER'S MEDIA

Like other artists, painters use a wide variety of tools and materials. Some of these are shown in Figure 3–12. How many of these can you identify? How many have you used?

Before a painter begins a work, he or she chooses a type of paint and an appropriate surface on which to work. The surface is the material to which the paint is to be applied. Canvas, paper, or silk are three examples. The look of a finished painting has much to do with the combination of media the artist chooses. A painting made by putting oil paint on canvas with a knife has a look very different from a painting made by putting watercolor on paper with a soft brush.

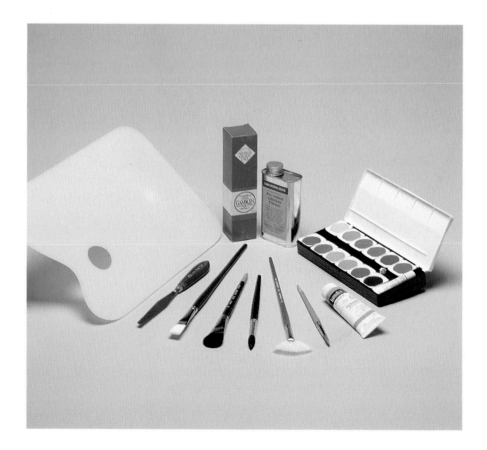

▶ **Figure 3–12 Some painting tools and media are shown at the right. What other media can you think of that are not shown here?**

All paints used in art are made up of three basic ingredients:

- **Pigment** is *a finely ground, colored powder that gives paint its color.*
- **Binder** is *a liquid to which the dry pigment is added.* The binder makes it possible for the pigment to stick to a surface. Linseed oil is the binder for oil paints. Gum arabic (**ar**-uh-bik) is the binder for watercolors.
- **Solvent** is *a liquid that controls the thickness or thinness of the paint.* Turpentine is the solvent in oil paints. Water is the solvent in watercolors. Solvents are also used to clean brushes.

STYLES OF PAINTING

When painters finish works of art, they usually sign their names to them. In a way, the signature of the artist is already there, in his or her individual style. **Style** is *an artist's personal way of expressing ideas in a work.* Style is like a snowflake or a fingerprint. No two are exactly alike, just like no two people have exactly the same handwriting. Two artists may start off with exactly the same media and end up with works that look totally different. Compare Figures 3–13, 3–14, and 3–15. In what ways are these three works alike? In what ways are they different? How do you think the thickness of the paint affected each work? How might you describe the style of each artist?

▲ **Figure 3–13** This artist experimented with many different styles of art before he came up with his own style. How would you describe that style? Explain your answer.

Wassily Kandinsky. *Improvisation Number 27: The Garden of Love.* Oil on canvas. 120.3 x 140 cm (47⅜ x 55¼"). Metropolitan Museum of Art, New York, New York. The Alfred Stieglitz Collection, 1949.

▲ **Figure 3–14   Henri-Charles Manguin was known as an open-air painter. This means that he did most of his work outdoors. He is best known for scenes that are near water.**

Henri-Charles Manguin. *Port Saint Tropez, le 14 Juillet*. Oil on canvas. 61.3 x 50.2 cm (24⅛ x 19¾″). The Museum of Fine Arts, Houston, Texas. The John A. & Audrey Jones Beck Collection.

Remember to check paints for safety labels. The labels *AP* (for Approved Product) and *CP* (for Certified Product) mean the paint does not contain harmful amounts of poisonous substances. An *HL* (for Health Label), on the other hand, warns that the paint contains poisonous ingredients and is dangerous to use.

✔CHECK YOUR UNDERSTANDING

1. What are the three types of ingredients found in every type of paint?
2. What is pigment?
3. What is an artist's style?

STUDIO EXPERIENCE

Experiment with different painting media. Gather an assortment of school acrylics and thick tempera paints, as well as tools for applying paint and a supply of white paper. In addition to different types of brushes, your painting tools might include painting knives, twigs with the ends bunched together into a brushlike effect, and even your fingers. Try one combination and then another, noting the effects of each. What kind of brush stroke do you get, for example, with a dry brush that has been dipped in thick paint? What happens when you use a wet brush dipped in the same paint? Does thinning the paint with water change its look on paper?

Share your observations with your classmates. Discuss similarities and differences in your results. Try to imagine how you could use these effects in a painting.

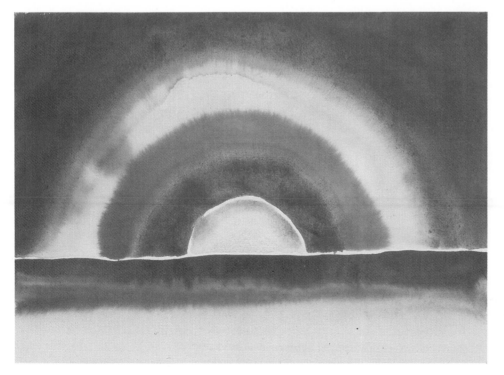

◀ **Figure 3–15 O'Keeffe "simplified" nature. Here she used a few wet watercolor shapes to capture the idea of sunrise over a desert.**

Georgia O'Keeffe. *Sunrise.* 1917. Watercolor. 22.5 x 30.2 cm (8⅞ x 11⅞"). Collection of Barney A. Ebsworth.

Experimenting with Pigment

Look again at the painting in Figure 3–15 on page **41** and at Figure 3–16 on this page. These were done by American artists, Georgia O'Keeffe and Edward Hopper. Notice from the credit lines that each painter used watercolor on paper. Yet the paintings look as if they were done with completely different media. In this studio lesson you will learn how one medium can be used to give such different results.

WHAT YOU WILL LEARN

You will be making a painting using watercolors on paper. You will experiment with changing the amount of solvent which, for watercolors, is water. Through this experiment, you will learn about the different effects painters are able to create using a single medium. (Figure 3–17 shows an experiment of this kind carried out by a student.)

WHAT YOU WILL NEED

- Watercolor paints and water
- Pencil and sheet of white paper, 9 x 12 inch (23 x 30 cm)
- Two watercolor brushes, one large and one small
- Tray or flat board larger than paper
- Paper towels and sponges

▲ **Figure 3–16** Edward Hopper painted this scene in watercolor. What emotion do you feel when you look at this painting? Hopper is noted for the loneliness portrayed in his work.

Edward Hopper. *Cottages at North Truro, Massachusetts*. 1938. Watercolor. 51.3 x 71.4 cm (20³/₁₆ x 28⅛"). Collection of Barney A. Ebsworth.

WHAT YOU WILL DO

1. Wet each cake of paint in the set with a few drops of water. This will allow the paint to begin to soften.
2. Write your name on the back of your paper with a pencil.
3. Using your large brush, wet the back of the paper with clear water. Make sure to wet the entire surface. Place the wet side of the paper on your tray or board. Now brush water on the front side of the paper. Be thorough, but do not let puddles form.
4. Load your small brush with color by rubbing it against one of the cakes of paint. Take time to dissolve the pigment. Then touch the paper in several places with the brush to make dots. What happens to the paint dots?
5. Clean your brush by swishing it around in the water. Blot it on a paper towel and load your brush with a second color. Draw lines on an unused wet area of the paper. What happens to the paint?
6. As your paper dries, add other colors to unused dry areas where the paint will not run. Concentrate on making some of your lines thick and some of them thin. (See Technique Tip **14**, *Handbook* **275**.) After a time, you will be able to paint over areas you have already painted since they have had time to dry.
7. When your paper is completely dry, share your work with your classmates. Discuss the different effects you have created.

- **Describe**   Point out areas in your work where the color is very weak. Describe the condition of the paper when you made these dots and lines. Point out dots and lines in your work where the color is very strong. Describe the condition of the paper when you made these dots and lines. Identify areas of your work where you painted over other colors.
- **Explain**   Tell what effect changing the amount of solvent will have in a painting. Tell how you think the artists of the works in Figures 3–15 and 3–16 arrived at such different results using the same medium.

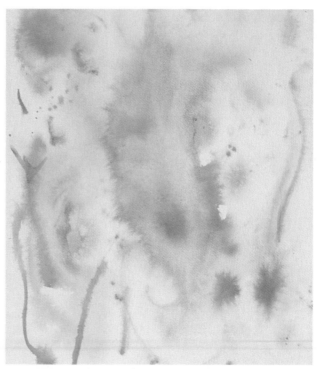

▲ **Figure 3–17   Student work. Watercolor painting.**

OTHER STUDIO IDEAS

- On another piece of paper, make a geometric pattern using just one color. Plan your work using what you have learned from the experiment above.

- •• Repeat the pigment experiment, but this time use school acrylics or tempera paints. Compare your results. (Both use water as a solvent.)

Sculpture

Have you ever made a sand castle or a snowman? If you have, then you have worked in sculpture. Sculpture is art that is made to occupy space. Sculpture is three-dimensional. **Three-dimensional** means *that an object has height, width, and depth*. (See Figure 3–18.) This is one way in which sculpture is different from the other kinds of art you have looked at so far. Although objects in a drawing or painting can look quite real, the work is flat, or two-dimensional. **Two-dimensional** means *that the work has height and width but not depth*.

▶ Figure 3–18 This artist is both a painter and a sculptor. She often uses "found" objects as the basis for her art. Name some of the found objects you see in this sculpture.

Nancy Stevenson Graves. *Zaga.* 1983. Cast bronze with polychrome chemical patination. 182.9 x 124.5 x 81.4 cm (72 x 49 x 32"). Nelson-Atkins Museum of Art, Kansas City, Missouri.

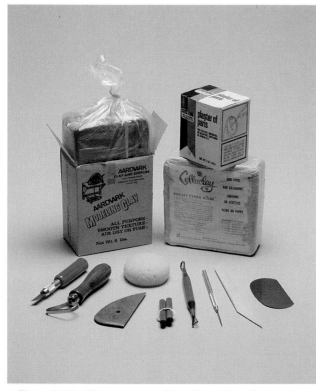

▲ **Figure 3–19** There are many kinds of sculpture tools and media. Can you name some other kinds not shown in this picture?

THE MEDIA OF SCULPTURE

An artist who works in sculpture is called a sculptor. Sculptors work with a great many materials and tools. One sculpture medium that you have probably used is modeling clay. Some others are shown in Figure 3–19. How many of these can you name? How many have you used?

Most sculpture is freestanding, or in the round. **Freestanding** means *surrounded on all sides by space*. Statues of people are examples of freestanding sculptures. Every side of a freestanding sculpture is sculpted and finished. In order to see the work as the sculptor meant it to be seen, you have to move around it. Notice that each view of the boy in Figure 3–20 reveals something the other views do not.

▲ **Figure 3–20** This young boy stands stiffly with his toys. This shows the stern rules of the tribe he belonged to. In a few years, he would be a soldier.

Unknown artist. *Figure of Standing Youth.* 400-300 B.C. Bronze and jade, Chinese Eastern Zhou Dynasty. 30 cm (11.8"). Museum of Fine Arts, Boston, Massachusetts. Maria Antoinette Evans Fund.

In addition to freestanding sculpture, there is relief sculpture. **Relief** is *a type of sculpture in which forms and figures are projected from the front only*. It is flat along the back. You can see large reliefs on buildings and small reliefs on items such as jewelry.

► Figure 3–21   Käthe Kollwitz produced powerful treatments of well-known subjects such as poverty and sorrow. She made social statements with her work. This is a self-portrait she executed when she was 69 years old.

Käthe Kollwitz. *Self-Portrait*. 1936. Bronze on marble base. 36.5 x 23.1 x 28.7 cm (14⅜ x 9⅛ x 11⅜"). Hirshhorn Museum, Smithsonian Institution, Washington, D.C. Joseph H. Hirshhorn, 1966.

▼ Figure 3–22   What is the center of interest in this work? Why? What do you think it means?

Marisol Escobar. *Poor Family I*. 1987. Wood, charcoal, stones, plastic doll. 198.1 x 396.2 x 213.4 cm (78 x 156 x 84"). Sidney Janis Gallery, New York, New York.

SCULPTING METHODS

There are four basic methods for making sculpture. These are:

- **Carving.** In carving, the sculptor starts with a block of material and cuts or chips a shape from it. Often a hard material like stone is used.
- **Casting.** In casting, the sculptor starts by making a mold. He or she then pours in a melted-down metal or some other liquid that will later harden. See Figure 3–21 for an example of bronze sculpture.
- **Modeling.** In modeling, the sculptor builds up and shapes a soft material. Clay and fresh plaster are two such materials.
- **Assembling.** In assembling, also known as constructing, the sculptor glues or in some other way joins together pieces of material. The sculpture in Figure 3–22 was made by assembling pieces of wood, charcoal, stones, and a plastic doll. This sculpture shows both additive and subtractive methods.

Modeling and assembling are known as additive methods of sculpting. In the additive method, the artist adds together or builds up the material. Carving is a subtractive method. In the subtractive method, the artist takes away or removes material.

━━━━ SAFETY TIP ━━━━

Be very careful when using cutting tools, such as scissors and knives. Pick these up only by the handle, never by the blade. When handing them to another person, offer the handle to the other person.

STUDIO EXPERIENCE

Using pieces of scrap styrofoam from beverage containers, trays, and packing materials, work in teams to create a freestanding sculpture. You may use both the additive and subtractive techniques to create this work. Use slots and tabs to hold the smaller pieces of your construction together. Straight pins, strings, and other joining devices can help you hold the larger pieces together. The size of these constructions depends upon the limits of your art room and the supplies you can collect. They may reach from floor to ceiling, or they may be 5 inches (13 cm) tall. If you are working with very large packing materials, you can carve them with scissors and utility knives. If you are making small sculpture pieces, you can cut the cups and trays with scissors into a variety of shapes.

✔ CHECK YOUR UNDERSTANDING

1. What is another term that has the same meaning as freestanding?
2. Name two media used by sculptors.
3. Briefly describe the four basic methods for making sculpture.
4. What is meant by the term additive as it is used in sculpture? Which two basic methods of making sculpture are additive?
5. What is meant by the term subtractive as it is used in sculpture? Which basic method of making sculpture is subtractive?

Creating with Mixed Media

The young artist who created the mixed media work in Figure 3–23 was creating a work of art which represented his life. He included objects and symbols that were important to him. The daffodil represents a summer spent studying art at the Daffodil Farm. The tiny figure of Pinocchio is from a drawing that his kindergarten teacher had framed for him. Near the center of the work there is a checkerboard. What do you think this might represent? Can you recognize any other symbols that give you more information about this young man?

He used different types of media to create this work. For example, graphite, colored pencil, and markers are some of the media he used. What others can you identify?

WHAT YOU WILL LEARN

You will create a mixed-media picture that represents something about your life. You may include a photo or sketch of yourself, but do not have it take up the whole work. As you create your work of art, experiment with a variety of media.

▲ **Figure 3–23** The artist worked on this mixed media piece for a year. It shows symbols of important events in his life. Can you identify some of the symbols?

Herbert Andrew Williams. *A Year in the Life of Herbert.* 1988. Mixed media. Private collection.

WHAT YOU WILL NEED

- Pencil and sketch paper
- Sheet of white paper, 12 x 18 inch (30 x 46 cm)
- Variety of media, including markers, paints, colored pencils
- Magazine, newspaper, and wallpaper scraps

WHAT YOU WILL DO

1. Make a list of people, places, objects and events that symbolize you and your life. Make rough sketches of these items. You may also add words. Notice that you can find the artist's name in Figure 3–23, but it is slightly hidden.

2. Look through magazines and newspapers for pictures and words that represent your interests, skills, and cultural background. If you decide to cut out a shape, cut neatly around the edge of the shape. Do you see the brown hand near the center of Figure 3–23? Notice how it has been carefully cut and outlined with colored pencil and black ink.

3. Select from the pieces you have cut and decide on the sketch you wiil use. Draw your final plan on the sheet of white paper.

4. Glue down the cut objects. Use any other media you wish to finish your work. (See Figure 3–24.)

5. Place your work on display with your classmates. Can you recognize your friends by the symbols they used?

- **Describe** List the media that you used in this work. List the symbols you included and explain how each symbol relates to you. Identify the media that you enjoyed working with and explain why. Identify any media that did not produce the results you wanted. Explain why.

▲ **Figure 3–24 Student work. Mixed media.**

OTHER STUDIO IDEAS

- Select one medium that gave you the most successful results. Determine a theme for your composition, such as a sporting event, school activity, or family outing. Plan the composition and complete it using the medium of your choice.

●● Create a mixed media work that represents your school, city, state, or country.

CHAPTER 3 REVIEW

BUILDING VOCABULARY

Number a sheet of paper from 1 to 13. After each number, write the term from the box that best matches each description below.

binder	print
edition	relief
freestanding	reproduction
medium of art	solvent
mixed media	style
pigment	three-dimensional
	two-dimensional

1. A material used to create an art work.
2. An image that is transferred from a prepared surface to paper or fabric.
3. Work that has height, width, depth.
4. A finely ground powder that gives paint its color.
5. Surrounded on all sides by space.
6. Use of more than one medium in art.
7. A work that has height and width.
8. A type of sculpture in which the image projects from only the front.
9. A photograph of a print.
10. An artist's personal way of expressing ideas in a work.
11. A liquid to which dry pigment is added.
12. A liquid that controls the thickness or thinness of the paint.
13. A series of prints all exactly alike.

REVIEWING ART FACTS

Number a sheet of paper from 14 to 18. Answer each question in a complete sentence.

14. Name two drawing media.
15. What is the first step in printmaking?
16. What is a group of identical prints called?
17. How is freestanding sculpture meant to be seen?
18. What type of sculpture is flat on the back?

THINKING ABOUT ART

On a sheet of paper, answer each question in a sentence or two.

1. **Summarize.** Look again at the photograph of the painting by Jan Steen on page **28**. How many painting media are shown in the work? How many sculpture media?
2. **Compare and contrast.** Compare the styles of the prints in Figures 3–9 and 3–10. What differences can you describe?
3. **Analyze.** Sculptors, like other artists, develop individual styles. How would you describe the styles of the sculptors for Figures 3–18 and 3–20?
4. **Analyze.** What method of sculpture would you be using if you whittled a tree branch? What method would you be using if you built a tower of building blocks that snapped together?

MAKING ART CONNECTIONS

1. **Language Arts.** Carefully study the Hopper painting in Figure 3–16. Try to imagine the mood of the event and what is happening in the painting. Describe the place and people shown. Use words such as color, line, shape, form, space, and texture. Write a few paragraphs about what is happening in the painting.
2. **Communication.** Find three examples of printmaking in your daily activities. Think about how this art form has developed into an important medium for communicating ideas. Share your examples with the class.
3. **Industrial Arts.** In 1440 a German printer named Gütenberg invented a printing press with movable type. The effect of this invention was profound. Trace the development of the printing industry from 1440 through the present.

LOOKING AT THE DETAILS

The detail shown below is from Jan Steen's *The Drawing Lesson*. Study the detail and answer the following questions.

1. This painting is of ordinary people and an ordinary situation. What message do you think Jan Steen was trying to communicate? What do you think he is telling us about the artist?
2. Look at the entire work on page **28**. Does this change or add to your answers to the previous questions? Explain.
3. Locate examples of drawing, printmaking, painting, and sculpture in this work.
4. How would you describe this artist's style?
5. Why do you think Jan Steen chose the media of painting instead of sculpture to communicate his message?

Jan Steen. *The Drawing Lesson.* 1665. Oil on wood. (Detail.) 49.3 x 41 cm (19⅜ x 16¼"). J. Paul Getty Museum.

▲ Cézanne is noted for the many landscapes he painted, but he also used people and everyday objects as sources of inspiration.

Paul Cézanne. *The Bay of Marseille, Seen from L'Estaque.* 1886–90. Oil on canvas. 80.8 x 99.8 cm (31⅞ x 39¼"). The Art Institute of Chicago. Mr. & Mrs. Martin A. Ryerson Collection.

The Elements of Art

When creating a work of art, an artist is faced with a number of questions. Look at the painting at the left. Think about how the artist answered the following questions:

- What colors will I use?
- Will the painting as a whole appear to be smooth or rough to the touch?
- Will the objects in the painting look flat and two-dimensional, or will they appear deep and realistic?

How an artist answers these and other questions determines how the finished work will look.

OBJECTIVES

After completing this chapter, you will be able to:

- Name the six elements of art.
- Identify the three properties of color.
- Use complementary colors in an art work.
- Name the different kinds of line.
- Explain the difference between shapes and forms.
- Explain the two ways we experience texture.
- Experiment with the elements of art.

WORDS YOU WILL LEARN

analogous colors	line variation
color wheel	monochromatic colors
complementary colors	motif
form	shape
hue	space
intensity	texture
line	value
line quality	

ARTISTS YOU WILL MEET

Constantin Brancusi	Elizabeth Murray
Paul Cézanne	José Clemente Orozco
Arthur G. Dove	Attilio Salemme
Alberto Giacometti	Miriam Schapiro
Käthe Kollwitz	Frank Stella
Piet Mondrian	Vincent van Gogh

The Language of Art

When you talk to someone or write a letter, you communicate. You share your ideas and feelings. You use words—either spoken or written—to get a message across.

Artists do the same thing. They do not express their thoughts and feelings in ordinary words, however. Instead, artists use visual images—things that we can see and sometimes touch—to "speak" to us.

In this lesson you will learn about the special "language" artists use when they communicate. You will also begin to see that an artist's success in communicating depends partly on his or her skill in using this language.

THE VISUAL LANGUAGE

Since earliest times people have used the language of art to speak to each other. This is clear from the discovery of cave paintings like the one in Figure 4–1. Such early art works show that humans were writing in pictures some 12,000 years before the invention of the alphabet.

You have probably heard it said that a picture is worth a thousand words. In a very real sense, this saying is true. To understand the relationship between words and pictures, first read the following paragraph:

> The frightened mother was locked in a terrible struggle with the phantom, who greedily eyed her child. "No!" the mother's wide eyes protested. "No—you can never have him!" As her heart raced wildly, the mother clutched her little boy to her body with the strength of 10 men. But no matter how hard she fought, little by little she felt her grip weaken. Slowly—ever so slowly—the child was slipping from her fingers. In the end, she was no match for the phantom. Death, she knew in that awful final instant, would soon claim another helpless victim.

Now look at Figure 4–2 with the title *Death and the Mother*. Notice the look of sheer terror on the mother's face. Notice the power in her

▶ **Figure 4–1** Humans long ago painted pictures of animals on cave walls and ceilings. What reasons might they have had for doing this?

Unknown. Cave paintings. Gallery of Prehistoric Art, New York, New York.

bulging arm as she holds fast to her child. What it took the writer 100 words to say, the artist has said in a single look!

▲ **Figure 4–3** Why might the artist have chosen to make the man so thin and angled?

Alberto Giacometti. *Man Pointing*. 1947. Bronze. 179.1 x 103.5 x 41.6 cm Base 30.5 x 33.1 cm (70½ x 40¾ x 16⅜″ Base 12 x 13¼″). The Museum of Modern Art, New York, New York. Gift of Mrs. John D. Rockefeller III.

It is often hard to tell one element from another when you look at a work of art. When you look at Figure 4–3, for instance, you do not see the elements of line (long) and texture (rough). Instead, you see the sculpture as a whole. Your eye "reads" the elements of line and texture together. And yet, it is the very blending of these elements that permits you to see the art work as the artist meant you to see it: a man pointing.

"READING" THE LANGUAGE

When you first learned to read, you did not start with a book. You began by reading a word at a time. That is how you will learn the language of art: one element at a time.

Because these elements are so important, the remaining lessons of this chapter will be devoted to a discussion of them. Once you have studied these elements you will know a good part of the art vocabulary.

✔ CHECK YOUR UNDERSTANDING

1. In what way can art be said to be a language?
2. What is an element of art?
3. Name the six elements of art.

▲ **Figure 4–2** How would you describe the look on the woman's face? Why is she terrified? Can you tell what she is clutching in her arms?

Käthe Kollwitz. *Death and the Mother*. 1934. Lithograph. Private collection.

THE VOCABULARY OF ART

You know that every language has its own word system, or vocabulary. Before a person can speak the language, he or she must know at least some of the words in its vocabulary.

The language of art, too, has a vocabulary all its own. Instead of words, however, the vocabulary of art is made up of six visual elements. An **element of art** is a *basic visual symbol an artist uses to create visual art*. These are color, line, shape, form, space, and texture. In much the way we put words together to form a sentence, the artist puts the visual elements together to make a statement.

LESSON 2

Color

Color is everywhere. It is in the orange-pink glow of the summer sky just before sunrise. It is in the rich reds and oranges of autumn leaves and in the long purple shadows that lay across the snow toward the close of a winter's day.

Color is even in our everyday language. "Green with envy," "feeling blue," and "red with rage" are English expressions that mention color.

In this lesson you will learn about the very important role color plays in art. You will learn how some artists have used color successfully. This knowledge of color can help you use it more creatively and effectively in your own art works.

TRAITS OF COLOR

Look up at the sun on a clear day and you see an almost blinding white light—or so your eye tells you. In reality, what you are looking at—but failing to see—are all the colors of the rainbow. When the sunlight shines on objects, some of the light is absorbed by the object. Some of the light bounces off. Color is what the eye sees when sunlight or some other light bounces off an object.

In the 18th century, Sir Isaac Newton organized the colors into a color wheel. The **color wheel** is *an arrangement of colors in a circular format*. See Figure 4–4. Later in this chapter you will learn more about the arrangement of the colors on the color wheel.

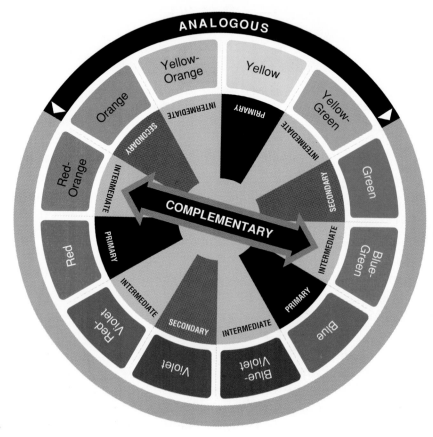

▶ **Figure 4–4   Color wheel.**

Sometimes artists use colors in bold and shocking ways (Figure 4–5). Sometimes they use them in quiet and serious ways (Figure 4–6 on page **58**). To achieve different results, artists must understand the three properties or traits of color. These are hue, value, and intensity.

Hue

Hue is *a color's name*. Red, yellow, and blue are the primary hues. They are always equally spaced on the color wheel. (See Figure 4–4.) They are called primary, or first, because they can be used to mix all the other colors but cannot themselves be made by the mixing of other colors.

◀ **Figure 4–5   What makes this painting bold? Do you think this is a successful painting? Why or why not?**

Miriam Schapiro. *High Steppin' Strutter I.* 1985. Paper and acrylic on paper. 203.2 x 138.4 cm (80 x 54½"). Bernice Steinbaum Gallery, New York. Given anonymously.

▶ **Figure 4–6   Why would this be considered a quiet painting? What gives it its serious quality?**

José Clemente Orozco. *Zapatistas.* 1931. Oil on canvas. 114.3 x 139.7 cm (45 x 55″). The Museum of Modern Art, New York, New York. Given anonymously.

The secondary hues are green, orange, and violet. The place of each on the color wheel — between the primary hues — tells which hues can be mixed to make it. To get orange, for example, you mix equal parts of red and yellow. Can you identify the colors that you would mix to obtain the remaining secondary hues?

Intermediate hues are made by mixing a primary hue with its neighboring secondary hue. When you mix the primary hue yellow with the secondary hue green, you get the intermediate hue yellow-green.

Value

You may have noticed that some colors on the color wheel seem lighter than others. The difference is one of value. **Value** is *the lightness or darkness of a hue.* Pale yellow is light in value and deep purple is dark in value.

You can change the value of a hue by adding black or white. In art, a light (or whiter) value of a hue is called a tint. Pink is a mixture of red and white. Pink could be called a tint. A dark (or blacker) value is called a shade. (See Figure 4–7.) Maroon is a mixture

of red and black. It could be called a shade. Be careful when using these terms. In everyday language, the word shade is often used to describe both light and dark values of a hue.

Intensity

Some hues strike the eye as bright and alive. Others appear dull or muddy. The difference is the color's intensity. **Intensity** is *the brightness or dullness of a hue.* A bright hue is said to be high in intensity. A dull hue is said to be low in intensity. Bright yellow is high in intensity. Mustard yellow is low in intensity.

Look again at the color wheel on page **56**. Notice that as you move away from green in the direction of red, the hue grows less intense. Red and green are **complementary colors,** *colors opposite each other on the color wheel.* Adding a hue's complementary color lowers the hue's intensity. (See Figure 4–7.) If you mix equal parts of two complementary colors, you get a neutral color such as brown or gray.

VALUES OF BLUE

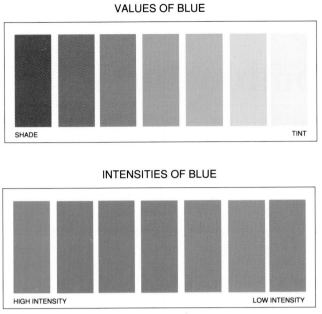

SHADE   TINT

INTENSITIES OF BLUE

HIGH INTENSITY   LOW INTENSITY

▲ Figure 4–7 Value and intensity scales.

COMBINING COLORS

Colors are like musical instruments. Just as each instrument has its own special sound, so every color has its own "personality." Combining colors in just the right way can lead to striking results. The following are some common color schemes that trained artists use:

- **Monochromatic color schemes. Monochromatic** (**mahn**-uh-kroh-**mat**-ik) **colors** are *different values of a single hue.* For example, dark blue, medium blue, and light blue is a monochromatic scheme. This type of scheme tightly weaves together the parts of an art work. A danger of a monochromatic scheme, however, is that it can bore the viewer.
- **Analogous color schemes. Analogous** (uh-**nal**-uh-gus) **colors** are *colors that are side by side on the color wheel and share a hue.* Violet, red-violet, red, and red-orange are analogous colors that share the hue red. Analogous colors in an art work can tie one shape to the next.

- **Warm or cool color schemes.** Red, yellow, and orange remind us of sunshine, fire and other warm things. For this reason, they are known as warm colors. Blue, green, and violet make us think of cool things, like ice and grass. They are known, therefore, as cool colors. When used in an art work, warm colors seem to move toward the viewer. Cool colors appear to move back and away.

✔ CHECK YOUR UNDERSTANDING

1. What are the three primary hues?
2. What is the difference between a tint and a shade?
3. What are complementary colors? Give an example.
4. What is a monochromatic color scheme?
5. Define an analogous color scheme.

Using Color Combinations

Artists use color schemes to create special effects in works of art. Color schemes can make a painting vibrate or make colors look brighter.

Look at Figure 4–8. Notice how Elizabeth Murray has used the red and green complementary color scheme to create this work. To give it variety she has experimented with values. Can you find a tint and a shade of red?

WHAT YOU WILL LEARN

You will create a complementary color design. You will create a motif, based on your initials. A **motif** (moh-**teef**) is *a unit that is repeated in a pattern or visual rhythm.* Plan the motif so that it touches all four edges of the paper. Then arrange the motif to form an interesting pattern. Paint all the letters with one color. Paint all the negative spaces with its complement.

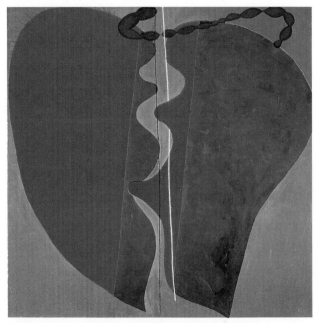

▲ **Figure 4–8** How does the artist's choice and placement of color affect the meaning of the painting?

Elizabeth Murray. *Join*. 1980. Oil on canvas. 337.8 x 304.8 cm (133 x 120"). Security Pacific Bank Collection.

WHAT YOU WILL NEED

- Pencil, sketch paper, eraser
- White paper, 4½ x 6 inch (11 x 15 cm)
- White paper, 9 x 12 inch (23 x 30 cm)
- Masking tape
- Tempera paint and two small brushes
- Paper towels

WHAT YOU WILL DO

1. Using sketch paper, draw different arrangements of your initials. In this design, an interesting shape is more important than the readability of the letters.
2. Select your best design. Using double lines, draw the letters on the smaller sheet of white paper. Be sure that the letters touch all four sides of the paper. (See Figure 4–9.)
3. Hold the paper up to a glass window with the letters facing out. You will see them backwards through the paper. Carefully draw over the lines on the back with a soft lead pencil. The lines on the back must go directly over the lines on the front. These lines will act like carbon paper.
4. You may arrange the motif any way that fits on the larger sheet of paper.
5. Place your motif on the larger sheet of paper. Hold it in place with a small piece of tape. Transfer the image by drawing over the lines of the motif. If you wish, you may flip the motif over and trace the mirror image.
6. Select a set of complementary colors. You may use primaries and secondaries, or you may use a set of intermediates such as red-orange and blue-green.

4.5"

6"

- **Describe** Explain what set of complementary colors you selected. Did your motif touch all four sides of the paper? Describe the pattern you created with your motif. Show where you painted all the letters with one hue and all the negative spaces with its complement.
- **Explain** Describe the effect that is created by painting the complementary colors side by side.

▲ **Figure 4–9** Letter motif arrangement.

7. Use one brush and one hue to paint all the letters in your pattern. Be sure the paint is dry before you paint the second color next to it.

8. Use a second brush to paint all the negative spaces with the complement of that hue. Nothing should be left white. If you do not have two brushes, clean your brush thoroughly before using another color. (See Technique Tip **10**, *Handbook* page **273**.)

9. Put your work on display with your classmates. Do all the complements have the same exciting visual effect? (See Figure 4–10.)

▲ **Figure 4–10** Student work. Motif design.

OTHER STUDIO IDEA

- Select a sheet of construction paper of a primary color. Cut out objects from a magazine that have the complementary color of your paper. Organize them into a design and glue them to the background paper.

Line

Think about how many times every day you see lines. You write words, numbers, and symbols with the help of lines. You use lines to draw pictures. The lines on a map help you find the best route from one place to another. You also feel lines—in the grain of a piece of wood or the veins of a leaf.

This lesson will focus on the importance of line as one of the six elements of art.

THE MEANING OF LINE

Take a pencil and move it across a sheet of paper. What happened? The moving point of the pencil made a path of connected dots on the paper. In other words, it made a line. This definition of **line**—*the path of a dot through space*—is a good one to remember. It reminds you that it takes movement to make a line. When you see a line, your eye usually follows its movement. A trained artist uses lines to control the movement of the viewer's eyes. Lines can lead the eyes into, around, and out of visual images in a work of art.

KINDS OF LINE

There are five main kinds of line: vertical, horizontal, diagonal, curved, and zigzag. When used in an art work, lines can communicate different messages or feelings to the viewer.

Vertical Lines

Vertical lines (Figure 4–11) move straight up and down. They do not lean at all. When you stand up straight and tall, your body forms a vertical line.

In art, vertical lines appear to be at attention. Artists use them to show dignity, formality, or strength.

Horizontal Lines

Horizontal lines (Figure 4–12) run parallel to the ground. They do not slant. When you lie flat on the floor, your body forms a horizontal line.

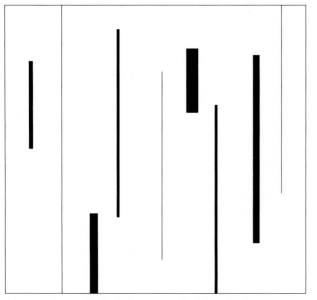

▲ **Figure 4–11** Vertical lines move straight up and down.

▲ **Figure 4–12** Horizontal lines lie parallel to the horizon.

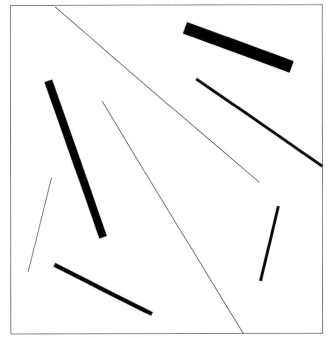

▲ Figure 4–13 Diagonal lines slant.

▲ Figure 4–14   Curved lines change direction gradually.

Horizontal lines in art seem at rest. Other words that come to mind in connection with them are quiet and peaceful. Horizontal lines make the viewer feel comfortable, calm, and relaxed.

Diagonal Lines

Diagonal lines (Figure 4–13) slant. They are somewhere between a vertical and a horizontal line. Imagine standing straight up and then, with your body stiff, falling to the floor. At any point during your fall, your body would form a diagonal line.

To the artist, diagonal lines signal action and excitement. Since they appear to be either rising or falling, diagonals sometimes make a viewer feel tense and uncomfortable. But when they meet and seem to hold each other up, as in the roof of a house, they appear firm and unmoving.

Curved Lines

Curved lines (Figure 4–14) change direction little by little. When you draw wiggly lines, you are actually linking a series of curves. Other forms that begin with curves are spirals and circles.

Like diagonal lines, curved lines, express movement, though in a more graceful, flowing way. The amount of movement in a curve depends on how tight the curve is. Notice how the painter, Vincent van Gogh suggests motion in his tree through the unusual use of curves (Figure 4–15, on page **64**).

Zigzag Lines

Zigzag lines (Figure 4–16, on page **65**) are made by combining different directions of diagonal lines. The diagonals form sharp angles and change direction suddenly.

Zigzag lines can create confusion. They suggest action and nervous excitement. Sometimes zigzags move in even horizontal patterns, like those at the top of a picket fence. These are less active than the jagged lines in a diagonal streak of lightning.

QUALITIES OF LINES

Lines may appear smooth or rough, continuous or broken, sketchy or controlled. The **line quality** describes *the unique character of any line.* Line quality is affected by either the tool or medium used to produce the mark, or by the particular motion of the artist's hands.

▲ Figure 4–15   How do the lines in van Gogh's painting direct your eyes? How is van Gogh's tree different from the usual idea of a tree?

Vincent van Gogh. *Cypresses*. 1889. Oil on canvas. 93.3 x 74 cm (36¾ x 29⅛"). Metropolitan Museum of Art, New York, New York. Rogers Fund, 1949.

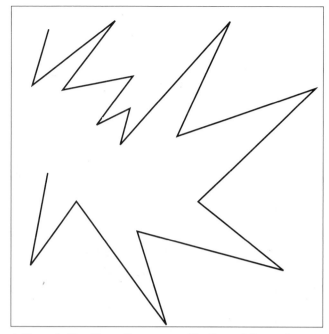

▲ **Figure 4–16** Zigzag lines are combinations of diagonals.

▲ **Figure 4–17** Line quality.

STUDIO EXPERIENCE

Draw a continuous curving line lightly with pencil on a sheet of white paper, 6 x 9 inch (15 x 23 cm). Begin the line on one edge of the paper and draw it wandering around the entire space of the page. Consider the line as the path of a flying insect. Let the line finish its path at a different edge of the paper. Use a black marker to trace your line. Create variations of thick and thin lines along your linear path to add visual balance to your composition.

Lines can also be varied. **Line variation** describes *the thickness or thinness, lightness or darkness of a line*. Thick and dark lines appear to be visually heavier than thin and light lines. Look at Figure 4–17 and identify the different quality of lines. What medium do you think was used to create each line?

✔**CHECK YOUR UNDERSTANDING**

1. What is the meaning of the term *line* as it is used in art?
2. Name five kinds of line.
3. Describe the way each of the five kinds of line causes a viewer of an art work to feel.
4. What affects line quality?

Shape, Form, and Space

The world we live in is made up basically of two things: objects and space. Each object—a car, an apple, a book, even you—has a shape or a form. Often you are able to pick out objects by their forms or shapes alone. Sometimes you can spot a friend in the distance just by recognizing his or her shape. With your eyes closed you could feel an object and tell that it has a round form.

Shape, form, and space are all closely tied to one another. In this lesson you will learn to read the meaning of these three elements.

SHAPE

In art a **shape** is *an area clearly set off by one or more of the other five visual elements of art.* Shapes are flat. They are limited to only two dimensions: length and width. A ball's shape is a circle. A shape may have an outline or boundary around it. Some shapes show up because of color. Others are set off purely by the space that surrounds them.

Shapes may be thought of as belonging to one of two classes:

▲ **Figure 4–18   What kind of unique worlds exist in your own imagination? Would you use geometric shapes in creating your unique world on paper?**

Attilio Salemme. *Inquisition.* 1952. Oil on canvas. 101.6 x 160 cm (40 x 63"). Whitney Museum of American Art.

▲ Figure 4–19   Do you like the organic shapes in this painting better than the geometric ones in Figure 4–18? Why or why not?

Arthur G. Dove. *Plant Forms*. 1915. Pastel on canvas. 43.8 x 60.6 cm (17¼ x 23⅞"). Whitney Museum of American Art, New York, New York. Purchased with funds from Mr. & Mrs. Roy R. Nueberger.

- **Geometric shapes.** These are precise shapes that look as if they were made with a ruler or other drawing tool. The square, the circle, the triangle, the rectangle, and the oval are the five basic geometric shapes. The strange world shown in Figure 4–18 is made up largely of geometric shapes.

- **Organic shapes.** These are not regular or even. Their outlines curve to make free-form shapes. Organic shapes are often found in nature. The objects in the painting in Figure 4–19 are based on organic, free-form shapes.

FORM

Like shapes, forms have length and width. But forms go a step further. They have depth. A **form** is *an object with three dimensions.* You are a three-dimensional form. So is a tree or a table.

Forms, too, are grouped as either geometric or organic. Examples of geometric forms are a baseball and a child's building block. Examples of organic forms are a stone and a cloud.

Shapes and forms are closely linked in art (Figure 4–20). The end of a cylinder is a circle. One side of a cube is a square. A triangle can "grow" into a pyramid.

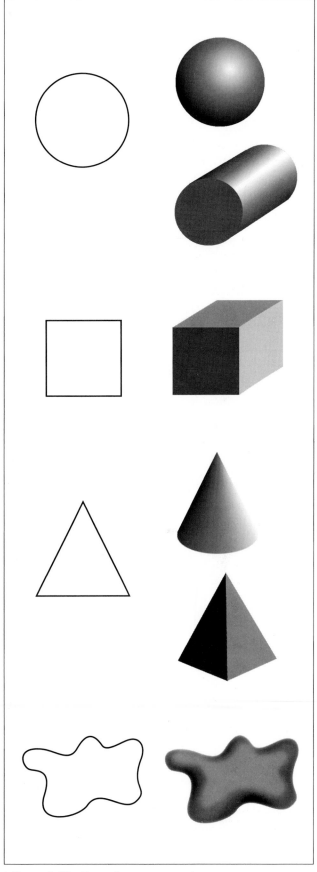

▲ Figure 4–20   Form-shape correspondences.

▲ **Figure 4–21** **Does seeing this sculpture make you want to walk around it and see it from different sides?**

Constantin Brancusi. *Mlle. Pogany II.* 1920. Polished bronze. 44.5 x 17.8 x 25.4 cm (17½ x 7 x 10"). Albright-Knox Art Gallery, Buffalo, New York. Charlotte A. Watson Fund, 1927.

SPACE

Space is *the distance or area between, around, above, below, and within things.* Space is empty until objects fill it. All objects take up space. You, for instance, are a living, breathing form moving through space.

Some kinds of art are three-dimensional. You may recall from Chapter 3 that sculpture is this kind of art. When a piece of sculpture is freestanding, as in Figure 4–21, we can move completely around it and see it from different sides.

Although drawings and paintings are created in two dimensions, they can be made to appear three-dimensional. Artists have developed techniques for giving the feeling of depth in paintings and drawings. These include:

- **Overlapping.** Having shapes overlap one another.
- **Size.** Making distant shapes smaller than closer ones.
- **Focus.** Adding more detail to closer objects, less detail to distant objects.
- **Placement.** Placing distant objects higher up in the picture, closer ones lower down.
- **Intensity and value.** Using colors that are lower in intensity and lighter in value for objects in the distance.
- **Linear perspective.** Slanting lines of buildings and other objects so they seem to come together in the distance.

✔ CHECK YOUR UNDERSTANDING

1. What is shape?
2. What are the two types of shape? Give an example of each type.
3. What is form?
4. What are the two types of form? Give an example of each type.
5. Name two techniques that artists use for creating a feeling of space.

Paper Sculpture Forms

Study the work in Figure 4–22. From the credit line, you can tell what media the artist, Frank Stella, used. You can also tell the size of the piece. Try to imagine a work of this size in your classroom. Do you think it could have been made with paper? In this studio lesson you will explore some of the ways that paper can be used to make sculpture forms.

WHAT YOU WILL LEARN

You will alter a flat two-dimensional shape of paper into a three-dimensional form. You will use paper sculpture techniques to create an interesting paper sculpture form.

WHAT YOU WILL NEED

- Scrap paper for experimenting
- Pencil and ruler
- Sheets of construction paper, 12 x 18 inch (30 x 46 cm)
- Scissors, knife, stapler
- White glue

WHAT YOU WILL DO

1. Using scrap paper, experiment with a variety of paper sculpture techniques. (See Technique Tip **21**, *Handbook* **278**.) This will show you some ways of working with paper. These techniques can be used for your paper sculpture.

▶ **Figure 4–22   Frank Stella's art was often displayed by attaching it to walls with heavy bolts.**

Frank Stella. *St. Michael's Counterguard.* 1984. Aluminum, fiberglass and honeycomb. 396.2 x 342.9 x 274.3 cm (156 x 135 x 108"). Los Angeles County Museum of Art. Gift of Anna Bing Arnold.

2. Using your large sheet of paper, begin your design. As you work, you may have to alter your plan to get the effect you desire. Include three paper sculpture techniques in your design.
3. You may cut into the paper, but do not cut it into two pieces. Use staples or glue to hold the paper in place.
4. Keep turning your sculpture so that it looks interesting from every point of view.
5. Display your paper form. (See Figure 4–23.)

- **Describe**   Tell what paper sculpture techniques you used.
- **Explain**   Tell how your two-dimensional shape was altered into a three-dimensional form. Tell how you used the paper sculpture techniques to complete your design.

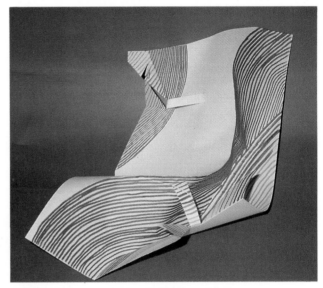

▲ **Figure 4–24   Student work. Paper sculpture.**

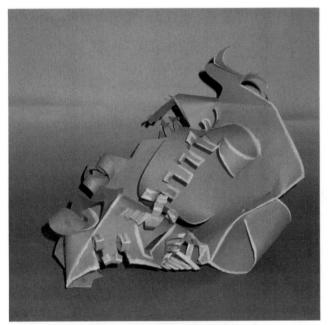

▲ **Figure 4–23   Student work. Paper sculpture.**

OTHER STUDIO IDEAS

- Experiment with scrap paper using the scoring and folding techniques you have learned to make a large bird. Attach a fine nylon filament to the center of the bird. You may have to attach more than one filament to position the bird the way you want. Suspend the bird from the ceiling or other high place so that it looks like it is flying.
- ● ● Build a paper castle using the paper sculpture techniques you have learned so far.

Texture

Rub your fingers lightly over this page. How would you describe the way it feels? **Texture** refers *to how things feel, or look as though they might feel, if touched.* No one needs to teach you about texture. You know what is rough and what is smooth. There are certain textures you find pleasant to the touch. Other surfaces you avoid touching because you do not like the way they feel.

In this lesson you will learn about the two ways texture works as an element of art.

TWO SIDES OF TEXTURE

Sandpaper, glass, a block of concrete—each has its own special texture, or feel. Have you ever tried on a piece of clothing—perhaps a sweater—that you thought looked itchy only to find it was not? Such things are possible because we experience texture through two of our senses. We experience texture with our sense of sight. We also experience it again—and sometimes differently—with our sense of touch.

▶ **Figure 4–25** How does your eye see the trees in this photograph? How do your fingers "see" them?

When you look at a photograph of tree bark or a seashell, you see patterns of light and dark (Figures 4–25 and 4–26). These patterns bring back memories of how those objects feel. When this happens, you are experiencing visual texture. The photograph is smooth and flat. It is your eyes that add the splintery coarseness of the bark or the satiny smoothness of the shell. Actual, or real texture, on the other hand, is what you experience when you touch the object itself, not the photograph. It is the message your fingers send to your brain.

STUDIO EXPERIENCE

Gather an assortment of fabrics and papers with smooth and rough textures. Look through a magazine for color pictures of smooth and rough visual textures and cut them out. Arrange these actual and visual textures on a small piece of cardboard. Cover all the background with textures. Your design should show contrasts of actual and visual, as well as smooth and rough textures. Glue down your design with white glue.

✔CHECK YOUR UNDERSTANDING

1. What is texture?
2. Through which two of our senses do we experience texture?
3. What is visual texture? What is actual texture?

◀ Figure 4–26 Why is the visual texture of the shell different from the actual texture of the photograph?

Painting a Landscape

Look at the painting of a tree by the Dutch artist Piet Mondrian (peet **mawn**-dree-ahn) in Figure 4–27. Does this look like a real tree? In this painting Mondrian used line quality and line variation to express the idea of a tree. Note how the artist also used color, shape, and texture to capture the idea of a tree.

WHAT YOU WILL LEARN

You will use the elements of color, line, shape, space, and texture to paint an unusual landscape. The landscape will have trees at different places in space. It will also show the underground roots of the nearest tree, plus different layers of soil and rock. (See Figure 4–28.)

WHAT YOU WILL NEED

- Pencil and sketch paper
- Tempera paint
- Soft and stiff brushes
- Mixing tray
- Water
- Sheet of heavy paper or illustration board, 12 x 18 inch (30 x 46 cm)
- Paper towels

WHAT YOU WILL DO

1. Take a walk outside or use your imagination to think of different landscapes. On scrap paper, make several pencil sketches of landscapes with trees. Show the branches clearly, but do not draw leaves.

▶ Figure 4–27 Are warm or cool colors used in this painting? How would you describe the lines used? Are the shapes geometric or organic? What has been done to give the work a rich texture?

Piet Mondrian. *Blue Tree.* 1909–1910. Oil on composition board. 56.8 x 74.9 cm (22⅜ x 29½"). Dallas Museum of Art.

2. Divide your sheet of white paper or illustration board horizontally into three equal parts with light pencil lines. In the top part, redraw lightly the best of your landscape sketches. The lines of the tree branches should be designed to make an interesting pattern of shapes. (Look again at Figure 4–27 for ideas.) The branches of the nearest tree should run off the top of your paper.

3. In the center part, draw the underground roots of the nearest tree. Use your imagination. The lines of the roots should add other interesting shapes.

4. In the bottom part, draw different layers of soil and rock. Once again, be as imaginative as you can.

5. Before painting your final work, experiment on scrap paper using stiff and soft brushes to create different textures. Dip the tip of the stiff bristle brush into the paint. Dab lightly at the paper. You should see bunches of dots. Drag the same brush across the paper for a fuzzy rough effect. Dip your soft brush into the paint. Dab it onto the paper making brush prints. Experiment with other techniques and develop your individual style.

6. Using tempera paint, mix your colors with white and black and with their complements to create different values and intensities.

7. Share your work with your classmates. Look for differences and similarities between your own landscape and those of other students.

EXAMINING YOUR WORK

- **Describe**   Point to the three trees and identify the roots of the nearest tree. Identify the different layers of rock and soil and describe how you made them different.
- **Explain**   Tell why you chose the colors you did. Show different lines, shapes, and textures in your work, and explain what media you used to create the differences. Explain how you created the illusion of space in your work.

▲ **Figure 4–28   Student work. An unusual landscape.**

OTHER STUDIO IDEAS

- Think about the characteristics and structures of trees you see during the winter season. Practice sketching a variety of trees using combinations of loosely drawn lines to build up the tree structures. Build up the trunk, limbs, branches, and twigs with straight, curved, and/or angular lines.

- ● Think about parks or forests and sketch an arrangement of trees with quick and spontaneous strokes of colored chalk or paint. Select three colors for the trees. Use a sheet of colored paper that works well as a background.

CHAPTER 4 REVIEW

BUILDING VOCABULARY

Number a sheet of paper from 1 to 15. After each number, write the term from the box that best matches each description below.

analogous colors	line variation
color wheel	monochromatic
complementary	colors
colors	motif
form	shape
hue	space
intensity	texture
line	value
line quality	

1. Colors opposite each other on the color wheel.
2. An area clearly set off by one or more of the other five visual elements of art.
3. Different values of a single hue.
4. The name of a color and its place on the color wheel.
5. An object with three dimensions.
6. The brightness or dullness of a hue.
7. The lightness or darkness of a hue.
8. Colors that share a hue and are side by side on the color wheel.
9. The distance or area around, between, above, below, and within things.
10. How things feel, or look as though they might feel, if touched.
11. The path of a dot through space.
12. A unit that is repeated in a pattern or visual rhythm.
13. Arrangement of hues in a circular format.
14. The unique character of any line.
15. The thickness or thinness of a line.

REVIEWING ART FACTS

Number a sheet of paper from 16 to 22. Answer each question in a complete sentence.

16. What is a risk of using monochromatic colors?

17. What effect can be achieved by using complementary color schemes?
18. How does a trained artist use line?
19. What are some adjectives that could be used to describe horizontal lines?
20. What is the difference between line quality and line variation?
21. What is the relationship between shape and form?
22. Describe one way you can create different textures, using paints.

THINKING ABOUT ART

On a sheet of paper, answer each question in a sentence or two.

1. **Analyze.** Imagine that you are helping paint a mural for the new school gymnasium. You have just finished painting a happy-looking section in red. You notice a student moving toward the section carrying a jar of green paint. What words of caution about the blending of colors might you pass along to this student?
2. **Compare and contrast.** In what ways are the elements of form and shape alike? In what ways are they different?

MAKING ART CONNECTIONS

1. **Science.** One way artists develop new images from subject matter is to change the distance from which they view it. As an object is viewed through the microscope, greater detail is observed and the image changes. Try drawing leaves and other objects while looking through the microscope.
2. **Language Arts.** Think about the color expressions used on page **56**. Explain what is meant by these expressions and why certain colors are used. List other color expressions that you can think of.

LOOKING AT THE DETAILS

The picture shown below is a detail from Paul Cézanne's *The Bay of Marseille, Seen from L'Estaque*. Study the detail and answer the following questions.

1. What techniques did Cézanne use to turn shapes into forms?
2. What are some things that this landscape communicates to you? Is it a quiet place? Is it a modern city or resort? Talk about color hues, intensity and value when explaining your answer.

3. Cézanne used both warm and cool color schemes. What effect does this have? How are the schemes brought together to create a unified whole?
4. How does Paul Cézanne's use of space differ from Elizabeth Murray's on page **60**? What effect does it have?
5. What do you think are some of the different ways color can affect a painting?

Paul Cézanne. *The Bay of Marseille, Seen from L'Estaque.* 1886–90. Oil on canvas. (Detail.) 80.8 x 99.8 cm (31⅞ x 39¼"). The Art Institute of Chicago. Mr. & Mrs. Martin A. Ryerson Collection.

▲ How do the colors and shapes in this work make you feel? What do they remind you of? What do you suppose the title of the work means?

Hale Woodruff. *Poor Man's Cotton*. 1944. Watercolor on paper. 77.5 x 57.2 cm (30½ x 22½"). The Newark Museum, Newark, New Jersey. Sophronia Anderson Fund.

CHAPTER 5

The Principles of Art

Have you ever looked at a work of art and found yourself wondering what the point of it was? Look at the painting at the left. Can you find any "rhyme or reason" to it? Why do you suppose the artist chose the colors, the lines, or the shapes he did?

If art has at times seemed puzzling to you, that is because every work of art is a "puzzle." Its "pieces" have been carefully combined. In this chapter you will learn about the guidelines artists use to make works of art.

OBJECTIVES

After completing this chapter, you will be able to:

- Define the term *principle of art*.
- Explain the three kinds of balance.
- Tell how artists use the principles of variety, harmony, emphasis, proportion, movement, and rhythm.
- Explain what unity does for an art work.
- Practice organizing elements and principles in original art works.

WORDS YOU WILL LEARN

balance	proportion
emphasis	rhythm
harmony	unity
movement	variety
principles of art	

ARTISTS YOU WILL MEET

Umberto Boccioni	Henri Matisse
Bernardo Daddi	Georgia O'Keeffe
William Glackens	Jean-Baptiste-Joseph
Robert Gwathmey	Pater
Alexei von Jawlensky	Michel Sittow
Jasper Johns	Vincent van Gogh
Wassily Kandinsky	Hale Woodruff
Jacob Lawrence	

The Language of Design

You know that speakers of any language follow rules of grammar. These rules govern the way words can go together to form sentences. The language of art also has rules. They are called **principles of art**, *guidelines that govern the way elements go together*.

The principles of art are: balance, variety, harmony, emphasis, proportion, movement, and rhythm. Like the elements, the principles in a work of art are hard to single out.

In this lesson you will meet the first of the principles of art, balance.

THE PRINCIPLE OF BALANCE

When you ride a bicycle and lean too far to one side or the other, what happens? You fall over. In riding a bike, balance is important.

Balance is important in art, too. In art, **balance** is *arranging elements so that no one part of a work overpowers, or seems heavier than, any other part*. In the real world, balance can be measured on a scale. If two objects weigh the same, the two sides of the scale will balance. If they do not, one side of the scale will tip. In art, balance is seen or felt by the viewer. A big, bold splotch of color off to one side of a painting pulls the viewer's eye there. It can

▲ **Figure 5–1** What kind of feelings might the formal balance of this church suggest? In what direction does the building seem to point? Why is this important?

Monastery of Oliva. Late 12th century. Oliva, Spain.

▲ **Figure 5–2** How different would this work have been if the artist had spread the figures around the picture?

Michel Sittow. *The Assumption of the Virgin.* c. 1500. Wood; painted surface. 21.3 x 16.5 cm (8⅜ x 6½"). National Gallery of Art, Washington, D.C. Ailsa Mellon Bruce Fund.

make the work seem lopsided. It can make the viewer feel uncomfortable.

Artists speak of three kinds of balance. These are formal balance, informal balance, and radial balance.

Formal Balance

Formal balance happens when one half of a work is a mirror image of the other half (Figure 5–1). Also called symmetrical balance (suh-**meh**-trih-kuhl), formal balance is the easiest type to notice. Because it is so predictable, using formal balance sometimes makes a work seem less interesting. This is not always the case. Look at the painting in Figure 5–2. Notice how the formal balance adds a feeling of quiet dignity to the work.

Informal Balance

In informal balance, two unlike objects are made to seem to have equal weight. The weight is suggested by the hues, values, intensities, and shapes of those objects. Also called asymmetrical balance (**ay**-suh-**meh**-trih-kuhl), informal balance often shows up in the way the artist has used color and shape. A small shape painted bright red will balance several larger shapes painted in duller hues. (See Figure 5–3.)

▲ **Figure 5–3** Where does your eye move first when you look at this picture? Why do you think this is so?

William Glackens. *Family Group.* 1910–1911. Canvas. 182.9 x 213.4 cm (72 x 84″). National Gallery of Art, Washington, D.C. Gift of Mr. & Mrs. Ira Glackens.

Informal balance is often used to create more interesting compositions. Arranging objects or elements informally can be very complicated, but can create visual interest when used skillfully.

Radial Balance

Radial balance happens when elements or objects in an art work are positioned around a central point. A flower with its petals spreading outward from the center is an example of radial balance in nature. The stained-glass rose window in Figure 5–4 is an example of radial balance in art.

▲ **Figure 5–4** An identical pattern is repeated several times in this cathedral window, nevertheless it holds our eye. Why?

Rose Window, Burgos Cathedral. 14th century. Burgos, Spain.

✔ CHECK YOUR UNDERSTANDING

1. Define principles of art.
2. List the principles of art.
3. What is balance?
4. Describe the three kinds of balance.

Formal Balance Cityscape

Look at the painting in Figure 5–5. This cityscape of New York City was painted by Georgia O'Keeffe. In many of her works she uses formal balance to give them a sense of dignity. To avoid boring the viewer, she uses approximate symmetry. That means that both sides of the work are not a perfect mirror image of each other.

The center of this painting is the Radiator Building. Notice that the top of the sky-scraper is symmetrical. However, the symmetry at the middle of the painting is not quite perfect. Do you see how the bright red rectangle catches your attention? It is balanced by the white and blue-green smoke on the opposite side.

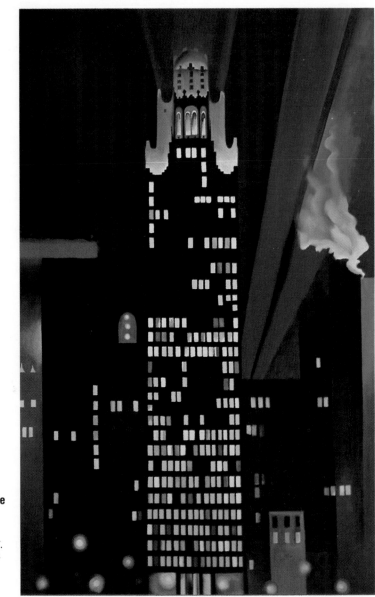

▶ **Figure 5–5 How is color used to achieve balance in this cityscape? How is shape and line configuration used?**

Georgia O'Keeffe. *Radiator Building—Night—New York.* 1927. Oil on canvas. 121.9 x 76.2 cm (48 x 30"). Carl Van Stieglitz Gallery of Fine Arts at Fisk University. Alfred Stieglitz Collection.

WHAT YOU WILL LEARN

You will create a night cityscape or a city scene, using formal balance. To make your work more interesting, you will use approximate symmetry. To create the nighttime effect that O'Keeffe captured, you will work with oil pastels on black paper.

WHAT YOU WILL NEED

- Pencil and sketch paper
- White chalk, gum eraser
- A sheet of black construction paper, 12 x 18 inch (30 x 46 cm)
- Oil pastels

WHAT YOU WILL DO

1. Do visual research. Study photographs of interesting city buildings, including skyscrapers. Make sketches of the buildings with the most interesting shapes. As you sketch the buildings, make changes that you think will make them more interesting. See how another student achieved formal balance in Figure 5–6.
2. Plan your composition. On your sketch paper make several plans for arranging your own city buildings using symmetry. Vary the sizes and shapes of your buildings. You may use one large building in the center, or you may have two almost equal shapes on either side of the center.
3. Choose your best plan and change it so that it becomes a design using approximate symmetry. Remember, to achieve approximate symmetry, your work must be almost symmetrical. Study O'Keeffe's painting in Figure 5–5 for ideas. Notice how she uses the dark blue rays of light to balance the large gray arched window. What effect is created by the yellow in some windows?

EXAMINING YOUR WORK

- **Describe**   Identify the sources you used for your inspiration. Describe how you changed the original shapes to make your own building shapes. Tell what colors you used to achieve a nighttime effect.
- **Analyze**   Tell how you created symmetry in your work. Identify the changes you made to achieve approximate symmetry.

4. Using the white chalk, draw your composition on the black paper. Press very lightly so that you can erase, if necessary, with the gum eraser without tearing the surface of the paper. If you press hard, the chalk may make a dent in the paper.
5. Add color with oil pastels. To keep the night effect, let the brightest colors come from the window shapes. (See Technique Tip 3, *Handbook* page **271**, for oil pastel techniques.)
6. Display your finished cityscape.

▲ **Figure 5–6   Student work. A formal balance cityscape.**

OTHER STUDIO IDEAS

- Use the same instructions to create a daytime effect on white or yellow paper.
- ●● Do a nighttime landscape using informal balance and the same materials.

Variety, Harmony, Emphasis, and Proportion

You may have heard it said that "variety is the spice of life." Variety is also the spice of art. The principle of variety and three others, harmony, emphasis, and proportion, make works of art interesting and pleasing to view. In this lesson you will learn how these principles are used by the artist to create art.

THE PRINCIPLE OF VARIETY

Imagine that you had to eat the same food every day for a whole year. Even if the food were your absolute favorite, after a while you would grow tired of it. You would long for other things to eat—even things you disliked—just for the change of pace.

▶ Figure 5–7   Point to the different colors in this painting. How many kinds of lines can you count? How many shapes? How many textures?

Henri Matisse. *Woman in a Purple Coat*. 1937. Oil on canvas. 81.3 x 64.1 cm (32 x 25¼"). The Museum of Fine Arts, Houston, Texas. John A. and Audrey Jones Beck Collection

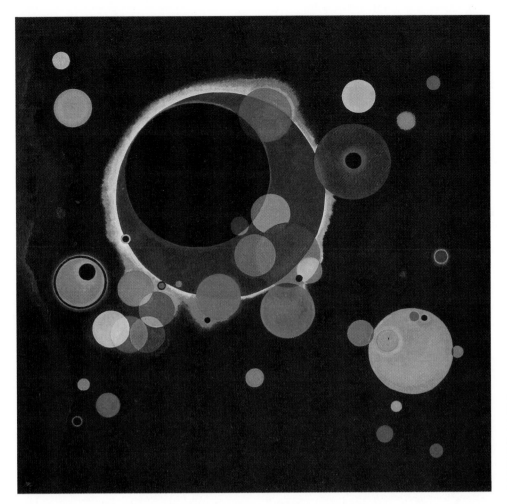

◄ **Figure 5–8 Which shape brings harmony to this work?**

Wassily Kandinsky. *Several Circles*. 1926. Oil on canvas. 140.3 x 141 cm (55¼ x 55⅜"). Solomon R. Guggenheim Museum, New York, New York. Gift of Solomon R. Guggenheim.

People need change to keep their lives interesting. The same goes for art. In art, **variety** is *combining one or more elements to create interest*. By giving a work variety, the artist heightens the visual appeal of the work.

Variety may be brought into play in many different ways. Light values of a color may be used to break the sameness of mostly dark values of that color. Straight lines can be a welcome change in a work made up mainly of curved lines. Which elements show variety in the work in Figure 5–7?

THE PRINCIPLE OF HARMONY

On the opposite side of the coin from variety is harmony. **Harmony** in art, as in mu-

sic, is *blending elements in a pleasing way*. Harmony is uncomplicated and soothing. Often artists use a small number of the same elements again and again, or in repetition, to bring harmony to a work of art. (See Figure 5–8.)

Skilled artists use the principles of harmony and variety together in different amounts to bind the parts of a work to the whole. Too much variety and too little harmony in a work can make it complicated and confusing. Focusing only on harmony, on the other hand, can make a work humdrum and uninteresting. Notice how the artist of the work in Figure 5–8 combines harmony and variety.

THE PRINCIPLE OF EMPHASIS

When people want to call attention to an important word in a sentence, they will underline it. Underlining a word makes that word stand out from the rest of the words in the message. It gives it emphasis.

Artists also use emphasis in their messages to viewers. In art, **emphasis** is *making an element or object in a work stand out*. The use of this principle helps the artist control what part of a work the viewer looks at first. It also helps the artist control how long the viewer will spend looking at each of the different parts. Emphasis can be created by contrast, or extreme changes in an element.

In the painting in Figure 5–9 several groups of figures are shown. One of these groups seems more important than the others. Can you identify that group? Can you tell why it caught your attention?

THE PRINCIPLE OF PROPORTION

Have you ever tried on a piece of clothing and found that it made you look shorter or taller than you actually are? Perhaps the problem was one of proportion. In art, **proportion** is *how parts of a work relate to each other and to the whole*.

▲ **Figure 5–9**   Besides value contrast, what techniques call attention to the group of people that includes the girl in white?

Jean-Baptiste-Joseph Pater. *Fête Champêtre*. 1730. Canvas. 74.6 x 92.7 cm (29⅜ x 36½"). National Gallery of Art, Washington, D.C. Samuel H. Kress Collection.

Look at the painting in Figure 5–10. Notice how the artist points out the main figures in the work by making them larger than the rest.

Proportion as an art principle is not limited to size. Elements such as color can be used in differing proportions. What is the key color in the work in Figure 5–11? What do you think was the artist's reason for using this color as he did?

▲ **Figure 5–11** What has the artist done to make the element of color stand out? What one color is used most?

Alexei von Jawlensky. *Portrait of a Woman*. 1910. Oil on panel. 53 x 49.5 cm (20⅞ x 19½"). The Museum of Fine Arts, Houston, Texas. John A. and Audrey Jones Beck Collection.

▲ **Figure 5–10** Which figures are the largest? Why are they larger than the other figures? Who are they? Who are the figures in the "supporting roles"?

Bernardo Daddi. *Madonna and Child with Saints and Angels*. 1330. Wood. 50.2 x 24.1 cm (19¾ x 9½"). National Gallery of Art, Washington, D.C. Samuel H. Kress Collection.

✔CHECK YOUR UNDERSTANDING

1. Name two ways artists can achieve variety in works of art.
2. How do artists achieve harmony in works of art?
3. What is emphasis? What two things does using this principle enable an artist to do?
4. What is proportion? How do artists use proportion?

Abstract Painting

Look at the painting in Figure 5–12. Notice how Robert Gwathmey has used the principles of variety, harmony, emphasis, and proportion. He has used a red color scheme to create harmony. Variety is introduced through different sizes and different shapes. Notice that the land, sky, and church are simple rectangles. The people are composed of geometric and free form shapes. Hands and feet are very small, arms are thin, and the shapes of the bodies vary.

As you study the painting you will notice that all the busy shapes in the foreground lead your eyes to the dark simple church on the horizon. Gwathmey emphasizes the church by isolating it and making it a different shape and a different value.

▲ **Figure 5–12** **How does the artist create depth and contrast in this painting?**

Robert Gwathmey. *Country Gospel Music*. 1971. Oil on canvas. 101.6 x 127 cm (40 x 50"). Terry Dintenfass Gallery, New York, New York.

WHAT YOU WILL LEARN

You will create an abstract painting using the principles of harmony, variety, and emphasis. You will use a variety of lines to draw shapes that vary in size from very large to very small. You will add harmony to your work by using different light and dark values of a single hue to paint the shapes and the negative spaces. You will emphasize a center of interest by painting one small shape the complement of the hue used.

WHAT YOU WILL NEED

- Pencil and sketch paper
- Sheet of white paper, 12 x 18 inch (30 x 46 cm)
- Colored chalk, gum eraser
- Tempera paints and thick and thin brushes
- Newspaper

WHAT YOU WILL DO

1. Make several sketches on your sketch paper to plan your composition. Decide how you will use a variety of lines to divide your paper into shapes. Using vertical, horizontal, diagonal, curved, and zigzag lines, vary the shape from large to small.

EXAMINING YOUR WORK

- **Describe** What hue did you choose for your monochromatic color scheme? What hue was the complement of that hue? Identify the lines you used to create shapes.
- **Analyze** How did you create a variety in your painting? Tell how color was used to create harmony. Identify the object of emphasis.

2. Select your best plan. Draw it, freehand, on the large white paper with a piece of colored chalk. If you need to make corrections, use the soft gum eraser so that you don't tear the paper.
3. Select one hue. Use black and white paint to create a variety of tints and shades of that hue. Select one shape to be the center of interest. Leave it white for now. Paint the rest of the shapes with your hue and tints and shades of that hue. See Technique Tip **12**, *Handbook* page **274** on mixing colors.
4. Paint the center of interest with the complement of the hue you used in your painting.
5. Place your work on display with your classmates. Can you find similarities and differences in the works?

OTHER STUDIO IDEAS

- Create a design for your painting using objects you like instead of abstract shapes. Harmonize the colors and introduce variety through size. Use a complementary color to create emphasis.
- • Create an abstract composition in construction paper using warm colors for your shapes. Select a sheet of colored construction paper that works well with the other colors. Cut as many shapes as you think you will need, varying the size of the shapes. Repeat some of the sizes for both shapes to create harmony. Arrange your shapes in several different positions until they balance and then glue them to the background sheet.

Movement and Rhythm

Have you ever thrown a rock in a pond and watched the concentric circles that followed? Have you traveled down the highway and watched the telephone lines passing by? These are two examples of movement and rhythm.

In this lesson you will learn about the principles of movement and rhythm.

THE PRINCIPLE OF MOVEMENT

You live in an age of special effects. When you go to the movies nowadays, you see strange life forms arriving from different galaxies. You see humans traveling backward in time or dancing with cartoon figures. These amazing sights and others like them are possible only through creative imaginations and special effects.

In art, special effects are nothing new. Artists have been using them for a long time. One of these effects is movement. **Movement** is *the principle of art that leads the viewer to sense action in a work or it can be the path the viewer's eye follows throughout a work.* Artists create movement through a careful blending of elements like line and shape. (See Figure 5–13.)

Through the principle of movement, the artist is able to guide the viewer's eye from one part of a painting to the next. Notice how the lines in Jean-Baptiste-Joseph Pater's painting in Figure 5–9 on page **86** carry your eye toward the girl in white. The trees and the people seem to be leaning toward her.

THE PRINCIPLE OF RHYTHM

Have you ever found yourself tapping your fingers or feet to the beat of a song? Songs can have catchy rhythms. Sometimes it seems as though we can feel these rhythms as well as hear them.

▶ **Figure 5–13 By repeating lines and shapes, the artist helps us see the movement of a speeding cyclist.**

Umberto Boccioni. *Study for Dynamic Force of a Cyclist I.* 1913. Ink wash and pencil on paper. 20.5 x 30.5 cm (8¹/₁₆ x 12"). Yale University Art Gallery, Connecticut. Gift of Societe Anonyme.

In art, we feel rhythms as well as see them. To the artist, **rhythm** is *the repeating of an element to make a work seem active*. Look at Figure 5–14. The artist uses rhythm to make his painting come alive. By carefully mixing shapes and colors, he gets your eye to move to the painting's "beat."

Sometimes, to create rhythm, artists will repeat not just elements but the same exact objects over and over. When they do this, a pattern is formed.

✔CHECK YOUR UNDERSTANDING

1. What is movement?
2. What is rhythm?
3. What does an artist create by repeating an object again and again?

▼ **Figure 5–14   Which element creates rhythm? Which element does the artist incorporate with the rhythm to give the painting a "beat"? How?**

Jasper Johns. *Between the Clock and the Bed*. 1981. Encaustic on canvas. 183.2 x 321 cm (72⅛ x 126⅜"). Museum of Modern Art, New York, New York. Given anonymously.

STUDIO EXPERIENCE

Draw five varying sizes of circles from small to large on a practice sheet of paper. Draw five different lengths and widths of a line (straight, curved, or zigzag) similar to the sizes of your circles on the same sheet. Do the same with a rectangle or square. Divide a sheet of white paper, 9 x 12 inch (23 x 30 cm) into three equal 4-inch (10 cm) sections. In the top section draw a row of circles like those on your practice sheet from small to large. Gradually widen the space between each circle. The last circle may appear to leave the page if only a part can be drawn. Below the circles, draw a repeat of this pattern with the lines and shapes from your practice sheet. Notice how the size and spatial changes appear to create movement and rhythm from left to right within the section. Create new patterns of movement and rhythm in the remaining two sections.

Creating Visual Movement

This painting by Jacob Lawrence has a strong sense of visual movement. The artist has used several special effects to create the feeling that the soldiers are surging forward. (See Figure 5–15.) First he used diagonal lines to form arrow-like movement to the right. Notice how the guns and hats slant down to the right, while the bodies of the soldiers slant up to the right. Second, he has repeated lines and shapes to create a visual rhythm that makes your eye move through the painting from left to right. The repetition of the waving vertical grasses balances the strong movement. This helps to rest the viewers' eyes.

WHAT YOU WILL LEARN

You will create a construction paper design using repeated silhouettes of one action figure. You will use visual rhythm to create a sense of visual movement. Use a cool color for the background and warm colors for the figures.

WHAT YOU WILL NEED

- One whole action figure cut from a magazine (sports magazines are good sources)
- Scissors and fine-tip marker
- One sheet of cool-colored construction paper, 12 x 18 inch (30 x 46 cm)
- Several pieces of warm-colored construction paper, 9 x 12 inch (23 x 30 cm)
- Pencil, eraser, and glue
- Envelope to hold cutouts, 9 1/2 x 4 inch (24 x 10 cm)

▶ **Figure 5–15 What are the elements used in repetition? How do they also provide harmony?**

Jacob Lawrence. *Toussaint L'Overture Series.* 1938. Tempera on paper. 46.4 x 61.6 cm (18¼ x 24¼"). Fisk University.

WHAT YOU WILL DO

1. Look through magazines and newspapers to find a whole body of an action figure. Be sure the figure is complete with both hands and feet.
2. Using a fine-tip marker, outline the figure. Then carefully cut out the figure by cutting along the outline. You will use this figure for the motif of your design.
3. Select a sheet of cool-colored construction paper. This will be used for your background. Select several sheets of smaller pieces of warm-colored construction paper. These will be used for the figures. (See Figure 5–16.)
4. Place the magazine cutout figure on a piece of construction paper and trace around it. Conserve paper by arranging the tracing on one side of the paper and using the other half for another cutout. Cut out five, seven, or nine figures or silhouettes. Keep them in the envelope until you are ready to use them.
5. Experiment with several arrangements of the silhouettes on the background. You may want to include the original magazine cutout to create a center of interest. The figures may overlap. When you have an arrangement that shows visual movement, glue it to the background piece of construction paper.
6. Display your design. Compare the designs with those of your classmates, and look for different rhythmic beats. Which designs have a strong sense of movement?

- **Describe**   Identify the action figure you selected. Did you cut it out carefully? What colors did you choose for the background? What colors did you choose for the cutout figures? Tell why, or why not, you chose to use the magazine cutout. Explain what kind of rhythm you created and how you achieved a feeling of visual movement.

▲ Figure 5–16   Student work. An action figure.

OTHER STUDIO IDEAS

- Do the visual movement problem above, but use complementary colors for the color scheme.

- • Create a rhythmic design, using geometric shapes, that has a strong sense of movement. Use cool colors for the shapes and a warm color for the background.

Unity in Art

When something breakable shatters—a vase, for example—it can never again be as it was. The pieces can be glued together, but the object will never be truly the same. The jagged seams will always be a reminder that the item is made up of separate parts.

When the pieces of an art puzzle are put together by a skilled artist, the seams do not show. The viewer cannot tell where one part ends and the next begins. The work has a oneness. It has unity.

UNITY IN ART

Unity is *the arrangement of elements and principles with media to create a feeling of completeness.* Unity in an art work is like an unseen glue. You cannot point to it as you can an element or principle, but you can sense it. You can also sense when it is missing. Look at Figure 5–17. The landscape below shows unity for many reasons. It seems to display a sense of completeness. Can you name the principles shown in this art work that make it have unity?

▲ **Figure 5–17** Van Gogh usually painted in brilliant colors with strong, passionate brush strokes. What do you think makes the painting show such a feeling of calmness?

Vincent van Gogh. *Garden of the Rectory at Nuenen.* Oil on canvas, mounted on panel. 53 x 78.2 cm (20⅞ x 30¾"). The Armand Hammer Foundation.

DESIGN CHART	PRINCIPLES OF ART					
	Balance	Variety	Harmony	Emphasis	Proportion	Movement/ Rhythm
Color: Hue						
Intensity						
Value						
Line						
Shape/Form						
Space						
Texture						

ELEMENTS OF ART

> UNITY

Note: Do not write on this chart.

▲ **Figure 5–18   Design chart.**

PLOTTING UNITY ON A CHART

Explaining how the parts of an art work fit together can be difficult. Using a design chart (Figure 5–18) makes the task easier. Notice that the chart shows the elements along the side and the principles along the top. Think of each square where an element and principle meet as a design question. Here, for example, are some questions that might be asked about hue.

- Is the balance of the hues formal, informal, or radial?
- Do the hues show variety?
- Is a single hue used throughout to add harmony?
- Is hue used to emphasize, or highlight, some part of the work?

- Is the proportion, or amount of hue greater or lesser than that of other elements?
- Does hue add to a sense of movement?
- Do hues repeat in a rhythmic way that adds action to the work?

Think about what questions you might ask about each of the remaining five elements.

✔ CHECK YOUR UNDERSTANDING

1. What is unity in art?
2. What does a design chart help you do?

BUILDING VOCABULARY

Number a sheet of paper from 1 to 9. After each number, write the term from the box that best matches each description below.

balance	proportion
emphasis	rhythm
harmony	unity
movement	variety
principles of art	

1. The rules that govern how the elements of art go together.
2. What a work has when no one part overpowers any other.
3. Mixing one or more elements for contrast.
4. Blending elements in a pleasing way.
5. Making an element or object in a work stand out.
6. The way parts of a work relate to each other.
7. The principle that leads a viewer to sense action in a work.
8. The repeating of an element again and again to make a work seem active.
9. Combining elements, principles, and media into an unbroken whole.

REVIEWING ART FACTS

Number a sheet of paper from 10 to 19. Answer each question in a complete sentence.

10. What kind of balance is shown in a work where one half mirrors the other?
11. What is another name for asymmetrical balance? For symmetrical balance?
12. Some artists think of radial balance as a complicated form of what other type of balance?
13. What can happen to a work when an artist overuses harmony?
14. What principle will an artist use to control which part of a work a viewer's eye sees first?
15. Is proportion in art limited to size of objects? Explain.
16. What principle will an artist use to carry the viewer's eye from one part of a work to the next?
17. What is a pattern?
18. What is another name for oneness?
19. What is a design chart used for?

THINKING ABOUT ART

On a sheet of paper, answer each question in a sentence or two.

1. **Extend.** What kind of balance is demonstrated by a design viewed in a kaleidoscope?
2. **Interpret.** How might an artist give emphasis to an object by using the element of line?
3. **Analyze.** Why might an artist choose to disobey the principle of proportion?
4. **Compare and contrast.** What do the principles of movement and rhythm have in common? How are they different?

MAKING ART CONNECTIONS

1. **Science.** Find examples from nature that represent formal, informal, and radial balance. Draw each example. Try looking at natural objects through a microscope and draw what you see. Group your drawings according to the type of balance. Think about the different principles of art. How do they relate to the designs found in nature?
2. **Industrial Arts.** Boccioni created *Study for Dynamic Force of a Cyclist I* (Figure 5–13, page **90**) in 1913. That same year Henry Ford introduced the conveyor belt assembly line. Find out what kinds of transportation were used at that time. Use repeated lines and shapes to create your own speeding vehicle from the same period.

LOOKING AT THE DETAILS

The detail shown below is from Hale Woodruff's *Poor Man's Cotton*. Study the detail and answer the following questions.

1. Would you describe this work as realistic? Why or why not?
2. The figures' garments are smooth and flowing and some of the faces are obscured and without detail. Why do you think the artist chose to omit certain details? For what purpose?

3. There is continuous, deliberate movement in this painting. How did Woodruff achieve this?
4. Which element or elements create rhythm in this work?
5. Do you feel a sense of unity in Woodruff's work? Why or why not?

Hale Woodruff. *Poor Man's Cotton.* 1944. Watercolor on paper. (Detail.) 77.5 x 57.2 cm (30½ x 22½"). The Newark Museum, Newark, New Jersey. Sophronia Anderson Fund.

▲ Would you view this painting differently if you knew when and where it was painted?
Would knowing something about the artist make a difference?

Berthe Morisot. *In the Dining Room*. 1886. Canvas. 61.3 x 50.0 cm (24⅛ x 19¾"). National Gallery
of Art, Washington, D.C. Chester Dale Collection.

You, the Art Critic

Life is full of new and enjoyable experiences. You hear a new song. You taste a food you have never before eaten. You see a piece of art that gives you a feeling of joy and excitement.

However, have you ever had the feeling, even after looking closely at a work of art, that you may be missing something? For example, when you look at the painting at the left, what do you see? Is there more you can learn about it to add to your understanding and appreciation of the work?

In this chapter you will learn about the steps you can take to answer these questions.

OBJECTIVES

After completing this chapter, you will be able to:
- Name the four steps used in art criticism.
- Explain how to describe objective and non-objective works of art.
- Define analyzing, interpreting, and judging.
- Apply art criticism to a work of art.

WORDS YOU WILL LEARN

analyzing	describing
applied art	interpreting
art critic	judging
art criticism	non-objective art

ARTISTS YOU WILL MEET

Pieter de Hooch	Berthe Morisot
Richard Estes	Raphael
El Greco	Milton Resnick
Grace Hartigan	Albert Pinkham Ryder
Barbara Hepworth	Andrew Wyeth

Describing Art Works

What do you think of when you hear the words art criticism? Do you think of someone saying they like a painting because the colors are vivid or the scenery is realistic? It is more than saying you like or do not like a piece of art. **Art criticism** is *the process of studying, understanding, and judging art works.*

A person who practices art criticism is called an **art critic**. Art critics learn as much as possible from all kinds of art work. They carefully study and examine works of art. They search for a meaning or message in the work. They gather facts that add to their understanding about the art work. Then this information is used to help them form judgments that can be supported with solid reasons.

You, too, can practice art criticism. You will find that it can help you:

- Examine and understand the art works of others.
- Study your own art works to determine how to improve them.
- Gain a better understanding and appreciation for all types and styles of art.

Every art critic has his or her way of doing things. By using the following four steps, you, also, can become an art critic. The four steps are:

- **Step 1:** Describing what is in the art work.
- **Step 2:** Analyzing how it is designed or put together.
- **Step 3:** Interpreting its meaning.
- **Step 4:** Judging its success.

In this lesson you will learn about the first of these steps, describing.

DESCRIBING OBJECTIVE ART WORKS

When you describe a work of art, you ask yourself the question "What do I see?" **Describing** is *making a careful list of all the things you see in the work.* In describing a work, you identify:

- The size of the work, the medium and process used.
- What people and objects you see and what is happening.
- The elements of art used.

In the describing stage, you report only the facts. You do not mention, for example, if the artist's use of many colors makes the painting confusing. That will come later in the judging stage.

Size, Medium, and Process

Describing the size and medium of a work is easy. You learned about credit lines in Chapter 2. The credit line gives the size, medium, and process used. In museums, this information appears on a card or paper near the work. Remember that the height of a work is always the first of the two numbers listed.

What is the size of Figure 6–1? What medium was used? What process was used?

Subject, Objects, and Details

Look again at the painting in Figure 6–1. A critic describing this work might begin by listing the people and other objects in it. Now it is your turn to be the art critic. How many figures do you see? Are all the figures the same distance from the viewer? Do some figures seem close to the viewer while others seem further away?

▲ **Figure 6–1** **What time of day or night is it? How are the figures dressed? What might this tell you about them?**

Pieter de Hooch. *The Bedroom.* c. 1660. Oil on canvas. 50.8 x 59.7 cm (20 x 23½"). National Gallery of Art, Washington, D.C. Widener Collection.

The critic would next tell what each figure was doing. The critic would note that the child has her hand on the door as though she has just entered. What other details might the critic mention? The critic might notice the quality of light entering the scene from the open door behind the child.

Finally, the critic would make a list of the furniture and other objects in the painting. What familiar pieces or objects do you see? Are there any that are unfamiliar?

DESIGN CHART	PRINCIPLES OF ART					
	Balance	Variety	Harmony	Emphasis	Proportion	Movement/ Rhythm
Color: Hue						
Intensity						
Value						
Line						
Shape/Form						
Space						
Texture						

ELEMENTS OF ART

UNITY

Note: Do not write on this chart.

▲ **Figure 6–2   Design Chart.**

Describing the Elements

The critic would next describe the way elements of color, line, texture, shape, and space are used in the work. To make it easier, the critic might make a checklist such as the one in Figure 6–2. On a sheet of paper, the critic would write the name of each element found in the work. Then next to each element, he or she would write a brief statement describing it.

As a critic, what hues can you identify in Figure 6–1? List them on the checklist. Then ask yourself what is the lightest value in the painting. Where is it found? Turning next to the element of line, you might ask whether the lines are thick or thin. You might then question the shapes. Are they flat two-dimensional shapes or are they solid, three-dimensional forms?

DESCRIBING NON-OBJECTIVE ART WORKS

How would you describe the painting in Figure 6–3? Would it make you feel uncomfortable because you cannot identify any objects? This type of work is called non-objective art. **Non-objective art** is *a work with no objects or subjects that can be readily identified*. Are such works passed over by critics?

Not at all! The critic's job, you will recall, is to describe what he or she sees. Since this work has no people, places, or objects, the critic will focus attention on the art elements. This is what the critic — or anyone else — will see in the work. This is called describing the formal aspects of a work.

How would you, the critic, describe the elements in this work? How many hues can you identify? Are the lines thick or thin? Are any straight lines used? What kinds of shapes are found?

The next time you look at a non-objective work of art and someone asks, "What do you see in that work?," point to the colors, lines, shapes, and other visual elements. Those were the concern of the artist. Concentrating on them will help you understand and appreciate the work.

▲ **Figure 6–3** **How did the artist use the element of space?**

Grace Hartigan. *The Far Away Places*. 1974. Oil on canvas. 228.6 x 166.4 cm (90 x 65½"). McNay Art Museum, San Antonio, Texas.

✔ CHECK YOUR UNDERSTANDING

1. What are the four steps of art criticism?
2. Describe one benefit of learning art criticism.
3. How can the credit line help you in describing art works?
4. What do you use to describe a non-objective work?

L E S S O N 2

Using Descriptive Techniques

Look at the painting by the Italian artist Raphael (**raf**-ee-l) in Figure 6–4. The man on horseback is Saint George. He is rescuing the woman in the red dress from a ferocious dragon. Do the figures and objects in the painting look real? What techniques has the artist used to get this result?

WHAT YOU WILL LEARN

In this studio lesson imagine that part of Raphael's painting is missing at the right side. Begin by making a description of this painting using the information on describing in Lesson 1. Then make a pencil drawing that continues the landscape in the painting at the viewer's right. Details of your drawing will reflect the ones in your description.

▶ **Figure 6–4   How is the element of space used differently in Raphael's painting than the one in Figure 6–3? What is the result?**

Raphael. *Saint George and the Dragon*. c. 1506. Oil on wood. 28.5 x 21.5 cm (11⅛ x 8⅜"). National Gallery of Art, Washington, D.C. Andrew W. Mellon Collection.

WHAT YOU WILL NEED

- Sheet of lined notebook paper and pencil
- Sheets of sketch paper
- Large sheet of white drawing paper

WHAT YOU WILL DO

1. Imagine that the right half of Raphael's painting of *St. George and the Dragon* is missing.
2. On your sheet of lined paper, describe what you see in this painting. Identify the figures and tell what each is doing. Pay special attention to details of the landscape. Notice how the artist used the elements of line, shape, and space.
3. Imagine the landscape as it might appear on the missing half. On sketch paper, practice sketching the half of the picture as you feel it would appear.
4. Use only lines and outlines of shapes in your drawing. Do not use shading. Create a feeling of deep space by having objects overlap. Distant objects should also be made smaller and with little detail.
5. Draw your completion of the landscape on a large sheet of white paper. Use your rough sketches and your description to guide you. Refer to the painting in the textbook. Match your sky, trees, flowers, and plants as carefully as you can. If you like, add another view of the city in the distance (Figure 6–5).
6. Share your work with your classmates. Look for differences and similarities between your own landscape and those of other students.

EXAMINING YOUR WORK

- **Describe**   Identify the trees, plants, rocks, and other objects in your work. Point to the place in your drawing where your trees and ground blend into the trees and ground in the painting.
- **Explain**   Referring to your description, identify the kinds of lines, shapes, and space found in the painting. Show examples of the same kinds of lines, shapes, and space in your drawing.

▲ Figure 6–5   Notice the city in the distance. What kinds of buildings would the city be made of?

Raphael. *Saint George and the Dragon*. c. 1506. Oil on wood. (Detail.) 28.5 x 21.5 cm (11⅛ x 8⅜"). National Gallery of Art, Washington, D.C. Andrew W. Mellon Collection.

OTHER STUDIO IDEAS

- Do a pencil sketch of a landscape you know well. Use at least two of the elements from the description you made for this lesson.
- ● Look through a magazine and find a picture of an outdoor scene which emphasizes one of the seasons. Cut out the picture and then cut the picture in half. Glue or tape the left half of the picture to your paper and continue the missing part using crayons or colored pencils.

Analyzing Art Works

Have you ever taken something apart to see how it works? In a way, that is what an art critic does in the second stage of art criticism. During this stage the critic analyzes by looking at the parts of the work to see how the whole was made.

ANALYZING ART WORKS

When you analyze a work of art, you ask yourself the question "How is the work organized?" **Analyzing** is *noting how the principles are used to organize the elements of color, line, texture, shape, form, and space.* Remember that some of the principles of art are balance, variety, and harmony. Can you name the other principles?

Look at the painting of *St. Martin and the Beggar* in Figure 6–6. To analyze this work, a critic might use a design chart like the one shown in Figure 6–2 on page **102**. The critic might notice the following:

- The painting is divided in half by an imaginary vertical line beginning with the right front leg of the horse (Figure 6–7). Trace the line upward with your finger from the right front leg of the horse, along the saddle blanket, through the center of St. Martin's breastplate, to his head. The different shapes are balanced on either side of this center line.
- Different values, textures, and shapes have been used to add variety to the picture. Can you point to different uses of each? How do these differences increase your visual interest?
- Other elements have been repeated to bring harmony to the work. What kinds of hues—warm or cool—has the artist used most? What kinds of lines are repeated more often—vertical or horizontal? What would happen if harmony had not been used?

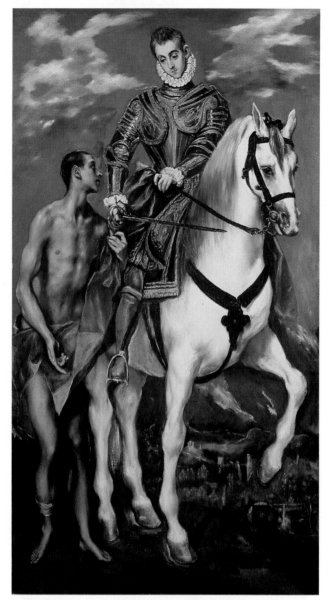

▲ Figure 6–6 How does texture and choice of color contribute to the realism in this painting? How do the shapes display proportion? Is there any movement in the painting? Where?

El Greco. *Saint Martin and the Beggar*. 1597/1599. Canvas. 193.5 x 102.8 cm (76⅛ x 40½"). National Gallery of Art, Washington, D.C. Widener Collection.

- The imaginary vertical line dividing the picture in half leads the viewer's eye directly to a single round shape. Can you find this shape? What else is done to emphasize the shape?

▲ Figure 6–7 (left) and Figure 6–8 (right)   What kind of balance is displayed on the left? What other technique did the artist use to emphasize the head of St. Martin?

El Greco. *Saint Martin and the Beggar.* 1597/1599. Canvas. 193.5 x 102.8 cm (76⅛ x 40½"). National Gallery of Art, Washington, D.C. Widener Collection.

STUDIO EXPERIENCE

Look back at Figure 6–4 on page **104**. Notice that the line of Saint George's lance leads the viewer's eye to the dragon. An imaginary line following the gaze of the saint also directs attention to the dragon. Look through a sports magazine for a photograph that shows action. Do a rough pencil sketch of the action scene. In your sketch, include lines that would lead a viewer's eye from one part of the scene to another. Your lines may be real (for example, the outstretched arm of a football player) or imaginary. Share your sketch with your classmates. See if your viewers can trace the lines in your sketch with their fingers.

- Many of the lines are used to direct the viewer's eye from one important point to another. Notice that one of the lines begins at the left side of the picture at the corner of St. Martin's cloak. It carries the eye upward, first to the head of the saint and then to the head of the beggar. (See Figure 6–8.)

You can use this same process for analyzing non-objective works. Look at the non-objective painting in Figure 6–9. Develop a design chart, and point out how the artist has used balance, variety, harmony, and the other principles to organize the elements in the painting.

✔CHECK YOUR UNDERSTANDING

1. What is the second step in art criticism?
2. What does an art critic do in the analysis stage of art criticism?
3. Why is a design chart helpful during analysis?

▲ Figure 6–9   Which hues are used for balance? Which ones for emphasis? Do they overlap? Which element provides harmony? Does it also add movement?

Milton Resnick. *Genie.* 1959. Oil on canvas. 264.2 x 177.8 cm (104 x 70"). Whitney Museum of American Art, New York, New York.

Interpreting Art Works

No two people see things exactly the same way. One person looks at a glass of water and sees it as half empty. Another person looks at the same glass and sees it as half full. What appears to be orange to you may look red to someone else.

People may, and often do, argue over their different views, or interpretations. In art, it is not unusual for two people to have different interpretations of the same art work. Since each interpretation can be based on different things found in the work, both can be right. When people share their opinions with other people, they learn something new about the work.

Interpreting is the third stage of art criticism. For the art critic, **interpreting** is *determining and explaining the meaning, mood, or idea of the work of art*. You will find that interpreting is the most exciting and creative part of art criticism.

INTERPRETING ART WORKS

When you interpret a work of art, you ask yourself two questions. One is "What do I believe is happening?" The other is "What idea, mood, or feeling does it suggest?"

Interpreting makes use of the facts and clues you gathered in the first two steps of criticism. But it also relies heavily on your ability to think things through and use your imagination. What you have done and seen in your life can also be important to your interpretation.

Look back at the painting in Figure 6–1 on page **101**. The artist has placed two people in the foreground. In step two of art criticism, a critic might have speculated this was done to emphasize these people. Now, in step three, the critic would ask questions that begin with who, what, where, when, why, or how. The answers to these questions help the critic arrive at an interpretation of the work.

INTERPRETING OBJECTIVE ART WORKS

Look at the child in the painting more closely (Figure 6–10). You be the critic. Who would you guess she is? How old would you suppose she is? What would you guess her feelings are? What clues can you find in the details to back up your theory?

Next, look back at the whole painting (Figure 6–1) on page **101**. Where is the woman looking? What does she seem to be looking at? (To answer this question, follow the line of her eye.) What is her expression?

Having answered these questions, a critic might give the following interpretation:

- The little girl in the work could be the daughter of the woman. (The woman is the right age to be the child's mother. They are in a bedroom of a house. The mother is looking fondly at the child.)
- The child is aglow with anticipation. (She looks as though she has just run in the house to tell her mother something.)
- She is carrying a ball and her cheeks are flushed. (She has been playing outside.)
- The background shows green trees and bushes in bloom. (A clue to the time of year, making it seem even more possible that the child has been playing outside.)
- The house is well-furnished and clean. The mother and child are well-dressed. (This indicates a certain level of social and economic status.)

In order to reach these conclusions, the critic would have to know about the customs and the way people lived in that period of history. Knowing clothing and architectural styles would also be important for interpreting art works.

INTERPRETING NON-OBJECTIVE ART WORKS

Pictures without subjects can also express ideas and feelings. Look at the painting in Figure 6–9 on page **107**. Notice how the overall pattern of lines and splashes of color creates a feeling of action and excitement in Milton Resnick's painting. Compare this with the feeling of calm stillness in the non-objective painting in Figure 6–3.

✔CHECK YOUR UNDERSTANDING

1. Define interpreting, as the term is used in art criticism.
2. What two questions do you ask yourself when you interpret a work?
3. Name three different sources of information a critic might use in an interpretation of an art work.
4. What words identify the six questions critics try to answer when interpreting a work of art?

Mood Chalk Painting

Look at the work in Figure 6–11. This seascape, or painting of the sea, was done by the American artist Albert Pinkham Ryder. Notice that the work is made up of simple shapes and few colors. No object is clearly shown. There is hardly any detail. Yet the quiet, calm mood of this moonlit scene is almost impossible to miss.

WHAT YOU WILL LEARN

You will use colored chalk to create another version of the seascape in Figure 6–11. Your version will include simple shapes of sailboats, the sea, the moon, and clouds. Repeat some of these shapes throughout the work to give it harmony. Your seascape, too, will focus mainly on mood. Yours, however, will express a mood opposite that of the original. Look at Figure 6–12 to see how a student captured an opposite mood from the original painting (Figure 6–11). You will choose four colors that help capture that mood. Repeating these colors will also add harmony to your work.

WHAT YOU WILL NEED

- Pencil
- Notepad
- Sketch paper
- Sheet of rough sandpaper, 10 x 12 inch (25 x 30 cm)
- Colored chalk

▶ **Figure 6–11   The artist who did this work lived as a hermit in New York City and only went out at night. He painted mostly from his imagination.**

Albert Pinkham Ryder. *The Toilers of the Sea*. 1880s. Oil on wood. 29.2 x 30.5 cm (11½ x 12"). The Metropolitan Museum of Art, New York, New York. George A. Hearn Fund.

WHAT YOU WILL DO

1. After looking at Ryder's seascape in Figure 6–11, brainstorm with your classmates to come up with words meaning the opposite of quiet and calm. Two possibilities are stormy and rough. Try to come up with at least four more words. Write these on your notepad.

2. On a sheet of sketch paper, lightly draw shapes of sailboats, the sea, the moon, and clouds. Keep your shapes simple, like those in Figure 6–11. Add no details beyond those in the original work.

3. Review the list of terms you copied. Think of colors that capture the mood expressed by these terms. Write the names of four of these colors on your notepad. Look back at your sketch. Think of changes you could make in line and shape that would help express the new mood. Make those changes. Again, do not add any new objects or details.

4. Transfer your sketch to the sandpaper. Color in your shapes with the four colors of chalk you chose. Limiting your colors to four will help add harmony to your work.

5. Compare your finished seascape with those of your classmates. Can you guess the mood of each work? Which most successfully expressed a mood?

═══ SAFETY TIP ═══

Chalk, which creates dust, should be used in a room with good ventilation. Those with breathing problems should wear a dust mask or avoid using chalk altogether. Crayon or oil pastels can be used instead.

EXAMINING YOUR WORK

- **Describe** Point out the shapes of sailboats, the sea, the moon, and clouds in your work. Tell whether you added shapes and details that were not in the original. Identify the four colors you chose. Explain how you used colored chalk to obtain different effects in your work.
- **Analyze** Explain how your use of the same simple shapes in your work gives it a feeling of harmony. Tell how your use of four colors repeated throughout the work added to the feeling of harmony.
- **Interpret** Tell what mood your work communicates to the viewer. Explain what you did to communicate a mood opposite that communicated by Ryder's painting.

▲ Figure 6–12 Student work. A mood chalk painting.

OTHER STUDIO IDEAS

- Create another mood seascape. This time, lightly wet the sandpaper before applying color. Explain what difference this technique makes in the look of the work.

- ● Create a city skyline using chalk on sandpaper. Decide what objects you will need to include. The work should be made up of simple shapes and colors. It should also express the same mood found in Figure 6–11.

Judging Art Works

It is the responsibility of every judge to be fair and open-minded. This is true of judges who rule over courts of law. And it is equally true of critics who judge works of art. Neither type of judge would ever hand down a ruling without first looking at all the facts. Neither would ever pass judgment without giving reasons.

In this lesson you will learn what goes into the final step of art criticism, judging.

JUDGING ART WORKS

When you judge a work of art, you ask yourself two questions. The first of these is: "Is this a good or successful work?" The second is: "Why is it good or successful?" **Judging** means *making a decision about a work's success or lack of success and giving reasons to support that decision.*

Ways of Judging a Work

Do you remember the three aesthetic views on art that you learned about in Chapter 2? Some art scholars, you will recall, feel art should imitate the real world. For them, a work succeeds if it looks real.

Others believe that what is most important about a piece of art is its composition. For them, a work succeeds if the artist has used the principles of art to combine the elements of art into an interesting whole.

Still others hold that what counts most is the mood or feeling a work expresses. For them, a work succeeds if the viewer shares this feeling or mood when seeing it.

The judgment that an art critic makes will depend on the aesthetic view he or she accepts. Look at the painting of the telephone booths (Figure 6–13). A critic from the first aesthetic view might praise the work because it is true to life. A critic from the second aesthetic view might admire the work for the

▶ **Figure 6–13 Would you consider this painting successful? Why or why not?**

Richard Estes. *Telephone Booths.* 1968. Oil on canvas. 121.9 x 175.3 cm (48 x 69"). Allan Stone Galleries, New York. Tissean-Bornemisza.

way the artist has created visual movement through the repetition of lines, shapes and color. A critic from the third aesthetic view might say the painting captures the existing mood of a busy city.

Not all critics limit themselves to one view of art. Many feel that accepting a single view carries the risk of missing some exciting discoveries. If a person accepts all three views, what judgments might he or she make about the sculpture in Figure 6–14? How would you personally judge the work?

JUDGING APPLIED ART

Art criticism can be applied to the study of all areas of art, not just paintings, sculptures, and other kinds of fine art. One other area that can be, and often is studied, is applied art. You may recall that **applied art** is *art made to be functional, as well as visually pleasing.* Designing details for jewelry or making decorative furniture are examples of applied art.

▲ Figure 6–15   Does the chair's appearance make you want to sit in it? Why or why not?

Verner Panton. *Stacking Side Chair*. 1967. PU-foam Baydur. 83.6 x 48.9 x 59.7 cm (32⅝ x 19¼ x 23½"). Museum of Modern Art, New York, New York. Gift of Herman Miller AG.

In using art criticism for works of applied art, critics use the same four steps: describing, analyzing, interpreting, and judging. At the final step, however, the rules change. The critic no longer evaluates a work purely in terms of its appearance. It must also be judged on how well the work does its job. A chair may look beautiful, but if it is uncomfortable to sit in, it is not successful. (See Figure 6–15.)

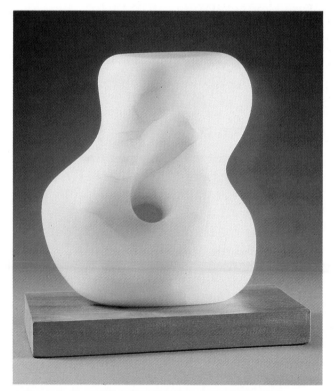

▲ Figure 6–14   Is this a "realistic" sculpture? What is its visual texture? What images does it evoke in your mind?

Barbara Hepworth. *Merryn*. 1962. Alabaster. 33.0 x 29.2 x 20.3 cm (13 x 11½ x 8"). National Museum of Women in the Arts, Washington, D.C. Wallace & Wilhelmina Holladay.

✔CHECK YOUR UNDERSTANDING

1. Define *judging*, as the term is used in art criticism.
2. What two questions do you ask yourself when you judge a work?
3. Describe briefly the three ways a critic can aesthetically view an art work.

Using Art Criticism

You have probably heard it said that experience is the best teacher. In this lesson you will discover the truth behind that saying. You will have the experience of using all four steps of art criticism on a single work.

The work you will criticize is the painting in Figure 6–16. Its title is *Christina's World*, and it was painted by an American artist, Andrew Wyeth.

DESCRIBING THE WORK

First, notice the size of the work and its medium. Try to imagine the full-size painting as it would look if it were in front of you right now. How might that affect the way you see the work?

Next, study the painting carefully. On a sheet of paper, write down every fact and detail you see. Use the following questions as a guide:

Subject

- What details about the girl's dress can you note?
- How would you describe the color and fabric of the girl's dress?
- Look at the folds in the dress. What do they tell you?
- Describe the color of the girl's belt.
- Look at the girl's hairdo. Notice the detail with which each hair is shown.
- Look closely at the girl's legs. What color are they? Is the color the same as that of her arms?
- Do you notice anything unusual about her arms or hands? Where is her left hand positioned?
- Look closely at the girl's posture. Where is all her weight resting?

Foreground

- Describe the girl's surroundings.
- In what direction do the blades of grass bend?
- How is the area where the girl is sitting different from the top of the hill?
- Describe the road.

Background

- How many buildings do you see and of what are they made?
- What facts can you gather from the background and grass? What colors are they?
- How are the buildings different?
- What color are the buildings? Do they look well-kept?
- How many chimneys do you see? Is there any smoke coming out of them?
- Do all the windows look the same?
- What color is the sky? How much of the picture is sky and how much is ground?
- What point of view do you think the artist is giving the viewer?

Design Elements

- What kinds of lines has the artist used for the buildings and for the line between the ground and sky?
- What lines are used for the girl?
- Describe the texture of the girl's dress, the grass, and the buildings?
- What kinds of colors do you see?

Try not to make guesses about the meaning of this work. Save your clues for later use.

◀ Figure 6–16   The vast area of grass is essential to the mood of the painting. Why? Where is the emphasis? Do you feel a sense of urgency?

Andrew Wyeth. *Christina's World*. 1948. Tempera on gessoed panel. 81.9 x 121.3 cm (32¼ x 47¾"). Museum of Modern Art, New York, New York.

ANALYZING THE WORK

What kind of balance has the artist used? What has been done to give the work variety? How is harmony achieved? Is anything in the painting emphasized? If so, what?

How does the artist control the way your eyes move through the work? Hold a ruler along the left slope of the roof on the biggest building. Where does the line lead your eye? Does the artist use accurate proportion to represent objects?

INTERPRETING THE WORK

Reread the clues you have gathered. What might the artist be telling you about the girl and about the world she lives in? When you imagined yourself in the girl's pose, did you feel the weight on your arms? Were your legs carrying your weight?

Why do you think the artist includes such a large area of ground in the work? Why has he shown separate blades of grass? How do you think the girl feels? Why do you think she feels this way? Whose house is it?

Do you think the title is appropriate? How does it help you interpret this work? Can you think of several adjectives that describe this work? What title would you give it?

JUDGING THE WORK

Tell whether the painting succeeds. Give the reasons why you feel as you do. Does the painting make you think? Why, or why not? Does it succeed in one of the following ways?

- It is lifelike.
- It uses the elements and principles to create an unusually interesting whole.
- It communicates a feeling or mood to the viewer.

Does the work succeed in more than one of these ways? Which ones? Explain your answer.

✔ CHECK YOUR UNDERSTANDING

1. List the four steps of art criticism.
2. List the three ways a critic could aesthetically view *Christina's World*.

BUILDING VOCABULARY

Number a sheet of paper from 1 to 8. After each number, write the term from the box that best matches each description below.

analyzing	describing
applied art	interpreting
art critic	judging
art criticism	non-objective art

1. The process of studying, understanding, and judging works of art.
2. One who practices the four steps in art criticism.
3. Making a careful list of all the things you see in a work of art.
4. A work with no objects or subjects that can be readily identified.
5. Noting how the principles in a work are used to organize the elements.
6. Explaining the meaning or mood expressed by an art work.
7. Telling if and why a work of art succeeds or fails.
8. Art made to be functional as well as visually pleasing.

REVIEWING ART FACTS

Number a sheet of paper from 9 to 13. Answer each question in a complete sentence.

9. Name the four steps of art criticism.
10. In addition to describing the people, objects, and events shown in a work of art, name two other things you could identify in a description.
11. In a credit line, which is given first — the height of a work or the width?
12. Which step of art criticism answers the question "How is the work organized?"
13. In which part of art criticism does a design chart come in handy? Briefly tell how it is used.

THINKING ABOUT ART

On a sheet of paper, answer each question in a sentence or two.

1. **Analyze.** Look at Figure 6–3 on page **103**. Which aesthetic view would you use when judging this work? Explain your answer.
2. **Analyze.** Why do you think it might be important to take the size of a work into account in a criticism? Why might the medium be important?
3. **Extend.** What problems could arise if one critic used another's description in his or her criticism of a work?
4. **Interpret.** Explain how two critics using the same four steps could come up with different interpretations and judgments of a work.

MAKING ART CONNECTIONS

1. **Social Studies.** The works of Andrew Wyeth (Figure 6–16) and Milton Resnick (Figure 6–9) were produced only 11 years apart, yet they are very different from each other. Investigate this period in history to determine how each artist's work may have been influenced by current events.
2. **Language Arts.** Select an object from nature. Look at it closely and write a description of the object as if you were describing a work of art. Use each element and principle of art at least once in your description. Try reading your description to a classmate without telling what it is you are describing. Have your classmate draw the object as you describe it.
3. **Social Studies.** Use a world map to locate where each of the artists in the chapter lived. Tell when they lived and what was happening in the world at that time.

CHAPTER 6 REVIEW

LOOKING AT THE DETAILS

The detail shown below is from Berthe Morisot's *In the Dining Room*. Study the detail and answer the following questions.

1. Describe the objects you see here. What do the surroundings tell you about the young woman?
2. Examine Morisot's brush strokes and use of color. How would you describe the artist's style?

3. Is the artist successful in creating a mood? If so explain what kind of mood you sense.
4. In interpreting the work, you may want to know where this woman lives. Does this detail assist you in answering that question? Why?

Berthe Morisot. *In the Dining Room*. 1886. Canvas. (Detail.) 61.3 x 50.0 cm (24⅛ x 19¾"). National Gallery of Art, Washington, D.C. Chester Dale Collection.

▲ **What objects or elements does the artist emphasize in this work? What elements does he use to bring harmony to the work?**

Pablo Picasso. *Three Musicians*. 1921. Oil on canvas. 200.7 x 222.9 cm (6′7 x 7′3¾″). Museum of Modern Art, New York. Mrs. Simon Guggenheim Fund.

Art History and You

As you have seen, you can discover a lot by looking closely at works of art. When you look at the painting on the left, what do you see? You might notice the geometric angles. You might also comment on the use of line and color.

As you look at art works, you may also have questions. For example, you may wonder whether the work is similar to others done around the same time. You may ask who painted it and when. These questions are among many you will learn about in this chapter. These questions explore the whys, whens, and wheres of art.

OBJECTIVES

After completing this chapter, you will be able to:
- Define *art history*.
- Tell what is revealed through each of the four parts of the art historian's job.
- Define *style*.
- Tell how time and place influence a work of art.
- Create works of art in the styles of different art movements.

WORDS YOU WILL LEARN

analyzing	interpreting
art history	judging
art movement	Madonna
collage	Renaissance
describing	style
Fauves	

ARTISTS YOU WILL MEET

Georges Braque	Claude Monet
Jasper Francis Cropsey	Pablo Picasso
Edgar Degas	Raphael
André Derain	Pierre Auguste Renoir
Sir Jacob Epstein	Georges Seurat
Giotto	Élisabeth Vigée-
George Inness	Lebrun
Judith Leyster	Maurice de Vlaminck
Fra Filippo Lippi	Clarence H. White
Henri Matisse	

Describing—Who, When, and Where

In a very real sense, no artist works totally alone. To understand any art work fully, you need to do more than just look at it. You need to look beyond it. You need to know when and where the work was done. You need to know something about the artist who did it. You need to know about his or her style of making art.

These and other kinds of information are the subject of art history. **Art history** is *the study of art from past to present*. Art history looks at changes that take place in the field of art over time. It also looks at differences in the way art is made from place to place. People who work in the field of art history are called *art historians*.

Like art critics, art historians use many different approaches when they study art. Art historians, however, go outside the art work for many of their clues. Their goal is not to learn *from* a work, as art critics do. Rather, it is to learn *about* a work.

▲ Figure 7–1 **This painting was originally done as an advertisement for the Delaware Lackawanna & Western Railroad. The artist was hired by the company's first president. Is it similar to advertisements you see today? Explain.**

George Inness. *The Lackawanna Valley*. 1855. Canvas. 86.0 x 127.5 cm (33⅞ x 50¼"). National Gallery of Art, Washington, D.C. Gift of Mrs. Huttleston Rogers.

ART HISTORY

In doing their jobs, art historians may use the same four-step system you read about in the last chapter. They describe, analyze, interpret, and then judge. As you will see, however, each of these terms has a different meaning to the art historian.

In this lesson, you will look at the first of these steps.

DESCRIBING A WORK

To art historians, **describing** is *telling who did a work, and when and where it was done.* Look at the painting in Figure 7–1. To begin, the art historian would look to see whether the artist had signed the work. Check the lower left corner. What name do you see there? Suppose the historian had never heard of G. Inness. He or she would then turn to an art history book. This source would reveal that George Inness was the name of two painters, a father and a son. It would also tell that both men lived and worked in America in the 1800s.

A little further exploration might turn up these facts:

- This painting was done by the father.
- It was painted in 1855.
- The painter was 30 years old at the time.
- He had studied landscape painting on his own in both America and Europe.

The historian might also come across this one especially interesting and important detail: George Inness had been taking formal art lessons for only one month when he began work on this picture.

Now it is your turn to be an art historian. Study the painting of the child with the watering can (Figure 7–2). But before you do, cover up the credit line with your hand.

Now can you identify the artist who painted this picture? Can you find his or her name on the work? It starts with the letter *R*.

▲ **Figure 7–2** Why do you suppose art historians are not lucky enough to have credit lines to help them?

Auguste Renoir. *A Girl with a Watering Can*. 1876. 100.3 x 73.0 cm (39½ x 28¾"). National Gallery of Art, Washington, D.C. Chester Dale Collection.

Can you make out the two numbers after the name? These are the last two figures of the year the work was painted. Where could you go to find out the artist's full name or to find out the century when this work was done? What other things would you try to find out?

✔CHECK YOUR UNDERSTANDING

1. What is art history?
2. What four steps do art historians use in their work?
3. Where might an art historian find details about an artist's life?

Making a Mixed Media Self-Portrait

As you study art history, you will find that many artists painted portraits of themselves. These portraits are called self-portraits. By studying self-portraits, you can find out what the artist looked like, what kind of personality the artist had, and something about when and where he or she lived.

Look at the painting below (Figure 7–3). What can you tell about the artist? When and where do you think she lived? How would you describe her personality? What other things in the picture give you insight into the artist's life?

▶ **Figure 7–3 How would you describe the personality of this woman? Identify things in the painting that tell you where she lived and when she painted.**

Judith Leyster. *Self-Portrait.* c. 1635. Canvas. 74.4 x 65.3 cm (29⅜ x 25⅝"). National Gallery of Art, Washington, D.C. Gift of Mr. & Mrs. Robert Woods Bliss.

WHAT YOU WILL LEARN

In this lesson you will imagine you are a famous artist. You will create a self-portrait using mixed media. Your self-portrait can be realistic or abstract. You will organize colors, lines, shapes, and textures to depict your personality and interests. The self-portrait should identify when and where you live and what your interests are. You will use the principle of emphasis to call attention to your strongest personality trait.

WHAT YOU WILL NEED

- Pencil and scrap paper
- Sheet of white paper, 10 x 12 inch (25 x 30 cm)
- Found objects: buttons, string, yarn, stones, cardboard, feathers, ribbon, shells
- Scissors
- Glue
- Crayons, colored pencils, or markers

WHAT YOU WILL DO

1. On a sheet of scrap paper, write down some of your personality traits, such as outgoing, confident, shy, unpredictable, athletic, or boisterous. List traits that give you a distinctive personality.
2. Determine if you will make a realistic or an abstract self-portrait. Think about a point of emphasis in the self-portrait. For example, you may wish to emphasize your eyes because you have an expressive and warm personality. Your smile might be a point of emphasis if you have a happy, outgoing personality.
3. On another sheet of paper, if you're making a realistic portrait, sketch an outline of your face. You may use a side or front view. Think of lightweight found objects

EXAMINING YOUR WORK

- **Describe**   Explain how your portrait tells something about your appearance. Point to the objects that show when and where you live and what your interests are.
- **Analyze**   Identify whether the self-portrait is realistic or abstract. Explain how color, lines, shapes, and textures have been used to express your personality and interests. Explain how emphasis has been used to highlight your strongest personality trait.
- **Interpret**   Explain how a viewer might describe your personality and interests.
- **Judge**   Tell whether you feel your work succeeds. Explain your answers.

that can be added to the picture that represent when and where you live and your interests.
4. Choose your best sketch and transfer it to the sheet of white drawing paper. Your portrait may run off the edges of your paper if you wish.
5. Take found objects and arrange them on the paper so they tell the viewer more about you. Using a small amount of glue, attach them to the paper.
6. When the glue is dry, add colors, shapes and lines using crayons, colored pencils, or felt markers.
7. Share your finished work with your classmates.

OTHER STUDIO IDEAS

- Create a mixed media portrait of a favorite friend.

- ● Create a mixed media portrait of a famous person, portraying some of the skills, events, or organizations the person is noted for.

Analyzing Artistic Style

No two people have exactly the same handwriting. Their writing styles may be similar, but one may use a slightly bigger loop on the *j*'s or cross the letter *t* using a line that is slightly longer.

The same is true of artists. Each artist works in a way that is at least slightly different from any other artist. These differences are the key to stage two of the art historian's job—analyzing.

ANALYZING A WORK

You will recall that in the describing stage the art historian looks for a signature on a work. Sometimes there is no signature. Sometimes the historian does not need one because the artist's style speaks as clearly as any signature. **Style** is *an artist's personal way of expressing ideas in a work*. You may remember that many times artists develop their style by studying the work of others. *Noting the style of a work*, or **analyzing**, is what the art historian does during the next stage.

▲ Figure 7–4   How are lines and hues combined to show depth? How does the mood in this painting differ from the mood in Figure 7–5?

Jasper Francis Cropsey. *Autumn on the Hudson River.* 1860. Canvas. 152.5 x 274.3 (60 x 108").
National Gallery of Art, Washington, D.C. Gift of the Avalon Foundation.

▲ **Figure 7–5 Which element do you think was most important to this artist? Which do you think was the least important?**

André Derain. *The River Seine at Carrieres-sur-Seine*. 1905. Oil on canvas. 70.7 x 110.7 cm (27⅞ x 43½"). Kimbell Art Museum, Fort Worth, Texas.

Look back at the landscape by George Inness on page **120** (Figure 7–1). An art historian might note that the painting shows a lifelike, or realistic style. Which of the landscapes shown in Figure 7–4 and 7–5 also shows a realistic style? What words might you use to describe the style of the other work?

ART MOVEMENTS

Sometimes *a group of artists with similar styles who have banded together* form an **art movement**. One of these had its beginnings early in this century in France. It was known as the Fauve (**fohv**) movement. Fauves is a French word meaning "wild beasts," and artists who developed the new artistic style were known as the Fauves. **Fauve** refers to the art movement in which the artists used *wild intense color combinations in their paintings*. The Fauves were not interested in doing realistic art. Instead, they emphasized the colors in their works as a way of increasing the visual and emotional appeal. The landscape in Figure 7–5 is an example of a work in the Fauve style.

In analyzing a work, art historians will try to decide if it fits into a movement. Look at Figures 7–6 and 7–7 and be the art historian. Which of these paintings is done in the Fauve style? What details can you point to that support your decision?

▲ Figure 7–6   Compare this work with Figure 7–2 on page 121. Both paintings were done by the same artist. What similarities and differences can you find between the two works?

Auguste Renoir. *Regatta at Argenteuil*. 1874. Canvas. 32.4 x 45.6 cm (12¾ x 18"). National Gallery of Art, Washington, D.C. Ailsa Mellon Bruce Collection.

► Figure 7–7   Does this sailboat scene have a different feel from the one in Figure 7–6? Compare the use of elements in each painting. How do they contribute to the overall effect?

Maurice de Vlaminck. *Sailboats on the Seine*. Oil on canvas. 54.6 x 73.7 cm (21½ x 29"). Metropolitan Museum of Art, New York. Robert Lehman Collection.

Look again briefly at Figures 7–6 and 7–7. Study the work in this pair that you decided was *not* in the Fauve style. This work also came out of a movement. The movement, called Impressionism, also had its start in France in the late 1800s. This painting was done by a leader of the movement, Pierre Auguste Renoir (pee-**air** oh-**goost** ren-**wahr**).

As an art historian, how would you describe this style of Impressionist painting? What kinds of colors do you think its members liked to use? What kinds of lines do you think they liked? Can you see how they tried to show the effects of sunlight on the subject matter? Did you notice how the choppy brush strokes were used to reproduce the flickering quality of sunlight? As you practice the skills of an art historian, you can turn to your school or community library to help you find the answers.

▲ Figure 7–8 The artist used dabs and dashes of paint in an attempt to show the flickering effect of sunlight on trees, shrubs, and other objects. Do you think the painting captures the look of a bright summer afternoon?

Claude Monet. *The Artist's Garden at Vetheuil.* 1880. Canvas. 151.4 x 121.0 cm (59⅝ x 47⅝"). National Gallery of Art, Washington, D.C. Ailsa Mellon Bruce Collection.

✔CHECK YOUR UNDERSTANDING

1. Define *analyzing*, as the term is used by an art historian.
2. What is style as it relates to art?
3. Describe the features of an art work done in the Impressionist style.

Painting in the Fauve Style

Look at the painting in Figure 7–9. This was done by Henri Matisse (ahn-**ree** mah-**tees**), the leader of the Fauves whom you met in the last chapter. Notice that the room in the work is free of corners and shadows. What else can you observe from this style?

▲ **Figure 7–9** **Which objects in the painting are painted in the most detail? Which are painted in the least detail? What reason might the artist have had for leaving certain objects less finished than others?**

Henri Matisse. *The Red Studio*. 1911. Oil on canvas. 181 x 219.1 cm (71¼ x 7′2¼″). Museum of Modern Art, New York. Mrs. Simon Guggenheim Fund.

WHAT YOU WILL LEARN

Paint an interior scene in the Fauve style of Matisse. Start with a rough sketch and choose a single bold color for the background and paint shapes in the room in other bold colors. Create harmony in your work by repeating certain line and colors throughout.

WHAT YOU WILL NEED

- Pencil and eraser
- Sheets of scrap paper
- Sheet of white paper, 9 x 12 inch (23 x 30 cm) or larger
- Watercolor paint in bold hues
- Two watercolor brushes, one large and one with very fine bristles
- Jar of water
- Paper towels

WHAT YOU WILL DO

1. On a sheet of scrap paper, do a pencil sketch of an interior scene, such as your bedroom, living room, or classroom. (Notice how much detail Matisse gives to the chair in the right foreground in Figure 7–9.) For other objects, sketch only the outline. (Notice the grandfather clock against the back wall in Figure 7–9.) Do not worry about proportion or whether your shapes seem realistic.

2. Using pencil, lightly copy your sketch onto the sheet of white paper. Sign your name in pencil to the back of the paper.

3. Choose three special hues of watercolor paint. Do not use brown or black. One color is to be the background of your work. The other two are to be used for

EXAMINING YOUR WORK

- **Describe** Tell what bold hue you have used as a background color. Identify the objects you have included in your interior scene.
- **Analyze** Tell how your use of line and color adds harmony to your work.
- **Interpret** Identify the adjectives a viewer might use to describe the colors in your work.
- **Judge** Tell whether you feel your work succeeds. What aesthetic view would you use to support your judgment?

the details. Soften the paint by adding a few drops of water to each.

4. Load your large brush with the color you have picked for the background. Using broad strokes, cover the sheet of paper with color. Do not worry about leaving streaks. Set your paper aside to dry.

5. When the paint is totally dry, begin to add objects using the remaining two colors. Use less water to make your colors as strong as possible. Use one of the colors to paint outlines. Use your small brush to make narrow lines. (See Technique Tip 4, *Handbook* page **271** for information on how to make thick and thin lines with a brush.) Use the other color to fill in shapes. Refer to your sketch as you work.

6. Allow your painting to dry totally. Share your finished work with your classmates.

OTHER STUDIO IDEAS

- Create another work in the Fauve style showing an interior scene. Do this work using oil pastels or colored markers and a sheet of construction paper in a light value of a primary or secondary color.

- ●● Do an oil pastel of an interior scene. This time, work in the style of the Impressionists. (See page **127**.) In preparing your pencil sketch, use the technique that seemed to give the best result in the studio experience on page **127**.

LESSON 5

Interpreting Time and Place

Our lives are shaped by when and where we live. Today we take cars and televisions for granted. People living a hundred years ago had neither of these inventions.

In art, too, time, place, and world events can have a great influence on an artist. Artists living in wartime may create works very different from those done in peacetime. Ethnic background often influences an artist's work as well. In art, time and place are central to the art historian's interpreting of works.

INTERPRETING A WORK

Do you remember the three questions art historians ask when describing a work? Two of those questions are "when?" and "where?" In stage three, art historians follow up on their answers to those questions. **Interpreting** is *noting how time and place affect an artist's style and subject matter.*

Sometimes historians interpret a work by studying the impact of time and place on its style. At other times, they focus mainly on the subject matter used. At still other times, an interpretation takes both style and subject matter into account.

Interpreting for Style

In the late 1800s a new branch of art was born. This branch was photography. Thanks to photography, familiar subjects could now be viewed from new and unusual angles.

The art of photography opened new doors for painters and other artists. Some began experimenting with new rules for making art. Figures in paintings were now pushed off to the side, as they were in photos. Parts of objects were sometimes cut off by the edges of the work. Compare the works in Figures 7–10 and 7–11. What words might an art historian use in interpreting the style of the painting?

Interpreting for Subject Matter

Today when people make news, their pictures often appear in the newspaper. If the news is big enough, their pictures may appear on television. Where do you think pictures of famous people appeared before there was photography or television?

▲ **Figure 7–10** This photograph originally appeared in a magazine called *Camera Work*. The magazine was run by Alfred Stieglitz (steeg-luhts), an important American photographer.

Clarence H. White. *Ring Toss*. 1903. Photograph. International Museum of Photography at George Eastman House, Rochester, New York.

◀ **Figure 7–11** How would you describe the artist's use of the principle of balance? What do you think art critics at the time may have said when they saw this work?

Edgar Degas. *Four Dancers*. 1899. Canvas. 151.1 x 180.2 cm (59½ x 71"). National Gallery of Art, Washington, D.C. Chester Dale Collection.

▼ **Figure 7–12** Among this painter's subjects were queens and other famous people. These days we know what leaders and famous people look like from photographs. Where else do we see their faces?

Marie-Louise-Élisabeth Vigée-Lebrun. *Theresa, Countess Kinsky*. 1793. Oil on canvas. 137.4 x 99.8 cm (54⅛ x 39⅜"). Norton Simon Art Foundation.

They appeared in paintings and other works of art. Figure 7–12 is a painting of one such person who was famous in the 1700s. The artist herself was well-known as a painter of portraits. These facts would be uppermost in the mind of an art historian interpreting this work. As an art historian, what questions might you ask about the subject in the painting? Where would you go for answers?

Portraits are not the only example of art that keeps records of people and events. Look once again at the landscape by George Inness (Figure 7–1 on page **120**). The work is a reminder of what railroads were like in the 1800s. It is also a record of an event in the artist's own life. This was the first time George Inness was paid for a painting. It marked a turning point in his career. An art historian might note both these facts in an interpretation of the painting. What other facts might an historian want to note?

Interpreting for Style and Subject Matter

A period of great awakening in the arts in Europe in the 1500s is known as the Renaissance (**ren**-uh-sahns). **Renaissance** is a *French word meaning "rebirth."* Before the Renaissance, artists were thought of as skilled craftspeople. Their work was no more important than that of carpenters or stone cutters. During the Renaissance, however, artists suddenly gained new prestige. This was partly because of the enormous talents of many artists of the period. You have probably heard of Michelangelo (my-kuh-**lan**-juh-loh) and Leonardo da Vinci (lee-uh-**nahr**-doh duh **vin**-chee). Both of these highly gifted artists worked during the Renaissance.

Another artist of the period whom you already met was Raphael. (In Chapter 6, you studied his painting *St. George and the Dragon* page **104**.) Look at the painting in Figure 7–13. An art historian interpreting this work

▶ **Figure 7–13** This is thought to be the most beautiful of the many Madonnas Raphael painted. It was painted shortly before Raphael began work on *St. George and the Dragon*.

Raphael. *The Small Cowper Madonna*. c. 1505. Wood. 59.5 x 44.0 cm (23⅜ x 17⅜"). National Gallery of Art, Washington, D.C. Widener Collection.

would notice two things. First, like most of Raphael's paintings, this one has a religious subject. Do you know the figures in the work? Reading about the Renaissance, an art historian might learn the following:

- The Catholic Church was a great patron of the arts.
- The Catholic Church hired artists to paint and sculpt scenes from the Bible.
- The art works were used to decorate churches.
- Most people living in the 1500s were unable to read.

Through these church paintings, the people were able to understand the story of Christ without reading about him.

The second thing an art historian might notice is that the painting has a religious figure as a central theme or subject. During the Renaissance, the Madonna became a theme for many works of art. A **Madonna** is *a work showing the mother of Christ.* The word madonna means "my lady." Raphael alone painted over 300 Madonnas. Figure 7–14 shows a Madonna by another Renaissance painter. Compare it with Raphael's Madonna (Figure 7–13). Notice the circles, or bands, framing the figures' heads. Do you know what these are called? How might you describe the looks on the faces of the figures? What other style features do the two works share? In what ways are the works different?

▲ **Figure 7–14** What differences do you see in the use of art elements and art principles between the two paintings shown on these two pages?

Fra Filippo Lippi. *Madonna and Child.* 1440/1445. Wood. 80 x 51 cm (31⅜ x 20⅛"). National Gallery of Art, Washington, D.C. Samuel H. Kress Collection.

✔CHECK YOUR UNDERSTANDING

1. Define *interpreting*, as the term is used by an art historian.
2. What use did portraits have in the past?
3. What is a Madonna?
4. What and when was the Renaissance? How were artists thought of before the Renaissance and during the Renaissance?

Time and Place Collage

Look at Figure 7–15. This type of art work is called a collage. A **collage** (kuh-**lahzh**) is *art arranged from cut and torn materials pasted to a surface.* Some of the materials in this collage are clues to the time and place in which it was created. Look at the piece of newspaper on the left side. Can you read any of the words? Do you know what language they are? Can you guess? Where might you go to find out when this newspaper was first printed? What would these facts reveal about when the artist worked?

WHAT YOU WILL LEARN

You will make a collage out of scrap paper (Figure 7–16). The principles of art will be used to combine the colors, textures, and shapes into a visually interesting whole. Your collage will give clues about life in America today.

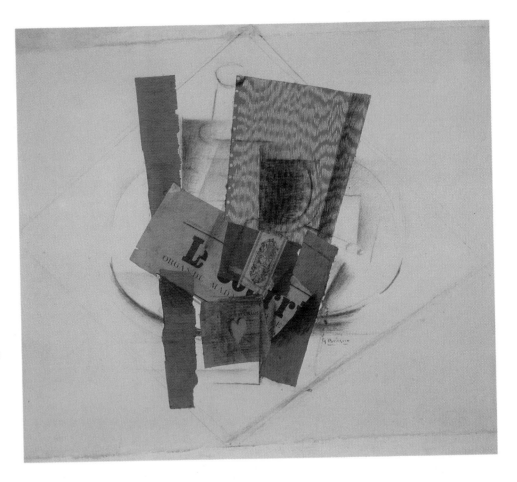

▶ **Figure 7–15　How many of the bits and pieces in this work can you identify? Do they add up to an interesting whole? Why or why not?**

Georges Braque. *Le Courrier.* Charcoal, gouache and printed paper collage. 50.6 x 57.8 cm (20¼ x 22¾"). Philadelphia Museum of Art. A. E. Gallatin Collection.

WHAT YOU WILL NEED

- Magazines and newspapers
- Scissors
- Pencil and sheets of sketch paper
- Poster board
- Slightly thinned white glue
- Small brush

WHAT YOU WILL DO

1. Turn through pages of newspapers and magazines. With scissors, clip out images that might depict life in America today. Use images of different sizes. You can use pictures or words from advertisements. Be as imaginative as you can in your choices.
2. Decide what materials will fill the spaces around your images. Again, be creative in choosing visually interesting colors, textures, shapes, and sizes. Clip the pieces out and set them aside.
3. Experiment with the pieces by arranging them on your poster board using the art principles. Pieces can overlap.
4. With the thinned glue and small brush, glue the pieces of your collage in place. Set your collage aside to dry.
5. *Optional.* You may want to use watercolor or tempera paint to help unify your composition. To do this, use a thin layer of paint to cover over some parts and accent others.

EXAMINING YOUR WORK

- **Describe**   Point to the images you clipped from newspapers or magazines. Tell what colors, textures, and shapes you chose.
- **Analyze**   Tell what principles you used to organize the elements into an interesting whole.
- **Interpret**   Tell what the images you chose reveal about life in America today. Point to images that show time, place, or both. Tell what overall feeling the viewer will have when seeing your work.
- **Judge**   Tell whether you feel your work succeeds. Explain your answer.

▲ **Figure 7–16   Student work. A time and place collage.**

OTHER STUDIO IDEAS

- Make a collage of things having to do with new food trends or your favorite food. Again, use magazine and newspaper clippings.

●● Make a collage of items promoting or representing your city or town.

Judging Historical Importance

What is the most important accomplishment that happened to you during the past week? What happened to you in the past month that was important? What event was an accomplishment during the past year? It is not likely your answer was the same for all three questions. For a few days doing well on a test or earning 20 extra dollars may seem like a big accomplishment. However, as days turn into months, your idea of what is important changes.

The same is true for art historians in the last stage of their work. In judging a work of art, they look at all aspects of the artist's work.

JUDGING A WORK

To art historians, judging is determining if a work of art makes a lasting contribution to the history of art. **Judging** is *deciding whether a work introduces a new style or if it is an outstanding example of an existing style*. It can also involve deciding whether a work makes a contribution to art by introducing a new style, technique, or a new medium.

Judging for Style

There are many ways in which pieces of art can make a contribution. One is by introducing a new style. Look again at Henri Matisse's painting of his studio (Figure 7–9) on page **128**. An art critic judging the painting would praise its bold colors. An art historian judging the painting would look beyond it. The historian would note how Matisse's use of bold colors influenced other artists and changed ideas about what is art. Do you remember the name of the art movement Matisse led? Do you remember what its members believed?

Look at the painting in Figure 7–17. It is a Madonna painted in the 1300s by an artist named Giotto (**jah**-toh). Is there anything in this work a historian would call new or striking? Is there any reason why the work should be judged important?

To the untrained eye today, Giotto's painting might seem stiff and awkward. To the art historian, however, there is more here than meets the eye. The historian would try to imagine himself or herself living in Giotto's time. Back then most Madonnas were like the one in Figure 7–18 on page **138**. True, this work does not look very realistic. But in the 1300s paintings seldom did. Pictures of religious figures were not meant to look real. They were painted to remind people of saints and prophets and to teach religious values. The golden lines in the drapery in Figure 7–18 were painted as a decorative pattern. No effort was made to make them look like real folds in real cloth.

The people in Giotto's day were shocked by Figure 7–17. His figures, compared with those in the typical Madonna, are lifelike. Although the traditional gold background is used, the figures do not appear flat. They give the impression of being rounded three-dimensional forms that stand out in space.

Now look again at Figure 7–18. The child in the work does not look or act like a real child. He seems to be giving his mother a lecture. Giotto's child, on the other hand, is more believable. He holds one of his mother's fingers as a real baby might.

Consider these points and tell how an art historian might judge this work. How would you judge it?

Giotto. *Madonna and Child*. c.1320/1330. Wood. 85.5 x 62.0 cm (33⅝ x 24⅜"). National Gallery of
Art, Washington, D.C. Samuel H. Kress Collection.

Judging for Technique

Another way a work of art can make a contribution is by introducing new techniques. Techniques are the ways an artist chooses to use a medium. This can be explained by taking a look at Figure 7–19. This painting was done by a French artist named Georges Seurat (suh-**rah**).

You can see by looking at Figure 7–19 that the technique used here differs from the technique used by other artists. Georges Seurat took a more scientific approach by combining thousands of dots of color. This made his paintings seem to shimmer with light. This is an example of how artists who use the same medium develop individual techniques.

◀ **Figure 7–18** **Paintings like this were thought to have great power. One famous Roman emperor carried one like it when he went into battle. These works were also thought to heal the sick and give sight to the blind.**

Byzantine XIII Century. *Enthroned Madonna and Child*. Wood. 131.1 x 76.8 cm (51⅝ x 30¼″). National Gallery of Art, Washington, D.C. Gift of Mrs. Otto H. Kahn.

▶ **Figure 7–19** **Is Seurat's technique successful in portraying the scene and conveying its mood? Where did he choose to concentrate on detail? Where is lack of detail displayed?**

Georges Seurat. *Sunday Afternoon on the Island of La Grande Jatte*. 1884-86. Oil on canvas. 207.6 x 308.0 cm (81¾ x 121¼″). The Art Institute of Chicago. Helen Birch Bartlett Memorial Collection.

▲ Figure 7–20 How would you describe the looks in the eyes of the two figures? What do these people seem to be feeling? Notice the mother's big feet. What other features has the sculptor used to make his subjects seem real?

Sir Jacob Epstein. *Madonna and Child*. Riverside Church, New York.

THE ART HISTORIAN AND HISTORY

If the historian's job is to look beyond works, should the historian look forward? Study the Madonna in Figure 7–20. This sculpture was done in the 1920s. It was finished 600 years after Giotto made his painting. Notice that this one is much more lifelike than Giotto's Madonna. The mother and child look like real people. They are similar to a mother and child you might meet on the street.

Does a work like this take away from the importance of Giotto's work? No. Changes in art happen little by little. Each age learns from and builds on advances made by earlier artists. A sculpture like this is made possible by the contributions of Giotto and others. Its creation is a testimony to the sensitivity and skill of artists who went before.

✔ CHECK YOUR UNDERSTANDING

1. Tell what the term judging means to an art historian.
2. What are two ways a work of art can make a contribution to the world of art?
3. How do changes in art happen?
4. Do artists learn from those who have created long before them?

CHAPTER 7 REVIEW

BUILDING VOCABULARY

Number a sheet of paper from 1 to 11. After each number, write the term from the box that best matches each description below.

analyzing	interpreting
art history	judging
art movement	Madonna
collage	Renaissance
describing	style
Fauves	

1. The study of art from past to present.
2. Identifying who did a work of art, and when and where it was done.
3. Noting an art work's style.
4. An artist's personal way of expressing ideas.
5. A group of artists with a similar style.
6. French art movement in which artists used wild blends of strong colors.
7. Noting the way that time and place affect an artist's style and subject matter.
8. A period of great awakening in the arts in Europe in the 1500s.
9. A work showing the mother of Christ.
10. A work made up of bits and pieces of objects pasted to a surface.
11. Deciding upon a work's place in art history.

REVIEWING ART FACTS

Number a sheet of paper from 12 to 20. Answer each question in a complete sentence.

12. In what ways is an art historian's approach to art different from an art critic's?
13. In describing a work of art, where does an art historian look first for an answer to the question "who"?
14. Why is style like a person's signature?
15. What did the Fauves believe in? When and where did they work?

16. What did the Impressionists believe in? Where did they work?
17. Where did pictures of famous people appear before the invention of photography?
18. Name two great artists of the Renaissance.
19. Name one way in which an art work might be judged as making a contribution to art history.
20. Explain how art works today often build upon the art works of the past.

THINKING ABOUT ART

On a sheet of paper, answer each question in a sentence or two.

1. **Extend.** Where else in a library besides art history books might you turn for information on an artist's life?
2. **Analyze.** Give an example of how time and place can affect style. How do time and place affect an artist's choice of subject matter?
3. **Compare and contrast.** How are describing and interpreting similar for an art historian? How are the two tasks different?

MAKING ART CONNECTIONS

1. **Home Economics.** Art history provides a look into the past to show us what people did, the things they used, and the clothes they wore. Look at the Renoir painting of the little girl on page **121**. Compare her clothing styles with the styles children wear today.
2. **Science.** Research methods used to date ancient artifacts and ways in which the art works contributed to a better understanding of the culture from which they came.

LOOKING AT THE DETAILS

The detail shown below is from Pablo Picasso's *Three Musicians*. Study the detail and answer the following questions.

1. At the turn of the century in Paris, Spanish born Pablo Picasso studied the works of the masters of his time, which included the Fauve artists and Impressionists. However, instead of merely imitating them, Picasso created a radically new and bold style, referred to as Cubism. Most of his fellow artists including Henri Matisse, disliked his work. What do you think are some of the reasons for this?

2. Compare this detail with the work of Henri Matisse on page **128**. What differences do you see? Would you consider Picasso's work as daring?

3. Does Picasso successfully organize the elements of art to create human forms? Explain.

4. Does it disturb you that the hands and faces are not realistically proportioned? Why or why not?

5. How does Picasso's Spanish heritage enter into this work?

6. As an art critic, how does knowing the time and place Picasso painted assist you in judging his work? What might be some other important considerations?

Pablo Picasso. *Three Musicians*. 1921. Oil on canvas. (Detail.) 200.7 x 222.9 cm (6'7 x 7'3¾"). Museum of Modern Art, New York. Mrs. Simon Guggenheim Fund.

▲ **NASA hired artists to make records of humans' first steps off the planet Earth. Do you know where those steps were? Why do you suppose NASA wanted artists to prepare such records?**

Paul Calle. *Gemini VI Astronauts*. Pencil on paper. 55.9 x 76.2 cm (22 x 30″). NASA.

Drawing

Have you ever heard someone say, "I can't draw"? Perhaps you have said it yourself. What you may not realize is that drawing is a skill. It can be learned just as dancing or playing a sport can be learned. With practice, you can use your drawing skills to express what you see in the world.

Look at the sketch on the left. What do you think the artist saw? With nothing more than a blank sheet of paper and a pencil, Paul Calle has created a detailed sketch. In this chapter you will find out how he made the astronauts and their equipment look so real.

OBJECTIVES

After completing this chapter, you will be able to:

- Name the three ways in which drawing is used in art.
- Define *shading*, and name four shading techniques.
- Make gesture drawings.
- Make contour drawings.

WORDS YOU WILL LEARN

blending	hatching
contour drawing	perception
crosshatching	shading
gesture drawing	stippling

ARTISTS YOU WILL MEET

Paul Calle	Henri Rousseau
Natalia Goncharova	Élisabeth Vigée-
Juan Gris	Lebrun
Rembrandt van Rijn	Leonardo da Vinci

The Art of Drawing

You have probably seen people doodling with a pencil. You may have done it yourself. If you have, you are not alone. Ever since you took a crayon in your hand and scribbled on paper, you have been drawing.

You can learn certain skills to help you improve your ability to draw. Look again at the drawing of the astronauts on page 142. Notice how the artist, Paul Calle (**kal**-ee), using just a pencil, made such dark shadows. Notice how he made some surfaces look soft and others smooth and shiny.

▶ **Figure 8–1** Does this drawing tell you simply how these people looked? How did da Vinci perceive this group of men? How does he convey this perception?

Leonardo da Vinci. *Five Grotesque Heads.* c. 1494. Pen on white paper. Windsor Castle, Royal Library of Her Majesty the Queen.

In this lesson you will learn about some of the uses of drawing. You will also learn a few drawing techniques. In later lessons you will get a chance to use these techniques.

THE USES OF DRAWING

Drawing has a great many uses in art. The three most important are to develop perception, to help plan projects, and to make a finished art work. **Perception** is *the ability to really see and study an object*.

Improving Perception

To an artist, looking and seeing are not the same thing. Looking is simply noticing an object as you pass by it. Seeing, or perceiving, is really studying the object. It is picking up on every line and shadow. It is observing all the details.

Through drawing, artists become better at perceiving. Many artists use sketchbooks to record their surroundings and to study objects. They use drawing to make preliminary studies for finished works. The Renaissance artist Leonardo da Vinci filled over a hundred sketchbooks with drawings. The drawings in Figure 8–1 come from one of them.

Planning Projects

Drawing is usually the first step in completing many art works and other projects. Rough sketches, or studies, are almost always done before creating a work in another medium, such as painting or sculpture. Design drawings for this year's fashions were made long before any fabric was cut. (See Figure 8–2.) Many creative people, such as stage designers, graphic designers, and architects must show presentation drawings for a client's approval. Once the drawing is approved, work can begin on the project.

▲ **Figure 8–2** Can you envision how this drawing would translate into an actual piece of clothing? What feeling do you think a viewer gets when looking at this work? Explain your answer.

▲ **Figure 8–3** Why do you think color was an important element for the artist? What guidelines did the artist have to consider before beginning this work?

Natalia Goncharova. *The City Square*. Design for scenery for the ballet Le Coq d'Or. Produced by Ballets Russes, Paris, 1914. Gouache, watercolor and traces of pencil on cardboard. 46.7 x 61.6 cm (18⅜ x 24¼"). Museum of Modern Art, New York, New York. Acquired through the Lillie P. Bliss Bequest.

Making a Finished Art Work

A third use of drawing is to make finished art works. These are sometimes used to illustrate books and magazines. The drawing in Figure 8–3 originally was used to show a stage design for a ballet. Now it is considered fine art. The picture of the astronauts on page **142** was done for the National Aeronautics and Space Administration (NASA).

Look more closely at Figure 8–3. Notice the fine detail the artist has chosen to show. Why do you think she made such a detailed drawing?

SHADING TECHNIQUES

Look once again at the drawing of the astronauts on page **142**. Here the artist creates a work so real it looks almost like a photograph. Do you know how this is done? One technique he uses to get this result is shading. **Shading** is *the use of light and shadow to give a feeling of depth*.

There are four basic shading techniques.

- **Hatching** is *drawing a series of thin lines all running parallel, or in the same direction*. Look at the shapes in Figure 8–4. Which show hatching?

- **Crosshatching** is *drawing lines that criss-cross each other.* Which shapes in Figure 8–4 show crosshatching?
- **Blending** is *smoothly drawing dark values little by little by pressing harder on the drawing medium.* Which shapes in Figure 8–4 show blending?
- **Stippling** is *creating dark values with a dot pattern.* Which shapes in Figure 8–4 show stippling?

(For more on how to use these shading techniques, see Technique Tip **6**, *Handbook* page **272**.)

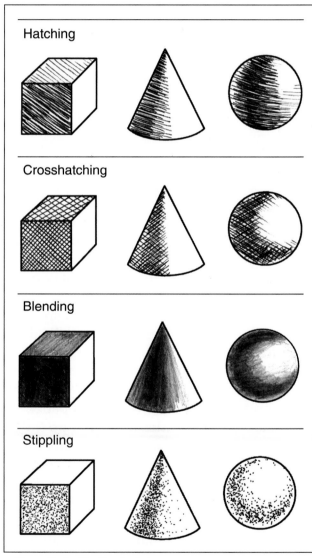

▲ **Figure 8–4   Shading techniques.**

✔CHECK YOUR UNDERSTANDING

1. What are three ways in which artists use drawing?
2. What is shading?
3. Name four techniques for shading. Describe each.

Gesture Drawing

Artists are able to freeze movement in a picture using a technique called gesture drawing. **Gesture drawing** is *drawing lines quickly and loosely to capture movement*. Look at Figure 8–5. This was done by the great Dutch painter Rembrandt van Rijn (**rem**-brant van **ryn**). Notice how the lines appear to have been made quickly to catch the action of the figure.

Using gesture drawing will help you break the habit of outlining everything you draw. In gesture drawing you use your whole arm, not just your hand. (See Technique Tip **2**, *Handbook* page **271**.)

▲ **Figure 8–5** **What appears to be in motion? How does detail enter into this?**

Rembrandt van Rijn. *Jan Cornelius Sylvius, The Preacher.*
c. 1644–1645. Pen and brown ink on laid paper. 13.3 x
12.2 cm (5¼ x 4¹³⁄₁₆"). National Gallery of Art, Washington, D.C.
Rosenwald Collection.

WHAT YOU WILL LEARN

You will make a series of 30-second gesture drawings using charcoal, graphite, or crayon. You will focus on the *movement* of the figure, not on the likeness of the person. Then you will make a large, slower sketch of a seated figure. Select one area of this figure to emphasize with details and shading. (See Figure 8–6.)

WHAT YOU WILL NEED

- Sticks of charcoal, soft graphite, or unwrapped crayon
- Sheets of white paper, 12 x 18 inch (30 x 46 cm)
- Pencil with a sharp point, and an eraser

WHAT YOU WILL DO

1. You and your classmates will take turns acting as the model. Models should pretend to be frozen in the middle of an activity. This may be an everyday action, such as sweeping the floor, or tying a shoelace. Dancing or acting out a sport are other possibilities. Each model will hold the pose for 30 seconds.
2. Using charcoal, graphite, or a crayon, begin making gesture drawings. You can fit several sketches on one sheet of paper. Make loose, free lines that build up the shape of the person. Your lines should be quickly drawn to capture movement.
3. After many 30-second drawings, make a slower gesture drawing of a seated model. Fill a sheet of paper. Select one area of the figure to emphasize with details and shading. Try a hand, a shoe, or a sleeve. (See Figure 8–7.)
4. When you are done, display your last drawing. Did your classmates choose the same detail to emphasize?

▲ **Figure 8–6** Which areas are strongly shaded? Which are not? Why?

Marie-Louise-Élisabeth Vigée-Lebrun. *La Princesse Barbe Gallitzin*. c. 1801. Graphite and chalk. Approximately 17.8 x 11.1 cm (7 x 4⅜"). National Museum of Women in the Arts, Washington, D.C. Gift of Wallace & Wilhelmina Holladay.

▶ **Figure 8–7** Student work. A gesture drawing with a detailed left foot.

OTHER STUDIO IDEAS

- Pretend you are a fashion illustrator for a local newspaper. Look through catalogs and do gesture drawings of the models in different action poses.

- ●● Look through a sporting magazine and find a picture of an athlete in motion. Tape the picture at eye level and do a gesture drawing of the athlete. Do the same drawings of the same athletes in different poses.

Contour Drawing

Look at Figure 8–8. Notice how lifelike the subject looks for a drawing made almost totally of line. A first step toward doing work like this is learning to do contour drawing. **Contour drawing** is *drawing an object as though your drawing tool is moving along all the edges and the ridges of the form.* This technique helps you become more perceptive. You are concerned with drawing shapes and curves.

In contour drawing, your eye and hand move at the same time. Imagine that the point of your pen is touching the edge of the object as your eye follows the edge. You never pick up your pen. When you move from one area to another, you leave a trail. Look at the model and not at the paper.

WHAT YOU WILL LEARN

You will make a series of contour drawings with a felt-tipped pen. First, you will draw different objects. Second, you will use your classmates as models. Finally, you will make a contour drawing of a classmate posed in a setting. (See Technique Tip **1**, *Handbook* page **271**.)

WHAT YOU WILL NEED

- Felt-tipped pen with a fine point
- Sheets of white paper, 12 x 18 inch (30 x 46 cm)
- Selected objects provided by your teacher

WHAT YOU WILL DO

1. Take one of the items from the collection on the display table. Place it on the table in front of you. Trace the lines of the object in the air on an imaginary sheet of glass. As you look at the object, you must concentrate and think. Notice every detail indicated by the direction and curves of the line.

▲ **Figure 8–8** Notice how the artist gives a feeling of form by changing the thickness of the line. What ways do you know of making lines thicker and darker?

Juan Gris. *Max Jacob*. 1919. Pencil on paper. 36.5 x 26.7 cm (14⅜ x 10½"). Museum of Modern Art, New York, New York. Gift of James Thrall Soby.

2. Make a contour drawing of the object on a sheet of paper using a felt-tipped pen. Do several more drawings on the same sheet of paper. Turn the object so you are looking at it from a different angle. Make another contour drawing. Keep working until your drawings begin to look like the object. (See Figure 8–9.)
3. Next, exchange objects with your classmates. Do a contour drawing of your new object. Work large, letting the drawing fill the page. Do not worry if your efforts look awkward. Complete several drawings of different objects.

4. Work with a partner. Take turns posing for each other. Each model should sit in a comfortable pose. The first contour will look distorted. Remember, you are drawing the pose. Work large and let the drawing fill the page.

5. Finally, make a contour drawing of one person sitting in a setting. Include background details. (See Figure 8–10.) You may stop and peek at the drawing. When you do, do not pick up the pencil. Do not take your eyes off the model while drawing.

6. Display the final drawing. Discuss how contour drawing has improved your perception.

EXAMINING YOUR WORK

- **Describe** Show the different kinds of contour drawings you did. Identify the media you used.
- **Analyze** Compare your first contour drawing to your last. Explain how using contour drawing has changed your perception skills.
- **Judge** Evaluate your final contour drawing. Tell whether you feel your work succeeds. Explain your answer.

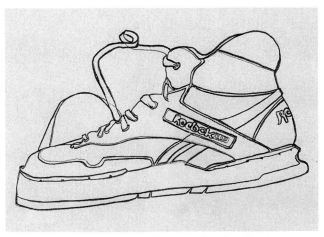

▲ **Figure 8–9** Student work. A contour drawing of a shoe.

▲ **Figure 8–10** Student work. This is an example of a contour drawing that shows background details.

OTHER STUDIO IDEAS

- Make a contour drawing of a chair in your classroom using crayons.

- ●● Use a piece of wire that bends easily and make a three-dimensional contour "drawing" of a foot or hand.

Presentation Drawing

Sometimes artists are called upon to do presentation drawings. Such drawings show a possible idea or design for a project. Figure 8–11 is a presentation drawing for the Washington Monument in Washington, D.C. It is one of many that were done by different artists. As you can see from the finished building (Figure 8–12), this design idea was not used.

Imagine you have been asked to design a set of wrought iron gates for the entrance to a zoo, botanical garden, or a playground.

WHAT YOU WILL LEARN

You will create a presentation drawing of a gate with two sides. The outside shape of the gate will be symmetrically balanced. To unify your design within the shape of the gate, create a symmetrical or asymmetrical design using lines and symbols that represent the place. Use the principles of rhythm and harmony to organize the lines.

▲ **Figure 8–11** How would you describe the mood of this design? What features help create that mood?

Robert Mills. *Rejected Sketch of Washington Monument.* The National Archives.

▲ **Figure 8–12** What features does this work have in common with the presentation drawing in Figure 8–11? In what ways is it different? Does it convey the same mood? Which of the two design ideas do you like better? Explain.

Washington Monument. Washington, D.C.

WHAT YOU WILL NEED

- Sheets of scrap paper
- Sheet of white paper, 12 x 18 inch (30 x 46 cm)
- Pencil and ruler
- Colored pencils or fine-line markers

WHAT YOU WILL DO

1. Choose a theme for your gates. Make some rough sketches of designs that symbolize the theme. On scrap paper, do rough pencil sketches showing different possible outline shapes for the symmetrical gate. Choose your best design, and set it aside.
2. Do rough pencil sketches of possible designs within the shape of the gate. Decide if the interior part of the gate will represent symmetrical or asymmetrical balance.
3. With a pencil, carefully develop your best idea. Use a ruler to make all the straight lines. (For information on the right way to hold a ruler, see Technique Tip **9**, *Handbook* page **273**.)
4. Fill in the two sides of your gate with your best designs. Again, use the ruler in drawing the design for the left side. Remember that repeating symbols can produce harmony.
5. Using the colored pencils or markers, add color to your presentation drawing. Use color to help give balance to the design.
6. Display your work. Discuss how students took different approaches to the assignment.

SAFETY TIP

When a project calls for the use of markers, always make sure to use the water-based kind. Permanent markers have chemicals in them that can be harmful when inhaled.

OTHER STUDIO IDEAS

- Make a presentation drawing for a new front door for your school. What mood do you want to capture in the finished work? Create the presentation drawing using colored pencils or fine-line markers.

- • Make a presentation model of a door using wire that bends easily. Do the decorations for the two sides separately. Fasten them to the outline of the door with transparent tape.

Fantasy Jungle

Look at the painting in Figure 8–13. It was done by Henri Rousseau (aan-**ree** roo-**soh**), a French painter famous for his imaginary jungles. The artist used real plants and other life forms as models in all his works.

WHAT YOU WILL LEARN

You will create your own imaginative fantasy jungle. You will study real leaves and plants as models for those in your work. Images of birds, animals, or reptiles will be based on photographs. You will do your finished work with oil pastels on colored construction paper. (See Figures 8–14 and 8–15.)

WHAT YOU WILL NEED

- Pencil and sheets of sketch paper or other plain white paper
- Sheet of colored construction paper, 12 x 18 inch (30 x 46 cm)
- White chalk and soft eraser
- Oil pastels

WHAT YOU WILL DO

1. With pencil on sketch paper, make detailed contour drawings of plants. These may be houseplants, flowers, or weeds.
2. On other sheets of sketch paper, make drawings of imaginary animals. They may be based on real birds, reptiles, and animals.
3. Using chalk, sketch the plan for your jungle on construction paper. Use the principles of harmony, informal balance, and emphasis. Pick a color of paper based on the mood your work will have. (Keep in mind differences of hue, intensity, and value.) Arrange your shapes and planned colors using informal balance. Keep other

▶ **Figure 8–13** The artist loved to spend time copying plants and animals from books. His finished works were a mixture of real-life images and images from his imagination. Which elements and techniques do you think give this painting the quality of a fantasy? Which ones display a sense of realism?

Henri Rousseau. *The Waterfall (La Cascade)*. 1910. Oil on canvas. 116.2 x 150.2 cm (45⅞ x 59"). Art Institute of Chicago. Helen Birch Bartlett Memorial Collection.

elements and principles, such as rhythm, in mind. As you draw, press lightly. That way, you will not tear the paper if you need to erase. Don't draw details so small that they can't be drawn with oil pastels.

4. Color your jungle. Use color contrast to create a strong center of interest or area of emphasis. Use different oil pastel drawing techniques. (See Technique Tip 3, *Handbook* page **271**.)

5. Display your work. Can you recognize what plants and animals your classmates used as models?

▲ Figure 8–14   Student drawing. A fantasy jungle.

EXAMINING YOUR WORK

- **Describe**   Identify the different plants in your fantasy jungle. Explain what real plants you used as sources. Explain what the imaginary animals were based on.
- **Analyze**   Show where you used informal balance to organize colors and shapes. Tell what principles you used to organize other elements.
- **Interpret**   Explain what kind of mood your work expresses. Tell what role background and foreground colors play in this mood. Tell whether your work has the look and feel of a fantasy jungle. Give your jungle a title.
- **Judge**   Tell whether you feel your work succeeds. Explain your answer.

▲ Figure 8–15   Student drawing. A fantasy jungle.

OTHER STUDIO IDEAS

- Do a second jungle scene using brush and ink only. Explain how you were able to capture the mood of an imaginative jungle without using color.
- ●● Draw your jungle with fine-line felt pens. Leave everything plain except your center of interest. Call attention to it by creating a strong contrast. Color it with bright colors, or give it the illusion of a three-dimensional form by shading it with one of the techniques you learned on page **147**.

CHAPTER 8 REVIEW

BUILDING VOCABULARY

Number a sheet of paper from 1 to 8. After each number, write the term from the box that best matches each description below.

blending	hatching
contour drawing	perception
crosshatching	shading
gesture drawing	stippling

1. The use of light and shadow to give a feeling of depth.
2. A shading technique using thin lines all running in the same direction.
3. A shading technique using lines that crisscross each other.
4. A shading technique in which dark values are added little by little.
5. A shading technique in which tiny black dots are accumulated.
6. Drawing lines quickly and loosely to show movement in a subject.
7. Drawing an object as though your drawing tool is touching the edge.
8. The ability to really see and study an object.

REVIEWING ART FACTS

Number a sheet of paper from 9 to 14. Answer each question in a complete sentence.

9. What are three main ways in which drawing is used by artists?
10. To an artist, how is looking at an object different from seeing it?
11. How does drawing help artists "see" better?
12. Name three ways in which drawing might be used to plan a project.
13. What is a name for the rough sketch an artist uses to plan a painting?
14. Name one place where drawings of finished works of art are used.

THINKING ABOUT ART

On a sheet of paper, answer each question in a sentence or two.

1. **Analyze.** Suppose someone said to you, "Drawing isn't real art. Anyone can pick up a pencil and make a drawing." How would you answer?
2. **Extend.** Why might the publishers of a book choose drawings rather than photographs as illustrations?
3. **Compare and contrast.** Which of the shading techniques you studied do you think gives the most realistic result? Which gives the least realistic result? Explain your answers.
4. **Interpret.** In what ways is using a rough or a thumbnail sketch similar to doing an outline for a piece of writing?
5. **Analyze.** Why do you think it is important to work quickly when doing gesture drawing? Why is it important to work slowly when doing contour drawing?

MAKING ART CONNECTIONS

1. **Science.** Scientists rely on photographs and detailed drawings to record and learn about the natural world. They sketch from observation and include unique features of their subjects. Study the work of scientific illustrators shown in science books, field guides, and magazines to see the type of images they use. Would Rousseau's paintings be useful to scientists studying plant and animal forms? Why or why not?
2. **Social Studies.** Starting with a drawing of your house and school, make a contour map showing the pathway of a short imaginary journey you plan to make. Include pictorial images to represent important landmarks. Show where you turn and how many blocks or miles you travel.

LOOKING AT THE DETAILS

The detail shown below is from Paul Calle's *Gemini VI Astronauts*. Study the detail and answer the following questions.

1. Calle used predominantly one shading technique. How does it relate to the sense of movement you see here?
2. Is Calle's organization of line successful? Why?
3. The window of the astronaut's headgear is dark and the viewer is unable to see a human face. Why do you think Calle avoided using the astronaut's face?
4. How do you think Calle perceived this astronaut?
5. How does the gear of the astronaut in front differ from the same gear worn by the astronaut behind him?
6. Can you think of some reasons for this difference?

Paul Calle. *Gemini VI Astronauts*. Pencil on paper. (Detail.) 55.9 x 76.2 cm (22 x 30"). NASA.

▲ The artist made a series of 15 woodblock prints to show scenes from the Bible. Do you know the story of the Four Horsemen of the Apocalypse? Notice the small letter D inside an *A* at the bottom. This is how Albrecht Dürer signed all his works.

Albrecht Dürer. *The Four Horsemen of the Apocalypse*. 1498. Woodcut. 30.9 x 20.8 cm (12 x 8"). Reproduced by courtesy of the Trustees of the British Museum, London.

CHAPTER 9

Printmaking

Artists are curious innovators. They never tire of looking for new challenges — new ways to create. Study the picture at the left. Notice the attention the artist has paid to detail. Notice the fierce looks on the faces of the riders. Notice how the horses seem to gallop across the picture.

The work would be remarkable if the artist had drawn it. But it was made using a technique far more technically involved than drawing with a pen or pencil. In this chapter you will learn more about the technique of printmaking and the media used in this process.

OBJECTIVES

After completing this chapter, you will be able to:
- Explain what printmakers do.
- Identify the three steps in printmaking.
- Name the four main methods for making prints and describe each of the methods.
- Make your own art work using different printmaking methods.

WORDS YOU WILL LEARN

brayer	printing plate
edition	printmaking
intaglio	registration
lithograph	relief printing
lithography	screen printing
monoprinting	serigraph

ARTISTS YOU WILL MEET

Albrecht Dürer	Pablo Picasso
Katsushika Hokusai	Janet Stayton
Doris Lee	Andy Warhol
Edvard Munch	

The Art of Printmaking

When you think of printing, newspapers might come to your mind. But printing has its place in art, too. In art, printing, or **printmaking**, is *transferring an inked image from one prepared surface to another.* Often the surface to which a printed image is transferred is paper.

THE HISTORY OF PRINTMAKING

Printmaking is nearly 2000 years old. The Chinese were among the first people to make prints. Later the Japanese developed printmaking into a fine art. (See Figure 9–1.) The remarkable work on page **158** is a print made toward the end of the 1400s. The artist was a German named Albrecht Dürer (**ahl**-brekt **dure**-uhr).

▲ **Figure 9–1** Do you think carving an image into wood may be more time consuming than painting it? What advantages do you think this artist may have seen in choosing wood as his medium?

Katsushika Hokusai. *View of Mt. Fuji from Seven-Ri Beach.* 1823-29. Colored woodcut. 25.7 x 38.1 cm (10⅛ x 15″). Metropolitan Museum of Art, New York, New York. Rogers Fund.

Prints may be made with many different media and techniques. Dürer's print began as an image carved in a wooden block. Ink was applied to the block, which was then pressed onto a sheet of paper. With the invention of the printing press in 1438, block prints were used for book illustrations.

THE PRINTMAKING BASICS

All prints are made using three basic steps. These steps, in the order in which they take place, are:

- **Making a printing plate.** A **printing plate** is *a surface onto or into which the image is placed*. In making a plate, the artist makes a mirror image of the final print. (See Figure 9–2.)
- **Inking the plate.** The artist applies ink. Often this is done with a **brayer**, *a roller with a handle*. For a multi-color print one plate is made for each color.
- **Transferring the image.** The paper is pressed against the inked plate. Sometimes this is done by hand. At other times a printing press is used.

Usually more than one print is made from a given plate. *A group of identical prints all made from a single plate* is called an **edition**. The artist will determine how many prints are made in an edition.

Creating a Print Edition

As each print in an edition is made, the artist studies it carefully. Each one that meets with his or her approval is signed and numbered in pencil. The number has this form: 11/50. The number on the right tells how many prints are in the edition. The number on the left tells that this particular print is the eleventh print made.

When an edition has been completed, the artist cancels or destroys the plate. This is done by disfiguring the plate so it can no longer be used.

▲ Figure 9–2   The invention of the printing press changed our world. Can you name some of the advantages?

✓ CHECK YOUR UNDERSTANDING

1. Define the term *printmaking*.
2. Name the three basic steps of making a print.
3. What does the number that appears on a print mean?

More About Printmaking

Printmaking is a popular art technique in today's world. Because prints are usually made in multiples, they are less expensive than paintings. People who might not be able to afford an original painting are often able to buy prints. Figure 9–3, a print by Edvard Munch, shows how stylized some prints can be.

PRINTMAKING

There are four main techniques artists use for making prints. They are relief printing, intaglio, lithography, and screen printing.

Relief Printing

You are probably already familiar with relief printing. If you have ever made a stamp print you have made a relief print. In **relief printing**, *the image to be printed is raised from a background* (Figure 9–4).

► **Figure 9–3   Does allowing the wood grain to show affect the feeling of the work? How? Does the title help you interpret the image?**

Edvard Munch. *The Kiss*. 1902. Woodcut, printed in grey and black, block. 46.7 x 46.4 cm (18⅜ x 18⁵⁄₁₆"). Museum of Modern Art, New York, New York. Gift of Abby Aldrich Rockefeller.

A popular medium in relief printing is carved wood. A print made by carving an image in a wooden block is called a woodcut. The print of the fierce riders on horseback on page **158** is a woodcut. Often woodcuts are done in color. When they are, a separate block, or plate, is made for each color. The blocks must be very carefully lined up during the printing process. If this is not done, the colors in the prints may overlap in the wrong places. This *careful matching up of plates in prints with more than one color* is called **registration**. How many blocks do you think were carved for the woodcut in Figure 9–3?

▲ **Figure 9–4** This drawing shows a woodcut being made. In the upper left corner you will see a detail that shows where the ink contacts the paper during the printing process.

Intaglio

A second technique for making prints is, in a way, the reverse of relief printing. **Intaglio** (in-**tal**-yoh) is *a printmaking technique in which the image to be printed is cut or etched into a surface* (Figure 9–5), rather than being

▲ **Figure 9–5** Look at the detail of the intaglio plate. How is it different from the woodcut detail?

raised from a background as in relief printing. In intaglio, paper is forced into the grooves that have been cut and scratched and which hold the ink. If you touch the surface of an intaglio print you can feel the buildup of the printmaking ink. One intaglio technique favored by many printmakers is engraving. In engraving, lines are scratched deep into a metal plate with an engraving tool.

Etching is another printing technique used by many artists. To make an etching, a metal printing plate is covered with a thin protective coating. The drawing is scratched through the coating with an etching needle. The plate is given an acid bath. The lines of the drawing are etched into the metal by the acid while the rest of the plate is protected by the protective covering.

▲ Figure 9–6   The illustration above shows a lithography stone as ink is being applied with a brayer.

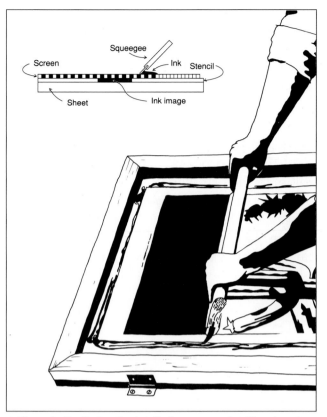

▲ Figure 9–7   Notice the detail of a screen print. How does it differ from the other printing plate details shown in Figures 9–4, 9–5, and 9–6?

▲ Figure 9–8   In this serigraph do you think some screens overlapped? Explain.

Doris Lee. *Untitled*. Serigraph on paper. 55.9 x 76.2 (22 x 30"). National Museum of Women in the Arts, Washington, D.C. Gift of Wallace and Wilhelmina Holladay.

Lithography

Have you ever noticed that grease and water don't mix? This fact is at the root of the printmaking technique called lithography. **Lithography** (lith-**ahg**-ruh-fee) is *a printmaking method in which the image to be printed is drawn on limestone, zinc, or aluminum with a special greasy crayon.* When the stone is dampened and then inked, the greased area alone holds the ink (Figure 9–6). Paper is pressed against the plate to make the print. *A print made by lithography* is called a **lithograph** (**lith**-uh-graf).

By using separate stones for each hue, lithographs may be printed in several colors. Lithography also allows the artist to use fine lines and blend values little by little.

Screen Printing

You have probably used lettering stencils at one time or another. The same basic idea is at work in **screen printing**, *a printmaking technique in which the artist transfers the design to the screen through various processes.* The area not to be printed is covered up with a special glue or sticky paper. (See Figure 9–7.) Ink is forced through the screen onto paper to make a print. *A screen print that has been handmade by an artist* is called a **serigraph** (**ser**-uh-graf).

Screen printing is the newest method for making prints. It was developed in the United States in this century.

To make a color serigraph, the artist makes one screen, or plate, for each color. Some serigraphs may have as many as 20 colors. How many colors can you find in the serigraph in Figure 9–8?

STUDIO EXPERIENCE

One of the hardest tasks facing a printmaker is thinking backwards. The printing plate, you will recall, must be a mirror image of the final print.

Each student in the class is to select a different letter of the alphabet. Once you have chosen a letter, place a thin sheet of paper over a thick pad of newspaper. Pressing down hard, draw your letter on the thin sheet of paper. Turn the paper over, and you will see your letter in reverse. Using the image as a model, carve a stamp from a cube of modeling clay. Apply paint to your stamp with a brush. On a sheet of paper, make a pattern by pressing your stamp several times. Does each image in your pattern look the same, or do they differ? Does this make your pattern more or less interesting? Explain your answers.

CHECK YOUR UNDERSTANDING

1. Name the four main techniques used for making prints.
2. Define the term *registration*.
3. Explain the difference between a lithograph and a serigraph.

Monoprints

Look at Figure 9–9. This is an example of a type of art print called a monoprint. **Monoprinting** is *a printmaking technique in which the image to be printed is put on the plate with ink or paint and then transferred to paper by pressing or hand-rubbing*. A monoprint plate can be used only once. The paint is absorbed into the paper, and the original image is gone.

WHAT YOU WILL LEARN

You will use a contour drawing process to make a monoprint drawing of a person. The image quality of the monoprint will help you understand the reversal process of printmaking. Create a mood within your work using the elements of line and color. The difference in line quality of a pencil line and a line made in a monoprint will become apparent. (See Figures 9–10 and 9–11.)

WHAT YOU WILL NEED

- Pencil and sheets of sketch paper
- Water-based printing ink
- Brayer
- Square of smooth vinyl flooring to be used as the printing plate
- Sheet of white paper the same size as or larger than the square of flooring

▶ **Figure 9–9 Notice how much this print looks like a painting. What differences can you see between finished monoprints and finished lithographs?**

Janet Stayton. *Yellow Promenade.* 1983. Oil on linen. 151.1 x 181.6 cm (59½ x 71½"). Pat Heesy Museum.

WHAT YOU WILL DO

1. Using pencil and sketch paper, make blind contour drawings of the model. When you are happy with your drawing, move on to the next step.
2. Squeeze ink onto the square of vinyl flooring. This is to be your printing plate. Spread the ink evenly with your brayer.
3. Place the sheet of white paper very lightly on your plate. Don't move it once it is down.
4. Supporting your hand so that it doesn't rest on the paper, use your pencil to draw a contour drawing that fills the paper. Be careful not to let anything but the pencil touch the paper. If a line looks wrong, draw it again. Do not, however, try to erase a line.
5. Starting at two corners, pull your paper carefully from the plate. Do not stop once you begin pulling. Place your paper, image side up, in a safe place to dry.
6. When the print has dried, display your work.

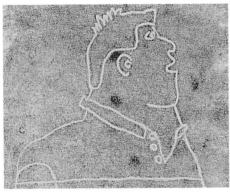
▲ Figure 9–10   Student work. A monoprint.

EXAMINING YOUR WORK

- **Describe**   Show where you used contour drawing to create an image of a person. Explain how the monoprint came out the reverse of your pencil drawing.
- **Analyze**   Explain how the quality of the monoprint line is different from a pencil line. Tell how you created contrast between the line of the print and the paper.
- **Interpret**   Tell what mood your work creates. Explain how the mood is different from one a simple line drawing would create.
- **Judge**   Tell whether you feel your work succeeds. Explain your answer.

▲ Figure 9–11   Student work. A monoprint.

OTHER STUDIO IDEAS

- Make an expressive drawing of a human head and face. Use a paper towel wrapped around your finger to draw this face on a plate. The removed ink will leave white lines on your print. Rub out solid areas for the cheeks, forehead, and chin. Make an impression of the print on a sheet of white paper.

- •• Create a series of three expressive faces and repeat the steps listed above. Try the first print of the face. Check and make any corrections. When you are satisfied, continue with the other two drawings. Compare your prints to see if they work well as a series.

Glue Prints

The techniques for making relief prints are almost endless. Did you know, for example, that you could make a printing plate from dried white glue? The work in Figure 9–12 was made using such a plate.

WHAT YOU WILL LEARN

You will make a printing plate from cardboard and dried glue. Lines and dots arranged in a radial design will be used. You will print an edition of three prints using water-based inks. Give your finished print a descriptive title.

▲ **Figure 9–12 Student work. A glue print.**

WHAT YOU WILL NEED

- White glue and newsprint
- Toothpicks and ruler
- Pencil and sheets of sketch paper
- Square of corrugated cardboard
- Water-based printing ink
- Brayer and vinyl floor square
- 3 sheets of white paper the same size or larger than the square of cardboard

WHAT YOU WILL DO

1. For practice, squeeze a thin line of glue onto a sheet of newsprint. You will notice that as it dries, it shrinks to form a line of fat dots. By pulling a toothpick from one to another, the dots can be connected again. This forms a new line. (See Figure 9–13.)
2. Using sketch paper, pencil, and ruler, plan a design with radial balance. Use straight lines and dots. Plan your design to fit your printing plate.
3. Transfer your design to the square of cardboard. Go over your lines with glue. Where your design shows lines, connect the shrinking dots to form them. Some lines may need a second coat of glue. When the glue has become clear, it is completely dry and the plate is ready to print.
4. Squeeze a small amount of ink onto a corner of the square of vinyl flooring. Roll your brayer into the ink, first in one direction, then in the other. Be sure that the brayer is well-coated and sticky with ink.
5. Transfer the ink to the cardboard print plate by rolling the brayer across your design in all directions.

6. With clean hands, place the sheet of white paper very lightly on your plate. Press it to the plate with the heel of your hand or a clean brayer. Pull the paper carefully from the plate. Set the print aside. If the plate is dry, add more ink. Make a second print, and then a third print.
7. When the prints are dry, use a pencil to write the title in the lower left corner of the white paper below the print. Sign your name in the lower right corner. In the center, record the number of the edition (3/3 means the third print in an edition of three).

EXAMINING YOUR WORK

- **Describe** Point out the lines in your print and show what parts of the design were made with dots. Identify each print in the edition. Show where you signed and numbered each print.
- **Analyze** Tell what kind of balance your design has. Explain how the drawing and glue print are different. Identify what is unusual about the lines and surface textures of the glue print.
- **Interpret** Explain what your title tells others about your print. Describe what type of mood or feeling you hoped to express in your print.
- **Judge** Tell whether you feel your work succeeds. Explain your answer.

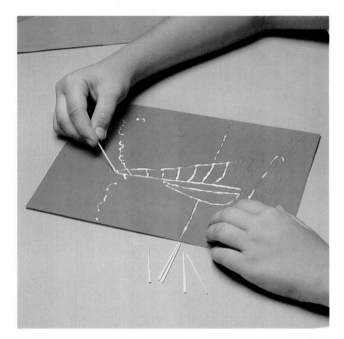

◀ Figure 9–13 The photo at the left shows the technique used to connect the dots as the glue dries.

OTHER STUDIO IDEAS

- Ink your plate and press a sheet of aluminum foil over it to create a relief design. Then carefully remove the foil from the plate. Explain how this print differs in appearance from the paper print.

- ●● Team up with a friend and plan a composition using two glue plates to make one print. Print each plate with a different color.

Linoleum Block Prints

Look at the print in Figure 9–14. This was done by the Spanish artist Pablo Picasso (**pah**-bloh pee-**kahs**-oh). The print was made from a relief carved in a section of linoleum. This material is softer than wood to cut. Notice the thin black lines in the gold area in the upper left corner. These show ridges left from cutting linoleum away in long strips. The artist has left them in to add to the visual interest of the work.

WHAT YOU WILL LEARN

You will create a linoleum block print using a clown as the subject. The main purpose of the print, however, will be to suggest a mood. You will use the elements of line and color to express this mood.

WHAT YOU WILL NEED

- Scrap pieces of linoleum
- Linoleum cutting tool with different sizes of blades
- Pencil and sheets of sketch paper
- Piece of linoleum, 4 x 6 inch (10 x 15 cm)
- Dark-colored marker and tape
- Carbon paper and crayon
- Inking plate and brayer
- Colored water-based printing inks
- Sheets of white paper

WHAT YOU WILL DO

1. Using a linoleum scrap, experiment with the different blades. Practice cutting thin lines and carving out large areas.
2. Using pencil and sketch paper, make rough sketches of a clown design. As you work, experiment with different moods. Remember that color and line can affect

▲ **Figure 9–14 Linoleum is softer than wood. This makes it easier to cut. Compare this work with the woodcut on page 158. What differences between the two types of print can you find?**

Pablo Picasso. *Seated Woman (After Cranach)*. 1958. Color linoleum cut, composition. 65.4 x 54.1 cm (25¹¹/₁₆ x 21⁵/₁₆"). Museum of Modern Art, New York, New York. Gift of Mr. & Mrs. Daniel Saidenberg.

mood. (See Chapter 4, Lessons 2 and 4.) Select the color ink you will use. Set aside your best design sketch.
3. Trace the outline of your linoleum block on a sheet of sketch paper. Draw your final design so that it touches all four edges of the block. Leave some shapes a solid color. Do not draw thin lines. Draw only the main lines of your clown face for now. You will add details later.

4. Hold your sketch up against a window. With a colored marker, trace over the lines you see through the page. (See Figure 9–15.) This will allow you to make a print that faces in the same direction as your drawing. Otherwise, you will end up with the mirror image of your design.
5. Place a piece of carbon paper on the linoleum. Place your design face down over the carbon paper. Trace over the lines with a pencil. Lift a corner of the carbon paper to be sure the image is transferring to the block. To keep the paper from slipping, tape the paper down.
6. Using the colored marker, color in all the areas on the linoleum that will not be cut away.
7. Using different blades, cut away the background. Remember that the background ridges can add interest to your print. As you cut, stop from time to time and make a crayon rubbing of your plate. This will help you identify areas that need further cutting.
8. Squeeze out some ink on the inking plate, and load the brayer. Roll the brayer over the linoleum block. Place the printing paper carefully on the block, and press the paper to the plate by rubbing it by hand or running it through a press.
9. Make an edition of five prints. Sign and number your prints and display one of them.

SAFETY TIP

Linoleum blades are very sharp and can cause serious cuts. Always cut away from your body and your other hand.

EXAMINING YOUR WORK

- **Describe** Point out the details you used to give the idea of a clown. Identify the details you included in the background. Explain why you used these details.
- **Analyze** Note which kinds of lines (horizontal, vertical, diagonal) and color (warm, cool, dark, light) you used.
- **Interpret** Identify the mood of your print. Explain how the lines and color you used helped to express this mood.
- **Judge** Tell whether you feel your work succeeds. Explain your answer.

▲ **Figure 9–15** This student is transferring the art image to the reverse side of the paper.

OTHER STUDIO IDEAS

- Make a colored tissue collage on a sheet of white paper. (See Technique Tip **27**, *Handbook* page **281**.) Print your clown design on the collage. Describe the new mood of your print.

- • Hand color one print with crayons or oil pastels. Do not use paints, because your ink is water based and it will run.

Silk Screen Prints

Screen printing is the easiest technique to use when making a print using many colors. Study the screen print in Figure 9–16. This was done by American artist Andy Warhol. How many different colors of ink do you think the artist used? How do the colors affect the mood of the work?

WHAT YOU WILL LEARN

You will make a screen plate out of cardboard, masking tape, and net fabric. You will block out a design with a wax crayon. The design will use the principle of rhythm to organize the element of shape. Give your print a title that describes the mood or feeling you want to capture. You will print an edition of three prints.

WHAT YOU WILL NEED

- Pencil and ruler
- Shoe box lid
- Utility knife and scissors
- Sheets of sketch paper
- Masking tape and nylon net fabric
- Wax crayon
- Colored water-based printing ink or school acrylic paint
- Squeegee or a piece of heavy-duty cardboard the size of the screen opening
- Sheets of white paper

▶ **Figure 9–16   What do we learn from the artist's mixing and matching of bold color? What does this tell you about the way color affects shape?**

Andy Warhol. *George Gershwin from Ten Portraits of Jews of the 20th Century*. 1980. Silk screen. 50.8 x 81.3 cm (40 x 32″). Ronald Frieman Fine Arts, New York.

WHAT YOU WILL DO

1. With pencil and ruler, measure a 3 x 5 inch (8 x 13 cm) square on the shoe box lid. Using the utility knife, carefully cut out the rectangle. Protect the table with a thick piece of cardboard.

2. Trace the size of the opening in the shoe box lid on sheets of sketch paper. Experiment drawing rhythmic designs that lead the eye around the space. One way to do this is by repeating shapes. Change the size, however, to add interest to these shapes. (See Figure 9–17.) Choose the best of your designs. Shade the space between the shapes with a pencil. Set your sketch aside.

3. Cut a rectangle of net fabric slightly larger than the opening. With masking tape, fasten the fabric securely to the inside of the lid. Cut a piece of cardboard that will fit inside the lid but cover the opening. The cardboard will act as a squeegee later.

4. Place the screen over your design. Hold it firmly in place. Pressing heavily with the crayon, plug the holes in the net over the shaded areas.

5. Place the screen over a sheet of white paper. Choose a color of ink. Squeeze a small amount of ink at the top of the screen. With your cardboard squeegee, pull ink from the top of the screen to the bottom. As you do, press down heavily.

6. Lift the screen carefully off the paper so as not to smear the ink. Make a second and third print.

7. Display one of your finished prints. Discuss any interesting textures you created.

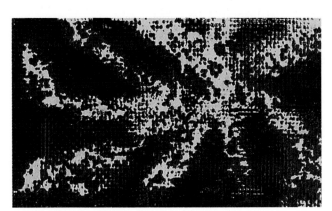

▲ Figure 9–17   Student work. A serigraph.

OTHER STUDIO IDEAS

- Make a screen print using crayon to draw a line design on the screen.

- ●● Borrow a classmate's plate. Using a second color of ink, add a second color to one of your dried prints. Line up the outlines of your print and the plate opening. Describe the result.

CHAPTER 9 REVIEW

BUILDING VOCABULARY

Number a sheet of paper from 1 to 12. After each number, write the term from the box that best matches each description below.

brayer	printing plate
edition	printmaking
intaglio	registration
lithograph	relief printing
lithography	screen printing
monoprinting	serigraph

1. The art of transferring an inked image from a prepared surface to another surface.
2. The surface onto which an image is placed.
3. A roller with a handle.
4. A group of identical prints all made from a single plate.
5. A technique in which the image to be printed is raised from the background.
6. The careful matching of plates in prints with more than one color.
7. A technique in which the image to be printed is cut or scratched into a surface.
8. A technique in which the image to be printed is drawn on limestone with a special crayon.
9. A print made by lithography.
10. A technique in which the image to be printed is drawn on a screen made of silk.
11. A screen print that has been handmade by an artist.
12. A technique in which the image to be printed is put on the plate with ink or paint and then transferred to paper by pressing or hand-rubbing.

REVIEWING ART FACTS

Number a sheet of paper from 13 to 18. Answer each question in a complete sentence.

13. What is inking? What tool is often used in inking?
14. What is meant by the numbers an artist writes on each print in an edition?
15. How does an artist "cancel a plate?"
16. What is a woodcut? What method of printmaking is used to make a woodcut?
17. Name one type of intaglio printing.
18. Which printmaking technique gives an edition size or number as 1?

THINKING ABOUT ART

On a sheet of paper, answer each question in a sentence or two.

1. **Analyze.** What reasons might artists have for canceling a plate at the end of an edition?
2. **Summarize.** Why is being able to "think backwards" important to a printmaker?
3. **Extend.** What problems might there be in making a glue print with an edition of 500?

MAKING ART CONNECTIONS

1. **Social Studies.** Look at the colored woodcut by Hokusai on page **160**. Mount Fuji, a volcano in Japan, appears in many works by Hokusai and other Japanese artists. Look for other art works showing the volcano and share them with the class. Why do you think this image plays such an important part in Japanese works of art?
2. **Science.** The printmaking technique called lithography is based on the fact that oil and water do not mix. What other substances don't mix? Find out why.

LOOKING AT THE DETAILS

The detail shown below is from Albrecht Dürer's woodcut *Four Horsemen of the Apocalypse*. Study the detail and answer the following questions.

1. Albrecht Dürer included many details in his work. What techniques did he use to make objects look like three-dimensional forms?
2. How does Dürer's choice of technique affect the mood of the work?

3. How do you think this image would change if the artist painted it in watercolor?
4. If you were to look at the original woodcut of this image, would it look the same? Explain.
5. What would you think about this image if you were told that it was done by a contemporary artist?

Albrecht Dürer. *The Four Horsemen of the Apocalypse.* Woodcut. (Detail.) 30.9 x 20.8 cm (12 x 8"). Reproduced by courtesy of the Trustees of the British Museum, London.

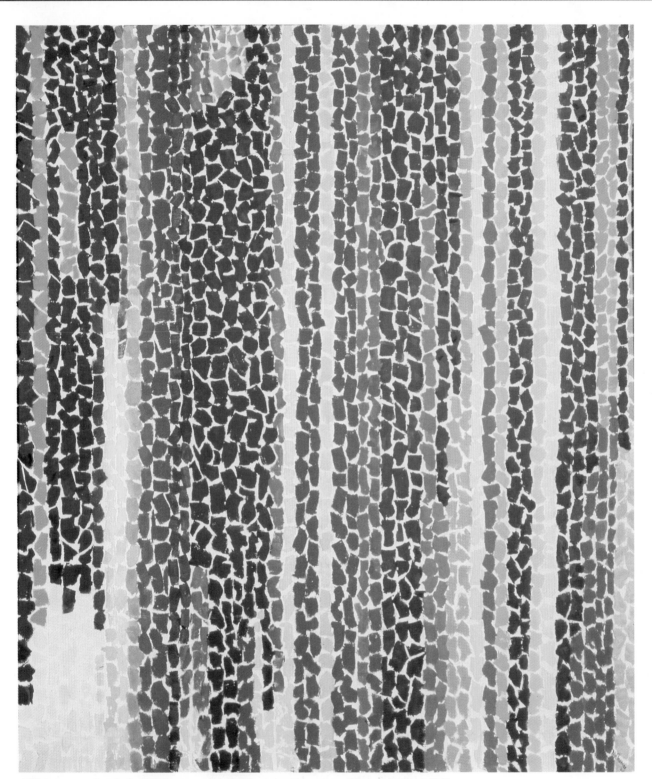

▲ The strong colors in the bands move up and down as well as across. They show the artist's strong feelings toward nature. Can you see a breeze moving over a sunlit garden? If not, what does the work say to you?

Alma Thomas. *Iris, Tulips, Jonquils and Crocuses*. 1969. Acrylic on canvas. 152.4 x 127 cm (60 x 50"). National Museum of Women in the Arts, Washington, D.C.

CHAPTER 10

Painting

The goal of writers is to make their words speak to the reader. The goal of artists is to make their images "speak" to the viewer. Look at Alma Thomas's painting at the left. Notice the size of the work. How big does that make each of the dabs of color? What hues has she used? Has she used any neutral colors? Has she changed the value of any hues? Can you relate the dabs of paint in her work to the title?

In this chapter you will learn about the many different techniques painters use. You will learn to use some of those techniques yourself.

OBJECTIVES

After completing this chapter, you will be able to:
- Name the basic ingredients of paint.
- Describe six important painting media.
- Make paintings using watercolors, school tempera, and school acrylic.

WORDS YOU WILL LEARN

acrylic	palette
binder	pigment
encaustic	solvent
fresco	synthetic paints
glaze	tempera
impasto	transparent
oil paint	watercolor
opaque	

ARTISTS YOU WILL MEET

Sonia Delaunay	Alice Neel
Lavinia Fontana	Diego Rivera
David Hockney	David Alfaro Siqueiros
Winslow Homer	Alma Thomas
Dong Kingman	Andrew Wyeth

LESSON 1

The Art of Painting

Most artists have stories about their first experiences with paint. They tell of blending beautiful, brilliant colors — and of ending up with a muddy mess! They tell of learning little by little how to make paints "behave."

In this lesson you will learn some of their secrets. You will learn to speak about color using the language of art.

THE HISTORY OF PAINTING

Do you remember reading about cave paintings in Chapter 4? Figure 4–1 on page **54** shows one such painting. Works like these date back as far as 15,000 B.C. Humans have been painting for nearly 17,000 years!

In the time since, many paint media and methods have been discovered. A large number of them are still in use.

PAINTING MEDIA

The basis of all paintings is, of course, the paint. Paint, you will recall, has three parts:

- **Pigment** is *a finely ground powder that gives every paint its color.*
- **Binder** is *a liquid that holds together the grains of pigment.*
- **Solvent** is *a material used to thin the binder.*

Every painting medium has its own unique quality. The best-known of these media are encaustic, fresco, tempera, oil paint, acrylic, and watercolor.

Encaustic

Some of the early paintings by the ancient Greeks and Romans were done using **encaustic** (in-**kaw**-stik), *a painting medium in which pigment is mixed into melted wax*. The wax, which is the binder, is kept liquid by

heat. Heat is the "solvent." Works that are painted with encaustic seem to glow with light.

Fresco

Another technique of applying paint, which also was developed long ago, is the one called fresco. **Fresco** (**fres**-koh) is *a painting medium in which pigment is applied to a wall spread with wet plaster*. The fresh plaster is applied to a small area of a wall and water-based pigments are painted quickly on the wet plaster. The paint bonds with the plaster, and when the plaster dries, the painting is part of the wall.

In fresco painting, the plaster itself is the binder. There is no solvent. Fresco painting was refined by Italian Renaissance painters and "rediscovered" in this century by Mexican mural painters (Figure 10–1).

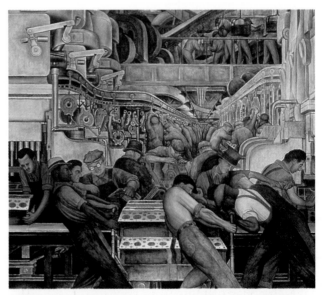

▲ **Figure 10–1** How would you describe the looks on the faces of these men? What part does the medium play in the artist's "statement"? Explain.

Diego Rivera. *Detroit Industry.* 1923–33. Fresco. North wall central panel. (Detail.) Founders Society, Detroit Institute of the Arts, Detroit.

▲ Figure 10–2   Why do you think this artist chose tempera as his medium? How might this same image differ if he had used watercolor?

Andrew Wyeth. *Christina's World*. 1948. Tempera on gessoed panel. (Detail.) 81.9 x 121.3 cm (32¼ x 47¾"). Museum of Modern Art, New York, New York.

▲ Figure 10–3   What is the visual texture of this work? How do you think the artist's application of oil paint contributes to its realism?

Lavinia Fontana. *Portrait of a Noblewoman*. c. 1580. Oil on canvas. (Detail.) 115.6 x 89.5 cm (45½ x 35¼"). National Museum of Women in the Arts, Washington, D.C. Gift of Wallace and Wilhelmina Holladay.

Tempera

Another very old medium is **tempera** (tem-puh-ruh), *a painting medium in which pigment mixed with egg yolk and water is applied with tiny brush strokes*. Tempera does not spread easily or blend well. Because of this, **transparent**, or *clear*, layers of color must be built up little by little. This can take time. Once dry, tempera is waterproof.

Tempera allows a painter to capture the details of a subject. Look at the portion of a painting, or detail, in Figure 10–2. Note how the artist shows highlights in the hair and in the individual blades of grass.

Notice, by the way, that this use of tempera is not the same medium as the tempera paint you use in school. The paint you use in your work is a poster paint.

Oil Paint

Oil paint is *paint with an oil base*. Oil paint was first used in the 1400s and has continued to be one of the most popular mediums used today.

Linseed oil is the binder for oil paint, and its solvent is turpentine. Oil paint dries slowly. This allows artists to blend colors right on the canvas.

Oil paint can be applied in *thick, buttery layers*, called **impasto** (im-**pahs**-toh), to make interesting textures. When applied thickly, oil paint is opaque. **Opaque** (oh-**pake**) means *that it does not let light pass through*. It can also be applied in a *thin, transparent layer*, called a **glaze**. A glaze allows dry color underneath to show through. Some painters make their works glow with light by building up layers of glaze. Look at Figure 10–3. Notice how the artist has blended the colors of the face so that they seem to melt together.

Watercolor

Once used only for sketches, watercolor has become a favorite medium of serious painters. **Watercolor** is *a painting medium in which pigment is blended with gum arabic and water*. Watercolor takes its name from its solvent. For the best results, watercolors are applied to good quality white paper. Blended colors are usually mixed on a palette before painting. A **palette** can be *any tray or plate where paints are mixed before use*. A white palette allows you to see what new mixed hues will look like against white paper before painting. A piece of white scrap paper can also be used to test colors for value and intensity before painting on good quality paper.

Watercolor can give a light, misty feel to paintings or they can be intense and brilliant.

Look at Figure 10–4. The artist, Winslow Homer, was among the first to use watercolor in finished works. Notice the amount of white paper he allows to show through. How do you think this affects the look of the work?

Acrylic

Advances in technology in the twentieth century have given artists new media choices. **Synthetic paints** are *manufactured paints with plastic binders*. They came onto the scene in the 1930s. The first artist to use a synthetic paint was a Mexican mural painter. His name was David Alfaro Siqueiros (dah-**veed** al-**far**-oh see-**care**-ohs). Figure 10–5 shows a detail from one of Siqueiros's early experiments. The work was done with quick-drying duco (**doo**-koh) paint.

▲ **Figure 10–4** Is there any movement in this work? How does it feel? Compare the visual texture of this painting with Figure 10–3.

Winslow Homer. *Return From the Hunt*. 1882. Watercolor. (Detail.) 40.6 x 53.3 cm (16 x 21"). Los Angeles County Museum of Art, Los Angeles. Paul Rodman Mabury Collection.

▲ **Figure 10–5** Do you find the look on this child's face troubling? Why? How do you think the medium helped the artist capture this mood?

David Alfaro Siqueiros. *Echo of a Scream*. 1937. Enamel on wood. (Detail.) 121.9 x 91.4 cm (48 x 36"). Museum of Modern Art, New York, New York. Gift of Edward M. M. Warburg.

One of the most widely used paints today is **acrylic** (uh-**kril**-ik), *a quick-drying water-based synthetic paint*. Acrylic paint first appeared in the 1950s. Not only does acrylic offer the artist a wide range of pure, intense colors (Figure 10–6) but it also is versatile. Like oil paint, it can be applied both thickly and in thin glazes. Acrylic paints can even be thinned enough to be sprayed in a thin mist with an airbrush. Acrylic is less messy to use than is oil paint because the solvent used for acrylic paint is water.

▲ **Figure 10–6** How does the artist's choice of color contribute to the mood of this painting?

David Hockney. *Les Mamelles des Tiresias*. 1980. Oil on canvas. (Detail.) 91.5 x 122 cm (36 x 48").

✔CHECK YOUR UNDERSTANDING

1. What are the three main parts of paint?
2. How is encaustic different from fresco? How is it different from tempera?
3. How is oil paint different from watercolor? How is it different from acrylic?
4. What is impasto? What is a glaze?
5. What is a synthetic paint? When did synthetic paints first appear?

Watercolor Painting

Look at the painting in Figure 10–7 by the artist Dong Kingman. He has captured a day in the life of an American city. Do you know what city it is? Is this just an ordinary day? How can you tell?

Take another look at the painting. What kind of paint did the artist use to create this work? What is unusual about his use of white paper?

▲ **Figure 10–7   What is the mood of this work? How does the medium help set the mood? How does the artist's attention to small details help?**

Dong Kingman. *Cable Car Festival.* 1988. Watercolor on paper. 76.2 x 55.9 cm (30 x 22″). Conacher Gallery San Francisco.

WHAT YOU WILL LEARN

You will make a watercolor painting in the style of Dong Kingman. The subject will be a festival that includes people and a setting. Pick an event similar to the one in Figure 10–7. Use bright colors to emphasize some part of the event in which people are having fun. Use lines and color to create a feeling of excitement. You will leave areas of your work unpainted.

WHAT YOU WILL NEED

- Pencil and sheets of sketch paper
- Watercolor paints
- Palette for mixing colors
- Container for water
- Thin and thick watercolor brushes
- Sheet of good quality white paper, pressed board, or watercolor paper, 12 x 18 inch (30 x 46 cm)
- Paper towels

WHAT YOU WILL DO

1. Brainstorm with your classmates to develop ideas for your work. Choose a festive occasion that is important to you, your school, or your community. Think of the particular part of the festival that represents the excitement. Think of special colors tied to the occasion and how those colors add to the festive mood.
2. Make pencil sketches to plan your work. Use line movements to create excitement. Choose your best idea.
3. Remember to set up all your supplies before you begin. Watercolor is a quick-drying medium.
4. Mix a light value of a watercolor paint on your palette. (You create light values with watercolors by adding more water to the

▲ **Figure 10–8   Student work. A watercolor painting.**

EXAMINING YOUR WORK

- **Describe**   Identify the festive occasion you chose to paint. Tell what part of the event you focused on. Tell what colors and kinds of lines you used.
- **Analyze**   Point to areas in which bright colors are used. Explain how these colors emphasize these areas. Explain how you created contrast.
- **Interpret**   Tell what words a viewer might use to describe the mood of your painting. Explain how color and line are used to create this mood. Give your work a title based on its mood.
- **Judge**   Tell whether you feel your work succeeds. What views of art would you use to defend your answer?

color you choose. This will allow more white from the paper to show through.) With the thin brush, draw your final sketch onto the sheet of good white paper. (See Technique Tip **4**, *Handbook* page **271**.)

5. Decide which area of your work you will emphasize and paint this area with your brightest colors. Paint other areas in contrasting dull colors. Leave large areas of the white paper showing. Do not paint in all your drawn objects. If you like, draw over some of your light lines with darker paint with a thin brush.
6. When your work is dry, display it. Discuss various ways classmates have achieved contrast and shown excitement using line and color.

OTHER STUDIO IDEAS

- Try drawing your work with colored pencil or crayon. Then wet the whole paper and paint it wet on wet. When it dries, add stronger color.

- ●● Notice how Kingman has used comedy in the work. Look at the little mice in the lower right corner. Notice the figure that is white, except for the brown legs. Find something you have finished, and add some unexpected things to it to create humor.

Non-objective Painting

Look at the painting in Figure 10–9. The artist, Sonia Delaunay, believed color was the most important art element. With her artist-husband, Robert, she explored the expressive quality of color. Notice the rhythmic movement of the shapes along diagonal lines. Notice also the soft edges of the shapes.

WHAT YOU WILL LEARN

You will make a painting that, like Delaunay's, is made up of the repetition of geometric shapes. Also like hers, yours will show rhythmic movement. You will use a primary- or secondary-color scheme. The background will be painted in black. (See Figure 10–10.)

WHAT YOU WILL NEED

- Pencil, sketch paper, and ruler
- Round shapes of different sizes, such as jar lids, or pre-cut cardboard patterns
- Paper towels
- Yellow chalk
- White paper, 12 x 18 inch (30 x 46 cm)
- Tempera paints, thin and thick brushes

► **Figure 10–9** Does your eye start at the top of this painting or at the bottom? Is the beat of the work a fast one or a slow one? Explain your answers.

Sonia Delaunay. *Colored Rhythm No. 698*. 1958. Oil on canvas. 114.3 x 87 cm (45 x 34¼"). Albright Knox Art Gallery, Buffalo, New York. Gift of Seymour H. Knox.

WHAT YOU WILL DO

1. Using pencil and sketch paper, plan your work. Using the ruler, draw a diagonal line across the paper from top to bottom. With the ruler, make squares and/or rectangles so that their sides rest on the diagonal. Use the circle patterns to make a series of circular shapes in different sizes. These should meet and cross the lines of the four-sided shapes. Repeating the different shapes will give a feeling of rhythm and movement to the design.

2. Using yellow chalk, draw your design on the sheet of white paper. Use the ruler and circle pattern. The edges of your shapes do not have to be perfect. Draw your design so that it touches at least three sides of the paper.

3. Choose a primary- or secondary-color scheme for the work. You may also use white. Repeat your colors in a way that adds to the sense of rhythmic movement.

4. Using the thin brush, paint the outline of each shape. Switch to the thick brush to fill in each shape with the same color you used for its outline. Since poster paints will run, be sure that one shape is dry before you paint a wet color next to it. (For more on using poster paints, see Technique Tip **13**, Handbook page **275**.)

5. When your work is dry, display it along with those made by other members of the class. Do any of the paintings look like yours? Are some completely different?

- **Describe**   Identify the diagonal line that organizes the shapes in your work. Point out and name the different geometric shapes you used. Explain which color scheme you chose.
- **Analyze**   Tell what colors and shapes you repeated to create rhythmic movement. Tell whether the "beat" of your work is steady or irregular. Show the path the viewer's eye follows through your work. Explain how you created contrast.
- **Interpret**   Tell what mood your work expresses. Give your work a title based on this mood.
- **Judge**   Tell whether you feel your work succeeds. Explain your answer.

▶ **Figure 10–10   Student work. Non-objective painting.**

OTHER STUDIO IDEAS

- Do the same project, but limit yourself to the repetition of one geometric shape, and vary the sizes.

- • Do the same project but limit the colors to a pair of complementary hues and black and white.

Expressive Painting

Sometimes artists use their works to speak about problems of the day. Look at the painting in Figure 10–11. It was done in 1940 by an American painter named Alice Neel. The patient in the painting is suffering from "T.B.," or tuberculosis. At the time of the painting, cases of tuberculosis were widespread in inner city ghettos. Its victims were, like the person in the painting, poor.

What statement about ghetto life and about being poor might the artist be making in this work? Which elements and principles has she chosen to punctuate her statement?

WHAT YOU WILL LEARN

You will learn to use social issues as content for a work of art. A social statement can be subject matter for art works. Select a social issue that faces the world today. You will paint a close-up view of people to illustrate this issue. Colors and heavy lines will be used to emphasize the mood of your work. Distorting the proportions of shapes will also add to this mood. Free-flowing, loose brushstrokes will be used to show movement and add texture. (See Figure 10–12.)

WHAT YOU WILL NEED

- Pencil and sheets of sketch paper
- School acrylic paints
- Shallow tray with sides to mix paints
- Water (as a solvent)
- Bristle brushes, varied sizes
- Sheet of heavy white paper, 12 x 18 inch (30 x 46 cm)
- Water (to clean brushes) and paper towels

▶ **Figure 10–11** What is the patient in the picture feeling? How does the artist help you feel the suffering? How does the medium help?

Alice Neel. *T. B. Harlem.* 1940. Oil on canvas. 76.2 x 76.2 cm (30 x 30"). National Museum of Women in the Arts, Washington, D.C. Gift of Wallace & Wilhelmina Holladay.

WHAT YOU WILL DO

1. Brainstorm with your classmates, and list social issues of the day. Some possibilities include pollution, teenage pregnancy, drug abuse, the homeless, and acid rain. Choose one that you know about and that truly concerns you.
2. Think about a way that you can create a painting that will make people think about the problem. How can you show its effect on people?
3. Make several pencil sketches for your composition. Use distortion and exaggeration to make your message strong. This is a painting, not a poster. Do not put any words in balloons for your people to speak. The visual image must carry the message. Select the best sketch.
4. Decide on a color scheme. Think about what colors will help express your feelings. How can you use strong contrast?
5. Pour a little of a light-value paint into the shallow tray. Add enough solvent to make a thin paint. Using your 1/4-inch (0.6-cm) brush draw the main shapes of your work on the sheet of white paper.
6. Paint your composition. Using your 1-inch (2.5-cm) brush, add deeper hues to the shapes. Do not try to smooth over the brush strokes. Let them show movement and create different textures. Use strong colors to emphasize the outlines of your shapes.
7. Put your work on display. Can you and your classmates read the themes in each others' statements?

EXAMINING YOUR WORK

- **Describe** Identify the person or persons in your work. Tell what problem you chose to speak about. Tell what statement you decided to make. Identify the colors and lines used. Identify places where different textures are used.
- **Analyze** Point to places where free-flowing, loose brushstrokes are used to show movement. Explain how the heavy lines and brush strokes add to the distortion, exaggeration, and contrast. Show where the proportions of shapes have been distorted.
- **Interpret** Tell what mood your painting expresses. Explain how the colors you chose help express this mood. Tell how distortion adds to the mood. Give your work a title that sums up its meaning.
- **Judge** Tell whether you feel your work succeeds in making a social statement. Tell whether it succeeds as a work of art. Explain your answers.

▶ **Figure 10–12   Student work. An expressive painting.**

OTHER STUDIO IDEAS

- Carry out this project combining magazine cutouts and paint.

●● Choose one hue, and paint your work using a monochromatic color scheme.

BUILDING VOCABULARY

Number a sheet of paper from 1 to 15. After each number, write the term from the box that best matches each description below.

acrylic	palette
binder	pigment
encaustic	solvent
fresco	synthetic paints
glaze	tempera
impasto	transparent
oil paint	watercolor
opaque	

1. A finely ground powder that gives every paint its color.
2. A liquid that holds together the grains of pigment.
3. A material used to thin the binder in paint.
4. A medium in which pigment is mixed into melted wax.
5. A medium in which pigment is applied to a wall spread with wet plaster.
6. A medium in which pigment mixed with egg yolk and water is applied with tiny brush strokes.
7. Paint with an oil base.
8. Thick, buttery layers of paint.
9. Clear.
10. A thin, clear sheet of paint.
11. A painting medium in which pigment is blended with gum arabic and water.
12. Manufactured paints with plastic binders.
13. Quick-drying water-based synthetic paint.
14. Does not allow light to pass through.
15. Light colored tray where paints are mixed before they are used for painting.

REVIEWING ART FACTS

Number a sheet of paper from 16 to 20. Answer each question in a few words.

16. What are the three parts of paint? What is the purpose of each part?
17. What is the solvent in encaustic? In fresco?
18. Why is tempera paint hard to use? What is an advantage of using it?
19. What fact about oil paint allows an artist to blend colors on the canvas?
20. Name two different techniques for applying oil paint. Tell what kind of results you get with each technique.

THINKING ABOUT ART

On a sheet of paper, answer each question in a sentence or two.

1. **Interpret.** What sort of paint do you think cave dwellers used to make their paintings? What sorts of tools do you think they painted with? Explain your answers.
2. **Analyze.** Do you think encaustic was an easy medium to use? Why, or why not?
3. **Compare and contrast.** Name some problems of doing frescoes that would not be true of other painting techniques.

MAKING ART CONNECTIONS

1. **Language Arts.** Discuss how artists use their art work to speak about problems or social issues. Write a paragraph describing what the artist was trying to say in *Echo of a Scream* on page **180**.
2. **Science.** Explore an interesting color illusion called an afterimage. Stare at a bright shape for a minute and then look away. What do you see? It's an afterimage of the same shape and size but a different color. Read about this occurrence and report to the class.

LOOKING AT THE DETAILS

The detail shown below is from Alma Thomas' *Iris, Tulips, Jonquils and Crocuses.* Study the detail and answer the following questions.

1. Do you think Alma Thomas could achieve the same effect in her painting if she used watercolors? Explain.
2. Which color draws your eye first? How does this color contribute to the "beat" of the painting?
3. In what way does the white background affect the image?
4. No two shapes in this painting are exactly the same, yet the image is organized. How did the artist achieve this effect?

Alma Thomas. *Iris, Tulips, Jonquils and Crocuses.* 1969. Acrylic on canvas. (Detail.) 152.4 x 127 cm (60 x 50"). National Museum of Women in the Arts, Washington, D.C.

JANE
Avril

H.Stern, Paris.

1899

▲ The artist was very careful about his work. He was even known to go into the print shop and mix his own colors.

Henri de Toulouse-Lautrec. *Jane Avril*. 1899. Color lithograph. 68.3 x 47 cm (26⅞ x 18½″). Free Library of Philadelphia.

Graphic Design

Artists, as you have seen, work and create in many different areas. Some artists paint. Others draw or sculpt. Others make prints.

The poster at the left is an example of yet another area in which artists work. This poster was done by a famous French painter, Henri de Toulouse-Lautrec. He was the first artist to create posters for commercial use. Most of his posters were used to advertise musical performances.

Artists working in commercial art use various art media and techniques to communicate their messages. In this chapter you will learn about this field.

OBJECTIVES

After completing this chapter, you will be able to:
- Explain what graphic design is.
- Describe jobs of different graphic artists.
- Identify layout and typeface.
- Design a logo, a comic strip, a concert poster, and a story illustration.

WORDS YOU WILL LEARN

editorial designers
graphic artists
graphic design
illustrators
layout
logo
typefaces

ARTISTS YOU WILL MEET

Victor Moscoso
Jeff MacNelly
Beatrix Potter
Theophile-Alexandre
  Steinlen
Henri de Toulouse-
  Lautrec
N.C. Wyeth

The Art of Graphic Design

There are artists at work all around you. Artists create the television commercials you view and the billboards you read. Some of the art work they create includes posters, packaging, magazine advertisements, and corporate symbols. There were even artists responsible for the graphic design of this book.

Artists who work in these areas are known as graphic artists. **Graphic artists** *work in the field of art known as graphic design.* **Graphic design** is the *field of art that uses pictures and words to instruct, or to communicate a specific message.* Look around your classroom. What graphic design symbols and images do you see?

GRAPHIC ARTISTS

Graphic artists work in a great many areas. Each area has its own special tasks and job title. Some of these areas are editorial design, illustration, advertising design, and sign making. Sometimes graphic artists work together as members of a larger creative team.

Editorial Design

The field of graphic design flourished in the 1500s. That was when the printing press was invented, making it possible to produce multiple copies of printed material at one time. People who arranged the words and pictures were similar to today's graphic artists.

Today these people are called editorial designers. **Editorial designers** are *graphic artists who arrange words and illustrations and prepare the material for printing.* Some editorial designers work on books, while others work on magazines and newspapers.

Planning the **layout**, or *the arrangement of words and pictures on a page*, is only one task of the editorial designer. Another is selecting the **typefaces**, or *styles of lettering for the printed material.* Figure 11–1 shows a typeface design based on an early typeface used many years ago in Europe. Today's editorial designers can choose from hundreds of typefaces. How many different typefaces can you find on this page? What differences can you spot among these styles?

abcdefghijklmnopqrstuvwxyz
ABCDEFGHIJKLMNOPQRSTUVWXYZ
1234567890 [&.,:;!?'""`=¶%/$£]

▲ Figure 11–1   Before Gütenberg invented the printing press, books were handwritten. Where do you think some of the first typeface styles came from?

▲ **Figure 11–2** Do you know this story? You may have heard it when you were small. How do illustrations like this help you visualize the personality of the characters?

Beatrix Potter. *Jemima Puddle-Duck.* 1908. Pencil, pen and ink, watercolor. Frederic Warne & Co., London.

Illustration

Have you ever used step-by-step drawings to put something together? If you have, you have used the same work habits of an illustrator. **Illustrators** are *graphic artists who create printed materials that explain or teach.* Many times illustrators work closely with editorial designers.

The color wheel on page **56** of this book (Figure 4–4) was drawn by an illustrator. So were the shaded shapes on page **147** (Figure 8–4). The drawing in Figure 11–2 was made to illustrate a children's book. When you look at Figure 11–3, you see the drawing of a technical illustrator. Notice the fine details that are included in the drawing.

Did you notice that each illustration listed above used a different art medium? Illustrators may use an airbrush, pen and ink, colored pencils, or watercolors to achieve the look they want. Today illustrators often use computers and other technology to create art.

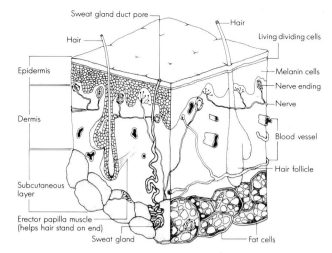

▲ **Figure 11–3** This is a drawing from a health textbook. How do drawings like this one help explain the lessons being taught?

Advertising Design

Other graphic artists specialize in advertising design. In this area the graphic artist communicates and creates a message in words and pictures to help sell or promote products or services.

Look again at the lithograph on page **190**. This was done by Henri de Toulouse-Lautrec to promote a concert by a well-known performer. Figure 11–4 shows an ad by another French printmaker of the 1800s. This one was for a company that made teas and chocolates. Notice that both artists used a combination of words and pictures. This is true of the work of graphic artists today.

Like editorial designers, advertising designers are concerned with layout and type styles. Some advertising designers work on newspaper or magazine ads. Others design commercials for television. The success of their work is measured by the impact the message has on the receiver. Can you think of an advertisement that has left an impression in your mind?

▲ Figure 11–4   What mood does the artist convey? Is it appealing? Is it appropriate for the company he is promoting? Why?

Theophile-Alexandre Steinlen. *Compagnie Française des Chocolats et des Thés*. 1899. Color lithograph. 76.2 x 101.6 cm (30 x 40"). Metropolitan Museum of Art, New York, New York.

▲ Figure 11–5   These are international signs intended to help travelers. Do the pictures quickly convey their messages? How does the artist's choice of color contribute to the sign's effectiveness?

▲ Figure 11–6   Notice how much information the designer has packed into these few words and symbols. Could a person unable to read tell what kind of business this was?

Rendered by John Sullivan. *Tailor's Shears* (Shop sign). c. 1935. National Gallery of Art, Washington, D.C.

Sign Making

You may not think of Figure 11–5 as an art work. Yet it was someone's job to choose a type style and size for the letters. Someone had to design the figures and pick a color combination for the signs.

The "someone" behind these choices was a graphic artist with the job title of sign maker. The art of making signs traces its roots to the earliest times. The sign in Figure 11–6 was made back during America's Colonial period. Can you tell what this sign is made of? Can you tell what kind of business the sign advertised?

▲ Figure 11–7   Student work. Letter collage.

STUDIO EXPERIENCE

Choose one of the 26 letters of the alphabet. Search through newspapers, magazines, and books. See how many different typefaces and sizes for this letter you can find. Cut examples of the letter from newspapers and magazine headlines. On a sheet of paper, make a collage based on the examples of your letter. To add interest to your collage, turn some of your letters upside down and some sideways. Try overlapping some of your letters. When you have an interesting arrangement, glue the letters to the background with white glue. If possible, photocopy your finished collage. Then add color using watercolors, crayons, or pastels. (See Figure 11–7.) (For more information on making a collage, see Technique Tip **28**, *Handbook* page **281**.)

✔CHECK YOUR UNDERSTANDING

1. What does an editorial designer do?
2. What is a layout? What is another term meaning "type style"?
3. What is the job title of a graphic artist who makes step-by-step drawings?
4. What are three art tools that an illustrator might use?
5. What do graphic artists who specialize in advertising do?

Designing a Logo

A **logo** is *a special image representing a business, group, or product.* All logos are one-of-a-kind shapes or pictures. Some contain letters or words as well. Figure 11–8 shows some well-known logos. How many of these have you seen? Do you know the business, group, or product each stands for?

Imagine you are a graphic artist for an advertising agency. You have been asked to create a logo for a space colony on a newly discovered planet. Imagine you were also asked to come up with a name for the colony.

WHAT YOU WILL LEARN

Working in a small group, you will create a logo for a new space colony. The logo should contain the name of the colony (or at least the name's initials). The logo should capture the idea that the space colony is a pleasant place to live. It should create a feeling that the settlers are living in their own backyard rather than out in space. You will use a variety of colors, lines, and shapes to help show this. These elements must be arranged using either formal or informal balance. See Figure 11-9.

WHAT YOU WILL NEED

- Pencil, eraser, and ruler
- Sheets of sketch paper
- Sheet of white paper, 9 x 12 inch (23 x 30 cm)
- Watercolor markers

WHAT YOU WILL DO

1. You have been selected to design a logo. The logo must include the name or initials of the space colony. Brainstorm with the class about what life might be like on the space colony. Will the colony be divided into neighborhoods? Will the colony be under a temperature-control dome? What kinds of jobs will the people have? What will they do for entertainment? Will they have TV?

2. Working by yourself, make rough pencil sketches for your logo. Think about different ways of showing the letters you chose to use. Think about what images you might use to stand for a space colony. Choose different lines and shapes to show that life in the colony is pleasant and comfortable.

▲ Figure 11–8   What do you think makes a logo successful? Why? What other logos can you think of that you see often? What companies or products do they stand for?

Logos courtesy of American Red Cross, Childreach Sponsorship, and Plan International USA.

3. Working neatly, draw your best idea onto the sheet of white paper. Use a ruler to draw the straight lines.
4. Color in your logo with the watercolor markers. Use colors that suggest the spirit of adventure experienced by people living in the colony.
5. Display your work. Look for similarities and differences between your work and those of classmates.

▲ Figure 11–9   Student works. Space colony logos.

OTHER STUDIO IDEAS

- Create pencil sketches for a logo for yourself. Include both type and visual elements. Select your best sketch and neatly draw it on paper 9 x 12 inch (23 x 30 cm).
- •• Do a logo for your school. Try to give depth to the logo. Use techniques of shading you have learned about to create the look of deep space.

Drawing a Comic Strip

Some graphic artists are storytellers. They tell their stories in connected boxes, or frames, made up of words and pictures. We know these strings of frames better as comic strips. Like a play, every comic strip has a cast of characters. When characters speak, their words often appear in outlined white spaces called balloons. (See Figures 11–10 and 11–11.)

Most "comic" strips are funny. Some, however, are not. Some are satirical, meaning that they poke fun at public figures and world events. Others are adventure stories or show suspense in some other way. Look again at Figure 11–10. Which kind of strip is this box from?

WHAT YOU WILL LEARN

You will create a comic strip made up of five or more boxes, or frames. Each box will be at least 5 inches (13 cm) square. The characters in your strip may be drawn in either a humorous or realistic way. Your strip may be funny, action-packed, or have a serious subject. If your strip is funny, the last frame should have the punch line. The lines and shapes will be used to add rhythm or movement to your strip.

WHAT YOU WILL NEED

- Notepad and pencil
- Sheets of sketch paper
- Eraser and ruler
- Sheets of white paper, 12 x 18 inch (30 x 46 cm)
- Black fine-line felt-tip marker
- Colored pencils, markers, or crayons
- Transparent tape

WHAT YOU WILL DO

1. Think about the people and situations you could include in your comic strip. Possibilities are school activities, fun with friends, or fantasy. Decide whether you will make your comic strip humorous or adventurous.
2. On your notepad, plan out your story. Identify the characters you will use. Decide what you will show them doing in the strip. Write out what you will have them say. Decide how many frames you will need to show the action.

▼ Figure 11–10 How does the illustration help you in interpreting the words?

Jeff MacNelly. *Shoe.* © 1989. Tribune Media Services, Inc.

3. Make rough pencil sketches of your characters. Use lines and shapes to show movement. Sketch the background. Practice drawing word balloons. Do a rough sketch for each one of the boxes that will be in your strip. Carefully print out the words each character will say. Number each frame.

4. Divide a sheet of paper, 12 x 18 inch (30 x 46 cm) into as many squares or rectangles as you will need. How many will you use? Will all the boxes be the same size, or will some be larger for emphasis? Use your ruler and pencil to draw the boxes. (See Technique Tip **22**, *Handbook* page **278** for information on measuring squares and rectangles.) Use extra sheets as needed. Use repetition of characters and environments to give the strip unity.

5. Working lightly in pencil, carefully draw your final sketches into the boxes. Print out your characters' words in balloons.

6. Go over all the lines and letters with the black fine-line marker. Color in your shapes with colored pencils, markers, or crayons. If you used more than one sheet, join the pages together with transparent tape.

EXAMINING YOUR WORK

- **Describe** Identify the characters in your strip. Tell who they are and what they are doing. Show that you used at least five boxes. Point to the different lines and shapes.
- **Analyze** Explain how the lines and shapes create rhythm or movement in your strip.
- **Interpret** Identify the mood of your strip. Tell what clues help the viewer understand this mood. If your strip was humorous, was the punch line in the last box effective?
- **Judge** Tell whether you feel your work succeeds. Explain your answer.

7. Display your work. Notice how classmates completed the assignment. Ask your classmates to read your strip. Can they understand your story? Can they recognize the theme?

◀ **Figure 11–11** What kind of balance does the comic strip at the left display? Explain.

Charles Schulz. *Peanuts.* © 1989. United Feature Syndicate, Inc.

OTHER STUDIO IDEAS

- Redraw your strip. This time, instead of adding color, use different values of India ink. Different values can be obtained by adding small amounts of water to India ink. Apply the India ink with a small brush. Does this change the mood of the work? Explain.

- ●● Have the whole class work together to plan a whole comic book. Each student will create one story for the book. When it is finished, protect the pages with lamination, and bind them into a book.

Designing a Poster

In music, as in art, different artists have different styles. The style of today's most popular rock group is different from that of yesterday's. Both are very different from the musical style of Mozart.

When graphic artists design concert posters for musical groups, they try to capture the musician's style. Their works often reflect one of the three views of art you have learned about. Look at the concert posters in Figure 11–12. Which of these is realistic? Which uses design composition alone to make its statement? Which expresses a feeling?

WHAT YOU WILL LEARN

You will invent a musician or musical group and choose the style of music your imaginary artist makes. Then you will design a concert poster for that artist. Decide on a title for the group. The poster will include the title of the concert and name of the artist. You will choose the medium or media to carry out the assignment. You will use the principles of balance, rhythm, and emphasis to organize the elements of colors, lines, shapes, space, and texture in your design. (See Figure 11–13.)

WHAT YOU WILL NEED

- Notepad and pencil
- Sheets of sketch paper
- Eraser and ruler
- Any or all of the following: broad-line and fine-line colored markers, crayons, collage materials (magazines, newspapers, scissors, white glue, small brush)
- Sheet of heavy white paper
- Transparent tape

▲ **Figure 11–12** **Describe the style of music of the top poster. If you were interested in rock and roll, would this poster interest you? What does the guitar symbolize to you? Explain.**

(TOP) Victor Moscoso. *Junior Wells and His Chicago Blues Band*. 1966. Offset lithograph. Poster. 50.5 x 35.6 cm (19⅞ x 14″). The Museum of Modern Art, New York, New York. Gift of the designer.
(BOTTOM) Ernie Friedlander Studios. 1990. Offset lithograph. 91.5 x 61 cm (36 x 24″). Portal Publications Ltd.

WHAT YOU WILL DO

1. Think of a musical style and name for your imaginary musician or group. Write the name on your notepad. Create a title for the concert poster. Write a short description of your group.

2. Create your own style or choose a style of lettering for the concert title and the artist's name. Decide where on the poster

each will appear and decide how large each will be. Sketch them in.

3. Plan how you will fill the remaining space. If you plan to use collage materials, find and clip images found in magazines and newspapers. Choose which aesthetic view of art you will take. Decide if you wish your work to look realistic, to make a statement with design alone, or to express a feeling or mood.

4. Working lightly in pencil, place your title lettering, artist's name and any other images on the poster. (See Technique Tip **5**, *Handbook* page **271**, which gives instructions on using a grid to enlarge letters and images.)

5. Using markers or crayons, color in the letters and images you have drawn. Using glue and brush, paste down any magazine or newspaper clippings you have chosen to add to your design.

6. Display your concert poster. Take a poll among your classmates. How many can tell the style of music your imaginary artist plays?

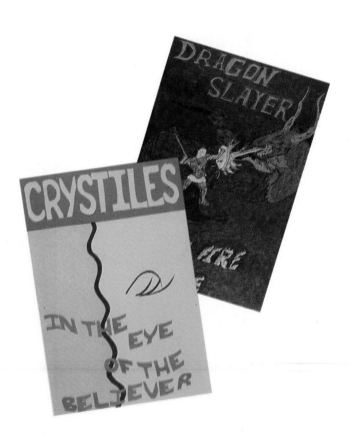

▶ Figure 11–13 Student works. Music concert posters.

EXAMINING YOUR WORK

- **Describe**   Point out the artist's name and the concert title. Tell what media you chose to make your concert poster. Identify the elements of art used in your design.
- **Analyze**   Tell which principles you used to organize the elements. Explain why you chose to use those principles.
- **Interpret**   Explain how your design helps a viewer understand the style of music of this group.
- **Judge**   Tell whether you feel your work succeeds. Identify the view or views of art you used when making this decision.

OTHER STUDIO IDEAS

- Create a compact disc cover for a real group or musician you like. Invent a title for the compact disc and individual song titles. Use a style that differs from the one you used above.

- ● Design a poster for an amusement park or a sporting event.

Illustrating a Story

Look at Figure 11–14. This is an illustration by N.C. Wyeth, a famous American story illustrator. Wyeth's illustrations made the stories he illustrated come alive for the readers. Do you know what famous story this Wyeth illustration comes from?

WHAT YOU WILL LEARN

Select an action story or poem you have recently read and liked. You will paint an illustration for an incident that took place in the story or poem. Your illustration will capture the setting, mood, and style of the whole work. You will decide whether your illustration will have formal or informal balance. You will decide whether to use realistic proportions for your figures or distortion. (See Figure 11–15.)

WHAT YOU WILL NEED

- Notepad, pencil, and eraser
- Sheets of sketch paper
- Paper towels
- Sheet of white paper, 12 x 18 inch (30 x 46 cm)
- School acrylic paint
- Bristle brushes, varied sizes
- Water

▶ **Figure 11–14** Would you describe the artist's style as realistic? What elements does he use to get this result? What principles does he use to organize those elements?

N. C. Wyeth. *Blind Pew.* 1911. Illustration from *Treasure Island* by Robert Louis Stevenson, Charles Scribner's Sons, Macmillan Publishing Company.

▲ Figure 11–15   Student work. A story illustration.

WHAT YOU WILL DO

1. Think about a short story, novel, or poem you have read and liked. Decide what scene from this work you want to illustrate using the main characters.
2. On the notepad, describe what the characters are doing. Write down information about their expressions, moods, and actions. List ways you will use color and the other elements of art in your painting. Decide whether the proportions of your figures will be realistic or exaggerated. Decide if you will use emphasis to

- **Describe**   Tell what story you have chosen to illustrate. Tell what is happening in the part of the work you have illustrated. Explain who the characters are. List the elements and principles used.
- **Analyze**   Tell whether your work has formal or informal balance. Point to and describe the proportions of your figures. Tell whether these proportions were used to make these figures look realistic or cartoon-like.
- **Interpret**   Explain how your illustration captures the setting, mood, and style of the story. Give your illustration a title and explain why you chose the title.
- **Judge**   Tell whether you feel your work succeeds.

make a figure or object stand out. Balance your illustration using either formal or informal balance.
3. Make rough pencil sketches for your painting.
4. Lightly sketch your plan on the good paper. Use your 1/4-inch (0.6 cm) brush and a light-value paint to draw the main shapes of your illustration on the sheet of white paper. Use your larger brushes to fill in shapes. Complete your painting.
5. Display your painting. Notice similarities and differences in the way you and classmates completed the assignment. Try to guess the titles of the different stories and poems illustrated.

OTHER STUDIO IDEAS

- Illustrate something you have written.
- ●● Work with the whole class. Choose one children's story and turn it into an illustrated book. Each student select a differ-

ent scene to illustrate. Protect the pages by laminating them, and bind them into a storybook for the little children to read at the library.

BUILDING VOCABULARY

Number a sheet of paper from 1 to 7. After each number, write the term from the box that best matches each description below.

editorial designers	layout
graphic artist	logo
graphic design	typefaces
illustrators	

1. The field of art that uses pictures and words to instruct, or communicate.
2. Graphic artists who arrange words and illustrations and prepare the material for printing.
3. The arrangement of words and pictures.
4. Styles of lettering.
5. Graphic artists who create printed materials that explain, teach, or decorate.
6. A special image connected with a business, group, or product.
7. People who work in the field of art known as graphic design.

REVIEWING ART FACTS

Number a sheet of paper from 8 to 14. Answer each question in a complete sentence.

8. Name four main areas of graphic design.
9. What invention spurred the beginning of the field of graphic design?
10. Name two tasks of an editorial designer.
11. What were lithographs by artists like Toulouse-Lautrec used for in the 1800s?
12. Name two places besides TV where you can see the work of advertising designers.
13. What kinds of graphic artists make step-by-step drawings?
14. Besides shapes or pictures, what do logos often contain?

THINKING ABOUT ART

On a sheet of paper, answer each question in a sentence or two.

1. **Analyze.** What kinds of products have you seen advertised both on TV and in printed form? In what ways are the two kinds of ads different?
2. **Extend.** How do you think the invention of the printing press affected the work of the sign maker?
3. **Extend.** In which kinds of books, science or history, do you think technical illustrations would be more useful? Explain your answer.

MAKING ART CONNECTIONS

1. **Drama.** Find out all you can about the theme and character of an upcoming play in your school or community. Design a poster advertising the play. Develop visual images that show what the play is about. Include information such as where and when the show will be given, the name of the organization producing it, the author, and how much tickets cost.
2. **Home Economics.** Collect an assortment of favorite recipes. Design and illustrate a cookbook. Work from direct observation of subject matter such as fresh fruits and vegetables, pots and pans, china, and cooking utensils.
3. **Physical Education.** Design a logo representing your favorite sport, create a poster design advertising an upcoming event, or design a school spirit T-shirt. Learn as much about the subject as possible. Observe and draw athletes in action, cheerleaders, mascots, and equipment used. Develop original imagery. Do not use existing images.

LOOKING AT THE DETAILS

The detail shown below is from a poster of the performer *Jane Avril*, done by the artist Henri de Toulouse-Lautrec. Study the detail and answer the following questions.

1. Examine the woman's hat. How do the elements of line and color affect the mood?
2. Knowing that this is only part of the work, where or how might you imagine to find the figure's legs?
3. Why do you think the artist chose this lettering style as opposed to a more formal one?
4. Imagine that you are walking down the street and you see several posters of advertisements, but only one catches your eye. What elements of art and principles of art would you expect to find in that one?

Henri de Toulouse-Lautrec. *Jane Avril*. 1899. Color lithograph. (Detail.) 68.3 x 47 cm (26⅞ x 18½"). Free Library of Philadelphia.

▲ The artist sculpted the work just before his first child was born. Notice the name of the work. What clues tell you how he felt the child would affect his relationship with his wife?

Henry Moore. *Family Group*. 1948–49. Cast 1950. Bronze. 150.5 x 118.1, base 114.3 x 75.9 cm (59¼ x 46½, base 45 x 29⅞"). Museum of Modern Art, New York, New York. A. Conger. Goodyear Fund.

CHAPTER 12

Sculpture

Like other artists, sculptors begin new projects by asking themselves questions. Here are some questions that faced the sculptor of the work at the left.

- What medium will I use?
- Will I create by adding to or taking away from?
- Will the work be realistic?
- Will the figures appear smooth or rough?

In this chapter you will learn about the different choices sculptors have when they create their art work.

OBJECTIVES

After completing this chapter, you will be able to:

- Name the four basic methods used by sculptors.
- Describe each method of sculpting.
- Define the terms *freestanding* and *relief.*
- Tell which sculpting methods are additive and which are subtractive.
- Create sculptures of your own using carving, modeling, and assembling.

WORDS YOU WILL LEARN

additive	high relief
assembling	low relief
carving	modeling
casting	relief
freestanding	subtractive

ARTISTS YOU WILL MEET

Jean Baptiste Carpeaux	Henry Moore
Clodion	Louise Nevelson
Naum Gabo	Georgia O'Keeffe
Alexandre Hogue	David Smith

The Art of Sculpture

When artists work with paints, they create the illusion of space in their works. It is the job of sculptors to create their works in space. Look at the painting in Figure 12–1. The objects in it seem to have roundness and depth. If you try to grasp one, however, your hand will bump up against flat canvas. The boy in Figure 12–2, on the other hand, has *real* roundness and depth. The work casts *real* shadows. It invites you to move around it. It invites you to see it from every side.

In this lesson you will learn about the many tools and methods sculptors use to create their art work. In later lessons you will use some of these tools and methods yourself.

THE BEGINNINGS OF SCULPTING

You may recall that the earliest artists, the cave dwellers, were painters. But did you know they were also sculptors? Stone, horn, ivory, and bone were some media used by these early sculptors. The sculpture in Figure 12–3, completed in 2600 B.C., is regarded by many to be one of the wonders of the world. Do you know in what country this remarkable work is found? Do you know what it is called? What medium was used to construct it?

► **Figure 12–1** Does this painting seem lifelike? How many different ways does the artist create a feeling of space?

Alexandre Hogue. *Drouth Stricken Area*. 1934. Oil on canvas. 76.2 x 107.9 cm (30 x 42½"). Dallas Museum of Art.

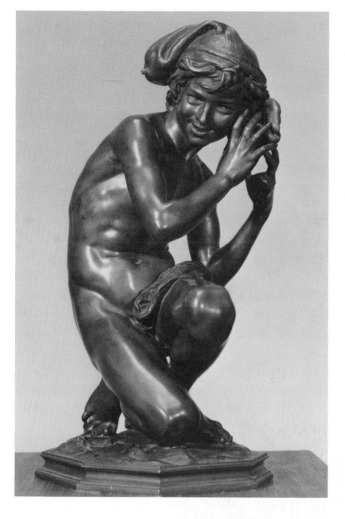

◄ **Figure 12–2** Notice how the work twists and turns in space. Does this make you want to move around the work?

Jean Baptiste Carpeaux. *Neopolitan Fisherboy*. 1857. Bronze with light brown patina. 34.6 cm (13⅝″). Allen Memorial Art Museum, Oberlin College, Oberlin, Ohio. Gift of Charles F. Olney.

▼ **Figure 12–3** At its highest point this sculpture is 65 feet (19.8 m) tall. The head is that of an ancient Egyptian king. The body is that of a lion. What statement could the Egyptians have been making?

Great Sphinx, Giza. c. 2600 B.C.

▲ Figure 12–4   Do you know the Biblical story in this carving?

The Annunciation. Estella San Miguel, Spain.

SCULPTING TECHNIQUES

Sculptors use four basic techniques in their work. These are carving, casting, modeling, and assembling. Some of these techniques are **additive**, *produced by adding to or combining materials.* Other techniques are **subtractive**, *produced by removing or taking away from the original material.*

Carving

Carving is *a sculpting method in which material is cut or chipped away.* The very first carvings were probably nothing more than figures scratched into a flat rock. Since then sculptors have learned ways of freeing images from great blocks of stone. Study the carving in Figure 12–4. It decorates the doorway of a church in Spain. The work has a religious subject. Do you remember any other art works you studied that have religious subjects?

In carving, sculptors end with less material than they start with. For this reason, carving is known as a subtractive method of sculpting.

Casting

Casting is *a sculpting method in which melted material is poured into a mold.* When the material cools it hardens and the mold is taken off. Often the material used is a metal such as bronze in a liquid form.

The art of casting bronze figures is over 3000 years old. The first people to do it were the Chinese. The Greeks and Romans later showed great skill in their bronze castings. Look again at Figure 12–2 on page **209**. Notice how lifelike the boy looks. Today artists still cast in bronze. The bronze statue that opened this chapter (page **206**) was cast by a leading sculptor of our century.

Modeling

Painters start off with blank canvases. Sculptors sometimes start off with blank space. By adding together bits of material, they create something where nothing was before. Such methods of sculpting are called additive methods.

Modeling, *a sculpting method in which a soft or workable material is built up and shaped,* is an additive method. The material used most often in modeling is clay. Like carving and casting, modeling is a very old method.

Assembling

Not all sculpting methods are old. A second additive method, known as assembling or constructing, came into being only recently. **Assembling** is *a sculpting method in which different kinds of materials are gathered and joined together.* Wood, plastic, wire, string, as well as found objects are some of the materials used to assemble sculpture. Glue, screws, and nails are a few of the materials used to join the objects together. Study

▲ **Figure 12–5** What elements and principles are blended to create a feeling of action in this work?

David Smith. *Cockfight-Variation.* 1945. Steel. 86.3 x 34.9 x 15.2 cm (34 x 13¾ x 6"). Whitney Museum of American Art, New York, New York.

▲ **Figure 12–6** The artist's father ran a lumberyard. How might that have affected her life's work?

Louise Nevelson. *Atmosphere and Environment.* 1970. Cor-Ten steel. 640.1 x 487.7 cm (252 x 192"). The Art Museum, Princeton University. John B. Putman Jr. Memorial Collection.

Figures 12–5 and 12–6. What materials were used to assemble each work of art? What tools did the artists use to construct their sculptural pieces? What does Figure 12–5 look like? How would you describe Figure 12–6?

✔ CHECK YOUR UNDERSTANDING

1. Name the four basic techniques of sculpting. Define each method.
2. Which technique of sculpting is called a subtractive technique? Why is it called this?
3. Who were the first people to do bronze casting?
4. Which two techniques of sculpting are called additive techniques? Why are they called this?
5. Name three media that can be used in assembling.

Carving a Plaster Relief

Sometimes sculptures are only partly enclosed by space. Such sculptures are called relief. **Relief** is *a type of sculpture in which forms and figures are projected from the front only*. Relief sculptures are flat along the back. They are meant to be viewed only from the front.

Sculptors speak of two kinds of relief sculpture. *Relief that stands out in space only slightly* is **low relief**. *Relief that stands out boldly from its background* is **high relief**.

In this lesson you will make a low relief sculpture using the method of carving.

WHAT YOU WILL LEARN

Using the method of carving, you will make a relief sculpture of a flower. Your work will show the flower close up. You will not try to make your flower realistic. Instead, you will concentrate on creating a unified design. Use radial balance and rhythm to organize the shapes and lines suggested by the flower. Use a variety of textures to make your design more interesting. Use line directions to make your flower express a certain mood, such as twisting wildly or swaying gently.

WHAT YOU WILL NEED

- Real flowers or photographs of flowers
- Pencil and sketch paper cut into sheets, 7 inches (18 cm) square
- Plastic bowl, cold water, mixing stick
- Molding plaster and vermiculite (vuhr-**mik**-yuh-lite)
- Pie pan lined with plastic, 9 inch (23 cm)
- Paper clip; assorted carving tools, such as knives, nails, files; fine sandpaper

▶ **Figure 12–7 How would you describe this flower? What elements and principles can you identify?**

Georgia O'Keeffe. *The White Calico Flower.* 1931. Oil on canvas. 76.2 x 91.4 cm (30 x 36"). Whitney Museum of American Art, New York, New York.

WHAT YOU WILL DO

1. Study the painting by Georgia O'Keeffe in Figure 12–7. It is one of many close-up looks at flowers the artist has painted. Notice that O'Keeffe has left out realistic details. Instead, she has focused on the flowing lines and curved surfaces to create an abstract design.

2. Using real flowers or photographs of flowers as models, make pencil sketches in the style of O'Keeffe. Focus on creating rhythm with the lines and shapes of stems and petals. Look for places where different textures can be used. Choose your best sketch. Set it aside.

3. Pour 3 parts cold water into a plastic mixing bowl. Mix in 3 parts molding plaster and 2 parts vermiculite. Using the stick, stir the mixture until it is smooth and creamy. When the mixture thickens slightly, pour it carefully into the plastic-lined pie pan. (See Technique Tip **19**, *Handbook* page **276**.)

4. After a few minutes you will notice the mixture begin to dry and set. Place a bent paper clip in it near the top center. Leave the looped end of the paper clip sticking out to serve as a hanger. When the mixture is dry and hard, grasp the plastic liner. Carefully lift the dried plaster mixture from the pan. Turn it so the clip side is down. Another name for your relief is a plaque (**plak**). A plaque is an ornamental tablet that is meant to be hung on a wall.

5. Transfer your flower design onto the flat part of the plaque. Using the knife, begin scraping away the plaque surrounding your design. The flower design should stand out from the background. Use smaller tools to carve the petals so they appear to overlap. Add texture to the leaves using the nail and other pointed tools. When you have finished carving, lightly sand the relief to give it a clean, smooth look.

6. Using the paper clip as a hook, hang your relief. Compare your work with those of your classmates.

EXAMINING YOUR WORK

- **Describe**   Point to the areas around your flower relief that you carved away. Show the petal shapes and lines you carved, and describe the texture you added.
- **Analyze**   Show where you used the principle of rhythm to organize the lines and shapes. Point to the variety of textures in your relief. Explain how you used the elements and principles to make a design that has unity.
- **Interpret**   Tell what mood your work captures. Explain which elements and principles help the viewer understand the mood.
- **Judge**   Tell whether you feel your work succeeds. Explain your answer.

SAFETY TIP

If you have breathing problems, tell your teacher. Dry dust from plaster and clay can be harmful. Wear a dust mask if necessary.

OTHER STUDIO IDEAS

- Do the above activity using corrugated cardboard. This time use the additive sculpture method to build your relief up from the flat base.

- ●● Make a plaster plaque as directed above and carve a relief design using symmetrical balance.

Modeling in Clay

Sculpture, you have read, uses space. Some sculptures use more space than others. Some are **freestanding**, or *surrounded on all sides by space*. Such works are also said to be "in the round."

The lively work in Figure 12–8 is a sculpture in the round. It was done by the French sculptor Clodion (**kloh**-dee-onh). When creating it the artist did not conform to limits of working on it from any one side. Instead, the artist kept turning the sculpture as work progressed. That way, Clodion was able to give equal attention to all sides. Study the work. Do you see the marks of the artist's fingers and tools on the surface? These help make the sculpture seem fresh and alive.

WHAT YOU WILL LEARN

Using the method of modeling, you will make a freestanding sculpture of an animal. You will build up the sculpture from a simple egg form. You will use texture to add harmony to the sculpture. Try to capture the personality of your animal by making it look gentle, friendly, or vicious.

WHAT YOU WILL NEED

- Pencil and sketch paper
- Piece of muslin or other smooth cloth
- Clay (a ball about the size of a grapefruit)
- Fork and slip (a liquid mixture of clay and water)
- Clay modeling tools

► Figure 12–8 The figure in the sculpture is a river god from mythology. Does the work give you a sense of water? Do you know any other characters from mythology? Which ones? How do you think they would be best shown in a sculpture?

Clodion (Claude Michel). *The River Rhine Separating the Waters.* 1765. Terracotta. 27.9 x 45.7 x 30.5 cm (11 x 18 x 12"). Kimbell Art Museum, Fort Worth, Texas.

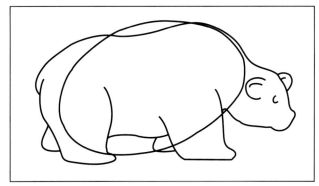

▲ Figure 12–9   Notice the oval shape of the bear's body. What other shapes do you see in this sketch?

WHAT YOU WILL DO

1. Look at the sketch of a bear in Figure 12–9. Notice how the rounded body of this animal has the form of an egg. Draw an egg outline similar to this one on a sheet of sketch paper. This will be the starting point for your own sculpture of an animal. Add legs, a head, a neck, and a tail to make an animal. Experiment with different animals. Begin each with an egg form. Choose your best sketch. As you sculpt, look back at the sketch from time to time.

2. Read the Technique Tip **17**, *Handbook* page **275**, about joining clay pieces. Working on a piece of burlap, divide your clay in half. Use one half to shape your egg form. Use the other half to make legs, neck, head, and tail. Using the fork, scratch lines on each part where it is to be attached to the egg. Wet each scratched surface with slip. Attach the parts firmly to the egg. Keep turning your sculpture as you work. Freestanding sculpture

EXAMINING YOUR WORK

- **Describe**   Tell what animal you sculpted. Point out details that make it easy to identify your animal. Point to the texture you used. Explain how this was done to suggest hair or fur. Explain what you learned about the strengths and weaknesses of clay as a sculpture medium.
- **Analyze**   Show how texture has been used to give harmony to your sculpture.
- **Interpret**   Show what features in your work would help a viewer understand the personality of your animal — friendly, fierce, gentle.
- **Judge**   Tell whether you feel your work succeeds. Explain your answer.

must look right when viewed from all angles. Avoid any fine details of clay that stick out. Keep your sculpture compact.

3. Finish your sculpture with a clay modeling tool. Do not use your fingers. Add details to your animal. Add an overall texture to give harmony to your sculpture. (*Hint*: A comb pulled or twisted across the surface will give a look of hair or fur.)

4. When your sculpture is firm but not dry, make a hole in the bottom. Hollow out the sculpture with a clay tool. This will keep it from cracking or exploding when it is baked, or fired.

5. Display your finished sculpture in a class "zoo."

OTHER STUDIO IDEAS

- Do a second clay sculpture, this time of an animal with a completely different personality. Compare it with your first sculpture. Are the different personalities easily identified?

- ● Do another clay sculpture, this time using a different geometric shape for the body. Use a cube, cone, sphere, or other shape.

Abstract Sculpture

Sculptures created through the method of assembling are often unique and daring. Look at Figure 12–10. Can you tell what materials the sculptor used? Can you tell what this sculpture is supposed to be?

This sculpture, by Naum Gabo, is abstract. Art work is abstract if you can recognize the subject of the work, but the object is portrayed in an unrealistic way. You probably can see that this sculpture represents a human head, but does it look real?

Imagine that this sculpture has been taken apart, and all of its pieces are laid in a pile in front of you. Would you be able to tell that these shapes represent the parts of a face? Imagine now that you are a sculptor. Could you assemble these same shapes to represent another kind of object?

WHAT YOU WILL LEARN

You will create an abstract sculpture using the method of assembling. You will use cardboard as a building material and glue as a joining material. Your sculpture will not be realistic. It will use a variety of geometric shapes and forms to express the idea of a bird, reptile, or amphibian. Design your sculpture with either a vertical or horizontal emphasis. When finished, paint the sculpture with a coat of black or white paint to give it harmony. (See Figure 12-11.)

WHAT YOU WILL NEED

- Pencil and sheets of sketch paper
- Sheets of corrugated cardboard cut from boxes
- Large scissors and white glue
- Tempera

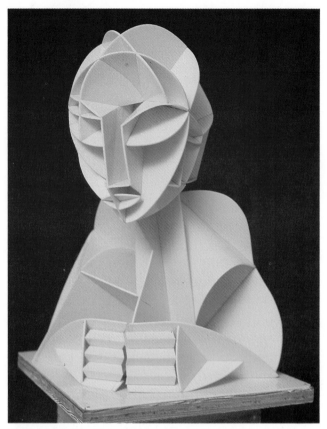

▲ **Figure 12–10** **The sculpture shows a human figure. Can you identify any features of this figure? Which ones? Why do you think this work was considered to be so daring when it was first seen?**

Naum Gabo. *Constructed Head No. 2.* 1916. Sculpture celluloid. 43.2 x 31.1 x 31.1 cm (17 x 12¼ x 12¼"). Dallas Museum of Art.

WHAT YOU WILL DO

1. Look through nature books to see the many variations of birds, reptiles, and amphibians. Choose one that has a variety of interesting shapes.
2. Make pencil sketches of your creature. Do several sketches until you have one that pleases you. You may want to combine the features of different types of birds, reptiles, or amphibians.

3. Make a revised pencil sketch of your creature using simple geometric shapes to symbolize the real shapes. Decide whether your sculpture will be horizontal or vertical.

4. Using scissors, cut a large cardboard shape as a base. Refer to your sketch to cut out smaller geometric shapes to form the body and features of your creature. You may cut the shapes in half, or in eighths. Think about different action poses. Is your creature standing still or twisting and turning? Is it sitting, lying down, or involved in some activity?

5. Assemble your work by gluing shapes and forms to each other. Work carefully. To see which angle works best, look at your sculpture from different angles before joining each new piece.

6. Paint your sculpture using either white or black. The use of a single color will add harmony to the work. Spray paint works especially well in this case.

SAFETY TIP

Use spray paint outdoors or in a room with good ventilation. Before spraying, place your sculpture inside a large cardboard box. This will contain some of the harmful fumes.

EXAMINING YOUR WORK

- **Describe** Identify the bird, reptile, or amphibian you chose as a starting point for your sculpture. Name the different shapes and forms you used in your work. Show shapes with different textures or patterns.
- **Analyze** Tell whether you used vertical or horizontal emphasis in your work. Point to the variety of shapes and forms you used. Explain how these add interest to your work. Explain how the use of a single black or white color adds to the harmony of the work.
- **Interpret** Give your work a title. Explain how the shapes you combined suggest a bird, reptile, or amphibian.
- **Judge** Tell whether you feel your work succeeds. Explain your answer.

▲ Figure 12–11 Student work. An abstract sculpture.

OTHER STUDIO IDEAS

- Create a second sculpture, this time combining found objects to represent an animal, bird, reptile, or amphibian. These odds and ends might include plastic spoons, soda straws, old door hinges, or other mechanical parts. Paint your sculpture black, white, or grey to emphasize the overall form of the sculpture.

CHAPTER 12 REVIEW

BUILDING VOCABULARY

Number a sheet of paper from 1 to 10. After each number, write the term from the box that best matches each description below.

additive	high relief
assembling	low relief
carving	modeling
casting	relief
freestanding	subtractive

1. A sculpting method in which material is cut or chipped away.
2. A term describing a sculpting method that takes away or removes material.
3. A sculpting method in which melted material is poured into a mold.
4. A term describing a sculpting method that adds together or joins bits of material together.
5. A sculpting method in which a soft or workable material is built up and shaped.
6. A sculpting method in which different kinds of materials are gathered and joined.
7. Surrounded on all sides by space.
8. Sculpture that is partly enclosed by space.
9. Sculpture that stands out in space only slightly.
10. Sculpture that stands out boldly from its background.

REVIEWING ART FACTS

Number a sheet of paper from 11 to 18. Answer each question in a complete sentence.

11. Name three sculpting media that have been in existence for thousands of years.
12. What are four sculpting techniques?
13. How old is the art of casting in bronze?
14. Who were the first people to do bronze castings?
15. What material is used most often in modeling?

16. Which method of sculpting is the most recent?
17. Name two building materials used in assembling. Name two fastening materials.
18. What is slip? What is it used for?

THINKING ABOUT ART

On a sheet of paper, answer each question in a sentence or two.

1. **Extend.** What kinds of materials do you think might be found in sculptures of the future? Explain your answer.
2. **Analyze.** Which two methods of sculpting could be used to create an ice sculpture? Describe how you would use each method. Tell why the two methods you didn't name would not work as well.
3. **Compare and contrast.** In what ways are the methods of modeling and assembling alike? In what ways are they different?
4. **Extend.** The term *terra cotta* means "baked earth." In which method of sculpting would you expect to find terra cotta used as a medium?

MAKING ART CONNECTIONS

1. **Science.** In this chapter you learned that early cave painters were also sculptors. In 1912 a cave, Tuc' d' Audoubert, was discovered in the French Pyrenees. Research more about this discovery and the artifacts associated with it.
2. **Social Studies.** Find examples of relief and freestanding sculptures in your community. Find out who or what the sculptures represent. Using a sketchbook and pencil, record what you see and take photographs of the works of art. Put together a journal using your drawings, photographs, and notes.

LOOKING AT THE DETAILS

The detail shown below is from Henry Moore's sculpture, entitled *Family Group*. Study the detail and answer the following questions.

1. This sculpture was made out of bronze. How can knowing the materials in a sculpture help you identify the technique the artist used?

2. The faces of the figures have little detail. How does this affect the visual texture of the work? How does it influence the interpretation of the work?

3. Do the positions of the figures' arms express a relationship? Explain.

4. Why do you think Moore chose to show detail in the fingers of the hand on the shoulder, but omitted detail in the child's feet?

Henry Moore. *Family Group.* 1948–49. Cast 1950. Bronze. (Detail.) 150.5 x 118.1, base 114.3 x 75.9 cm (59¼ x 46½, base 45 x 29⅞"). Museum of Modern Art, New York, New York. A. Conger. Goodyear Fund.

▲ Notice the materials mentioned in the credit line. What do you know about these materials? Can they be easily obtained? What challenges face the craftsperson who works with materials such as these?

Unknown. Chilkat Blanket. c. 1900. Woven cedar bark, mountain goat wool, fur. American Museum of Natural History, New York, New York. Courtesy of Department of Library Services.

CHAPTER 13

Crafts

Have you ever made or bought a special, hand-crafted item? Look at the blanket at the left. What materials did the artist use to create it? What details do you see in the work? All over the world there are people who make items that are not only functional, but are also works of art.

In this chapter you will learn what art works of this type are called. You will learn how — and by whom — they are made.

OBJECTIVES

After completing this chapter, you will be able to:

- Define the terms *crafts* and *craftsperson*.
- Describe the crafts of weaving, glassmaking, and ceramics.
- Identify the different conditions of clay.
- Make a clay bowl, a slab pot, a woven wall hanging, and paper jewelry.

WORDS YOU WILL LEARN

crafts	loom
craftsperson	pottery
fibers	slab
fired	slip
glassblowing	warp
glazed	weaving
kiln	weft

ARTISTS YOU WILL MEET

Elizabeth Garrison	Tommye M. Scanlin
Kim Keats	Pat Steadman
Kimiko	Margaret Tafoya
Dextra Q. Nampeyo	Louis Comfort Tiffany
Bob Owens	Ann Renee Weaver
Jane Pleak	and Tony Mann

The Art of Crafts

Before there were machines, everything that people used was made by hand. Fabric to make clothing was woven by hand. Plates, bowls, and pots to cook with were made by hand. At that time, artists worked not only out of a wish to create, but also out of necessity. These artists considered the useful function of the item. They also considered the beauty or the aesthetic qualities of the object. In many cases, their items were works of art.

An artist who made such useful and aesthetically pleasing goods was — and still is — called a craftsperson. A **craftsperson** is *someone who has become an expert in an area of applied art. The different areas of applied art in which craftspeople work* are called **crafts**.

▶ **Figure 13–1** This quilt was created to celebrate Georgia's 250th birthday. Everything on the quilt symbolizes one part of the state. Can you tell which part by studying the symbols?

Elizabeth Garrison. *Georgia*. 1983. Quilt. 120 x 157.5 cm (48 x 63"). Private collection.

CRAFTS

Today there is a renewed interest in all types of crafts. Look at the quilt in Figure 13–1. It was not made to cover a bed. Instead, it was designed and created by a craftsperson to hang on a wall. Crafts have increased in popularity because people appreciate the one-of-a-kind, well-made product.

Today, as in the past, craftspeople use many different media. Some work in wood (Figure 13–2). Others work in metals, (Figure 13–3). Still others work in fibers, fabrics, glass, and clay.

▲ **Figure 13–4** This one-of-a-kind basket is made of natural materials. How does the craftsperson create unity in the work?

Kim Keats. *Banded Tulip Basket*. 1986. Wisteria and dyed reeds. 33 x 68.6 x 35.6 cm (13 x 27 x 14″).

▲ **Figure 13–2** What makes these blocks special? How are they different from the kind made in factories?

Ann Renée Weaver and Tony Mann. *Alphabet Blocks in Case*. Brazilian Mahogany, non-toxic paints and finishes and brass hardware. Case, 7 x 41.3 x 15.2 cm (2¾ x 16¼ x 6″). Blocks, 4.8 x 4.3 x 4.4 cm (1⁷⁄₁₀ x 1⁷⁄₁₀ x 1¾″).

Weaving

Weaving is *a craft in which fiber strands are interlocked to make cloth or objects.* The basket in Figure 13–4 and the mask in Figure 13–5 are examples of the weaver's art.

▲ **Figure 13–3** How would you imagine it would feel to wear this helmet? In what ways would it be different if it were made out of fabric?

Unknown. *Parade Sallet in the Form of a Lion's Head*. Steel, gilt bronze, silver, semi-precious stones. 28.3 cm (11⅛″). Metropolitan Museum of Art, New York, New York. Harris Brisbane Dick Fund.

▲ **Figure 13–5** The Iroquois wove these masks from corn husks. What does this fact reveal about the habits of the tribe?

Iroquoian. *Husk Face Mask*. National Museum of American History, Smithsonian Institution.

The first weavers used twigs, reeds, and grasses as fibers. **Fibers** are *any thin, thread-like materials*. Today fibers are spun from animal hairs, such as wool, plant materials, such as cotton, and manufactured materials.

Cloth weaving is done on a loom. A **loom** is *a frame or machine that holds a set of threads that run vertically*. These are called the warp threads. The weaver passes threads from a second set under and over the first set. These threads are called the weft. This creates a pattern and locks the threads together. Today some artists work on computerized looms. In factories computers are programmed to control the weaving machines (Figure 13–6).

▲ **Figure 13–6** What are the advantages of using a loom as opposed to hand weaving?

Courtesy of American Weaving Association.

Glassmaking

The practice of melting sand to make glass is thousands of years old. So is the art of glassblowing. **Glassblowing** is *the craft of shaping melted glass by blowing air into it through a tube*. One of the most famous glass-makers of the recent past was Louis Comfort Tiffany. The son of a New York jeweler, Tiffany found a way of making unusually handsome glass patterns. Notice how the luminous color swirls seem to flow through the vase in Figure 13–7. Today glassblowers experiment with designs that, like much art of the day, are daring.

▲ **Figure 13–7** Tiffany set up a glass factory in 1885. The goal of the company was to make stained glass windows. The company began making pieces like this one from leftover glass.

Louis Comfort Tiffany. *Vase.* c. 1900. Favrile glass. 52 x 13 cm (20½ x 4¾"). Museum of Modern Art, New York, New York. Gift of Joseph H. Heil.

Ceramics

Ceramics is another craft. Ceramic pieces are any objects made from clay and hardened by fire. Clay is a natural material found in the ground all over the world. **Pottery** is *the craft of making objects from clay*. You may think of pottery as bowls and dishes, but it can also be statues, masks, or anything else made out of clay.

The making of clay pots goes back to ancient times. Today craftspeople use many of the same techniques that were used many centuries ago.

Making pottery starts with preparing the clay. Water is added to the clay so that it is wet enough to be worked easily. Potters have special words for the different conditions of the clay:

- **Plastic clay** is clay that is wet enough to be worked but firm enough to hold its shape.
- **Leather hard clay** is clay that is still damp but is too dry to shape. It can be carved or joined together with slip.
- **Slip** is *clay that has so much added water that it is liquid and runny.* It is used as glue to join pieces of clay together. It is also used in decorating a finished work.

When working clay by hand, there are special methods that have been developed to shape the clay. Some of these are called pinching, coiling, and slab building. In the studio lessons that follow you will have a chance to try these techniques.

Clay can also be shaped by throwing it, which means turning it on a rapidly spinning wheel called a potter's wheel. This helps make a smooth, symmetrical piece. Some works combine both methods.

After the clay is shaped, it must be **fired**, or *hardened by heating in a kiln.* A **kiln** is *a special piece of equipment used to fire ceramics.* It can get as hot as 3000°F (1650°C). Before clay

▲ **Figure 13–9** How would the mood and feel of this work be different if it were not glazed? Why do you think the artist chose to glaze it?

Kimiko. *Vase.* 1990. Ceramic glazeware. 46 cm (18"). Private collection.

has been fired in a kiln, it is called greenware. After it has been fired, it is called bisqueware (**bisk**-ware).

Sometimes bisqueware is **glazed**, or *coated with a mixture of powdered chemicals that melt during firing into a hard, glasslike finish.* The glaze is spread on the pottery and the item is fired a second time.

Pottery does not always have to be glazed. Some of the best pottery, like terra cotta, is unglazed (Figure 13–8). However, if it is to hold food or liquid, it must be glazed with nontoxic glazes to keep the clay from absorbing the moisture. (See Figure 13–9.)

▲ **Figure 13–8** This piece is terra cotta. Do you think this piece would have been more effective in a different medium? Explain.

Bob Owens. *Alpha Wolf.* 1990. Terra cotta sculpture. 36 x 41 x 30 cm (14 x 16 x 12"). Home Federal Savings, Gainesville, Georgia.

✓ CHECK YOUR UNDERSTANDING

1. What is a craftsperson? Define the term *craft*.
2. What is weaving? What is the name of the machine on which cloth is woven?
3. What is glass made of? What is glassblowing?
4. How is slip used?
5. Describe the difference between plastic and leather hard clay.
6. What is the difference between greenware and bisqueware?

Clay Bowl

Look at Figure 13–10. This is a piece of pottery that was handbuilt by Margaret Tafoya. Her work was done without the use of a potter's wheel. You also can make a container, such as a glass, mug, or bowl in the same way. Before you begin, concentrate on the form of the object. Identify the rim, body, and foot of the vase. Notice how the area lifts from the bottom to give shape and support to the container.

WHAT YOU WILL LEARN

You will make a small container by the pinch method. Make all the sides with even thickness and smooth the rim of the bowl and add a foot to the base. You may decorate it by pressing found objects into its surface. You may add pieces and coils of clay to create rhythmic, repeated patterns. (See Figure 13–11.)

WHAT YOU WILL NEED

- Sheets of newspaper or cloth
- Clay and slip
- Container of water
- Clay and clay scoring tools
- Plastic sheet or bag
- *Optional:* found objects, such as buttons, weeds, and pieces of broken toys

WHAT YOU WILL DO

1. Spread sheets of newspaper or cloth over your work area. Pinch off a small piece of clay. Dip one finger in the water and wet the piece. Set it aside for later. It may be used for decorating.
2. Form your clay into a ball by rolling it.
3. Hollow out the ball of clay by pressing your thumbs into the center while gently squeezing the clay between your thumbs

▲ **Figure 13–10** **This piece is a reflection of a Native American style. How might this vase be different if the artist created it on a potter's wheel?**

Margaret Tafoya. *Jar.* Santa Clara Pueblo, New Mexico. c. 1965. Blackware. 43 x 33 cm (17 x 13"). National Museum of Women in the Arts, Washington, D.C. Gift of Wallace & Wilhelmina Holladay.

on the inside and your fingers on the outside. Form it into the shape you want your container to have.

4. Gradually thin the sides and bottom of your pot with your thumbs and fingers. Make the walls and bottom smooth and even. Fix any small cracks in the clay by pressing and smoothing it out with your fingers and thumbs.

5. Wet your fingertips or use a damp sponge to smooth the top rim of your bowl.
6. Roll out a coil, or rope, of clay about 1/2 inch (13mm) thick. Turn your bowl upside down. Join your coil to the bottom to make a foot, or stand, for your work.
7. Decorate the surface of the bowl with a rhythmic pattern while the clay is still damp. Press your found objects into the surface of the bowl to create a pattern. Use your fingers to support the inside of the bowl while you make your impression. Add a second pattern by joining some small pieces of clay to your work. (See Technique Tip **17**, *Handbook* page **275**, for hints on joining clay pieces.)
8. Cover the piece loosely with a plastic sheet or bag. This will help it dry evenly and keep it from cracking. Remove the plastic when the clay is leather hard. When your work is completely dry, it is ready to fire.
9. *Optional*: Apply glaze and fire your work a second time. Do not apply glaze to the bottom of your piece. If you do, it will stick to the shelf in the kiln.

SAFETY TIP

Some older glazes are made with lead, which is poisonous. Be sure to use a nontoxic glaze on your work. If you're not sure whether or not a glaze is nontoxic, check with your teacher before using it.

EXAMINING YOUR WORK

- **Describe** Show that the sides of your container have an even thickness and that the rim is smooth. Point out the ring of clay you added to the bottom to create a foot. Point out the found objects and pieces of clay rope you added as a design.
- **Analyze** Describe the texture of your bowl's surface, and explain what you did to change the surface texture. Tell whether you used found objects and strips of clay to create a feeling of rhythmic repeated pattern.
- **Interpret** Tell whether your bowl is functional or a purely decorative item.
- **Judge** Tell whether your bowl succeeds as art. Explain your answer.

▲ **Figure 13–11** **What kind of balance is displayed by the design on this piece?**

Dextra Q. Nampeyo. *Jar.* c. 1920. Hopi polychrome pottery. 22.2 x 35 cm (8¾ x 13¾"). The Thomas Gilcrease Institute of American History and Art, Tulsa, Oklahoma.

OTHER STUDIO IDEAS

- Use the pinch method to make a clay bell. Poke a small hole in the top of the bell big enough to thread a string through. Form a small bead with a hole going through the center. Then make a thin clay clapper with a small hole at the top for the string. Dry and fire these clay pieces. See your teacher for assembling instructions.

Slab Container

An easy way to make ceramic objects is by using clay slabs. A **slab** is *a slice or sheet of clay*. The slab method works especially well when you are building an object with straight sides. Figure 13–12 shows a work made from slabs.

Slabs can be cut into any shape. The slab method can also be used to make cylinders. In this case, the slab must be curved while the clay is still flexible to avoid cracking. If you want to build a straight-wall rectangular box, the slabs must be dry, but not quite leather hard.

WHAT YOU WILL LEARN

You will use the slab method and proper joining techniques to make a container shaped like a cylinder. This can be used as a vase, pencil holder, or jar. You will decorate the surface of the container with designs cut from another slab. The designs may be flowers, animals, letters, or other objects made with geometric forms and shapes. (See Figure 13–13.) Be sure that the decorative designs are in proportion to the size of the container. Your container will be glazed inside and out.

WHAT YOU WILL NEED

- Sheets of newspaper or cloth
- Two guide sticks, each about 1/2 inch (13 mm) thick
- Clay and slip
- Rolling pin, pipe, or smooth jar
- Ruler
- Needle tool or open paper clip
- Container of water
- Scoring tools or fork

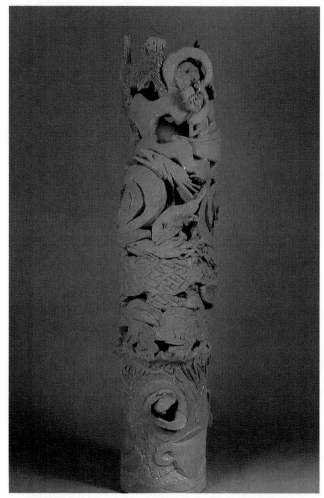

▲ **Figure 13–12   Can you tell where some of the different slabs come together?**

Jane Pleak. *Summertime Totem*. 1987. 129.5 x 35.6 x 35.6 cm (51 x 14 x 14"). Ceramic redware. Private collection.

WHAT YOU WILL DO

1. Spread sheets of newspaper or cloth over your work area.
2. Place the guide sticks on the cloth 6 inches (15 cm) apart. Place the clay between the guide sticks. Flatten it with the heel of your hand. Resting the rolling pin, pipe, or jar on the guide sticks, roll out the clay. This will help keep the thickness of the slab even.

3. Using the ruler and needle tool, measure and lightly mark two rectangles on the slab. One should be 6 x 10 inches (15 x 25 cm), the other, 5 inches (13 cm) square. Any mistakes can be wiped away with your fingers. Cut out the rectangles using the needle tool. Save the scraps. Keep them damp.

4. Bend the longer slab into a cylinder. Join the edges by scoring and using slip. (See Technique Tip **17**, *Handbook* page **275**.) Wet your fingers and wipe away any cracks in the surface of the cylinder.

5. Using the needle tool, trim one end of the cylinder so it will stand straight. Stand the cylinder, trimmed end down, on the 5-inch (13 cm) square slab. With the needle tool, lightly and carefully trace around the base of the cylinder. Remove the cylinder, and cut out the circle you have drawn. Join the cylinder and circle to form your container.

6. Cut design shapes of your choice from the leftover clay slab. Using the joining techniques you used to form the cylinder, apply the slab designs to the surface of the container. Allow the container to dry slowly. When it is at the greenware stage, fire it.

7. Apply glaze to every surface but the bottom, and fire the container a second time. If you want the container to hold water, pour a small amount of glaze in the container. Swirl it around the bottom and sides. Keep turning the container as you pour the excess glaze out so that it will cover the inside completely.

EXAMINING YOUR WORK

- **Describe** Show that the surface of your container is smooth and free of cracks. Tell whether your container is glazed inside and out. Describe the designs you added.
- **Analyze** Point out the shapes you used to decorate your container. Tell whether your decorations are in proportion to the size of your container.
- **Interpret** Tell how you would use the container.
- **Judge** Tell whether your work succeeds as applied art. Explain your answer.

▲ **Figure 13–13** Student work in progress. A slab container.

OTHER STUDIO IDEAS

- Use the slab method to make a container shaped like a rectangle. You will need four slabs, two measuring 10 x 3 inches (25 x 8 cm), and two measuring 10 x 2 inches (25 x 5 cm).

Making a Weaving

Look at the tapestry weaving in Figure 13–14. It was woven on a floor loom. The craftsperson dyed the threads before weaving. She wanted to control the color scheme, as well as the shape and texture.

Like all work done on a loom, this one is made by interlocking fibers. *The threads attached to the loom* are known as **warp** threads. *The threads pulled across the warp* are the **weft** threads. The weft threads are passed over and under the warp threads to lock the two sets of fibers together.

WHAT YOU WILL LEARN

You will make a fabric wall hanging using a cardboard loom and yarns, strings, and found fibers. You will use a variety of textures and limit the colors to a monochromatic or analogous color scheme.

WHAT YOU WILL NEED

- Ruler, pencil, scissors, and transparent tape
- Sheet of heavy cardboard, 12 x 18 inch (30 x 46 cm)
- Spool of strong, thin thread
- Different colored yarns and strings
- Found materials that can be used as fibers, such as grass, strips of paper, and used film
- Tapestry needle
- Comb
- Wooden dowel

WHAT YOU WILL DO

1. To make your loom, hold the ruler along the top edge of your cardboard. With the pencil, mark off every 1/4 inch (6 mm).

▲ **Figure 13–14** Describe some of the elements and principles of art the artist incorporated into her weaving.

Tommye M. Scanlin. *Cat Dreams*. 1988. Hand dyed wool tapestry. 55.9 x 86.4 cm (22 x 34"). Private collection.

Using the scissors, make a cut about 1/2 inch (13 mm) deep at each mark. Do the same thing along the bottom of the cardboard.

2. Tape the end of your thread to the back of the cardboard. Bring the spool to the front, passing the thread through the top left notch. Pull the spool down to the bottom of the loom. Pass the thread through the bottom left notch and around to the back. Move one notch to the right. Pull the thread through and up the front

of the loom. Keep working until you reach the last notch. (See Figure 13–15.) Bring the spool to the back. Cut the thread, and tape the end.

3. Decide which color scheme you will use. Select fibers you will use for your weft. Choose textures to add interest to your wall hanging.

4. Thread one of your thinner yarns through the eye of the tapestry needle. Start to weave at the bottom of your loom. Move the yarn across the warp, passing over one thread and under the next. (Figure 13–16.) Keep working in this over-and-under manner. When you reach the end of the warp, reverse directions. If you wove over the last thread, you must weave under when you start the next line of the weft. Do not pull the weft too tight. Curve it slightly as you pull it through the warp. This is called ballooning.

5. After weaving a few rows, pack the weft threads tightly with the comb. The tighter the weave, the stronger the fabric will be. Experiment with different weft fibers.

EXAMINING YOUR WORK

- **Describe**   Describe how you made the loom. Explain how you attached the warp threads to your loom. Explain ballooning. Why did you use it? List the weaving techniques you used.
- **Analyze**   What color scheme did you choose? Explain how you added a variety of textures to your weaving.
- **Interpret**   In what setting might you hang this weaving?
- **Judge**   Tell whether you feel your work succeeds. Explain your answer.

6. Be sure to end with another inch (2.5 cm) of thin, tightly-packed fiber. Break the tabs of your loom to slip the weaving off the cardboard. Fold the weaving over the dowel and stitch your weaving together, using a long piece of yarn and a tapestry needle.

7. Make a hanging loop by tying the ends of a piece of string to each end of the dowel.

▲ **Figure 13–15**   Notice the series of vertical lines. These are the warp threads.

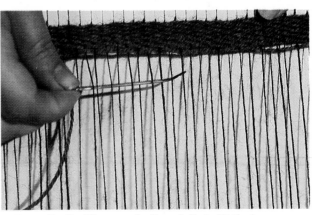

▲ **Figure 13–16**   These are the threads that will display your image. What are these threads called?

OTHER STUDIO IDEAS

- Make a table placemat for a favorite holiday. Choose the colors that best symbolize that holiday.

- ●● Experiment with weft and warp materials of differing textures and weights, incorporating found objects as you go to create a wall hanging.

Jewelry

Some art is made to be worn. An example of this kind of art appears in Figure 13–17. We call this art, and the craft of making it, jewelry.

Cave dwellers wore jewelry made of colorful shells and feathers. Today people wear jewelry made of precious stones and metals. Look once more at the necklace in Figure 13–17. From what stones and metals is this item made?

WHAT YOU WILL LEARN

You will make a piece of paper jewelry with a particular wearer in mind. You will paint your jewelry with watercolors. You will choose either geometric or free-form shapes for your design. You will make a pendant, a pin, or a pair of earrings (Figures 13–18 and 13–19). The item must harmonize with the size and clothing style of the person for whom it is intended.

WHAT YOU WILL NEED

- Pencil and sheets of sketch paper
- Sheet of heavy watercolor paper, 9 x 12 inch (23 x 30 cm)
- Sheets of scrap paper
- Scissors
- Watercolor paints and brushes
- White glue
- Pin or earring backs
- Straight pin
- Polyurethane spray

WHAT YOU WILL DO

1. Identify the person for whom the piece is intended. Decide whether you will make a pin, a pendant, or a pair of earrings. Make pencil sketches experimenting with different shapes for your jewelry.

▲ **Figure 13–17   What kind of balance is displayed in this work? Why does this kind of balance work for creating a necklace?**

L. L. Lee. *Native American Necklace*. 1990. Turquoise and silver. From the collection of John and Sue MacLaurin.

You may use either geometric or free-form shapes. Transfer your best sketches to the sheet of heavy watercolor paper. Set the paper aside.

2. On scrap paper, experiment with different colors and techniques for applying watercolor paints. (To review the different techniques, see Technique Tip **14**, *Handbook* page **275**.) If you are making the jewelry for yourself, think of your favorite colors. If the jewelry is to be a gift, think about the tastes of the person you have in mind.

3. Tear or cut out the paper shapes.

4. Paint your finished shapes. Make sure the colors you choose work together to create a feeling of harmony.

5. When the paint is dry, attach the pieces to a pin or earring backs with glue. If you are making a pendant, poke a hole near the top with the straight pin.
6. If you want to waterproof the jewelry, use polyurethane (pahl-ee-**your**-uh-thane) spray. *Make sure your teacher is present during this step.*
7. Display your finished jewelry. Note ways in which it is like and different from jewelry made by your classmates.

═══ SAFETY TIP ═══

Polyurethane sprays can be harmful if inhaled. Use these sprays in rooms that are well ventilated. Use them only when an adult is present.

▲ **Figure 13–18** What shape and kind of balance is shown in this piece?

Ann Renee Weaver. *Paper Jewelery Pin.* 1989. Paper towels, white glue, opalescent acrylic, and textile paint. 7.6 cm (3″) diameter. Private collection.

EXAMINING YOUR WORK

- **Describe** Tell what type of jewelry (pin, pendant, earrings) you have made. Identify the materials you used to create the jewelry. Tell what colors you have chosen.
- **Analyze** Tell whether you have chosen geometric or free-form shapes. Explain whether the colors and shapes you chose will harmonize with the size and clothing style of the wearer.
- **Interpret** Tell whether the jewelry will appeal to the individual for whom it was made. Explain why.
- **Judge** Explain whether you feel your work succeeds as applied art. Explain your answer.

▲ **Figure 13–19** Student work. Three sets of paper earrings.

OTHER STUDIO IDEAS

- Add other materials to your paper jewelry. Try fabric, buttons, string, or feathers, for example.

•• Make a pin out of clay using the clay working techniques in Lesson 3.

BUILDING VOCABULARY

Number a sheet of paper from 1 to 14. After each number, write the term from the box that best matches each description below.

crafts	loom
craftsperson	pottery
fibers	slab
fired	slip
glassblowing	warp
glazed	weaving
kiln	weft

1. Someone who has become an expert in an area of applied art.
2. The areas of applied art in which craftspeople work.
3. A craft in which strands of fiber are interlocked to make cloth or objects.
4. A frame used for weaving threads.
5. The craft of shaping melted glass by blowing air into it through a tube.
6. The craft of making objects from clay.
7. Hardened by heating in a kiln.
8. Any thin, threadlike materials.
9. Clay that has so much added water that it is liquid and runny.
10. A slice or sheet of clay.
11. Coated with a mixture of powdered chemicals that melt during firing into a hard, glasslike finish.
12. A special oven used to fire ceramics.
13. Threads attached to a loom.
14. Threads pulled across those already on the loom.

REVIEWING ART FACTS

Number a sheet of paper from 15 to 21. Answer each question in a complete sentence.

15. What kinds of things did the first weavers use as fibers?
16. What is glass made of?
17. Who is Louis Comfort Tiffany? For what is he famous?
18. What are ceramics?
19. What are the different conditions of clay called?
20. Describe how clay pieces are joined in making pottery.
21. What method of claymaking is best for designing objects with straight sides?

THINKING ABOUT ART

On a sheet of paper, answer each question in a sentence or two.

1. **Interpret.** What information would you need to have before accepting a drink out of a homemade ceramic cup?
2. **Extend.** Name two ceramic objects that would be best made using the slab method. Name two that would be best made using the pinching method. Give reasons for your choices.

MAKING ART CONNECTIONS

1. **Science.** Clay is the result of a certain type of rock decomposition. Research where clay is found and find out what is added to make it easier for artists to use. Report your results to the class.
2. **Industrial Arts.** Choose one of the products discussed in this chapter and find out how a similar product might be produced in industry. Explain how the industrial methods differ from those of an individual craftsperson.

LOOKING AT THE DETAILS

The detail shown below is from a Chilkat Blanket woven by a member of the Tlingit, a tribe of Native Americans who live in British Columbia. Study the detail and answer the following questions.

1. Notice the precision of line and well-displayed harmony in this detail. Knowing that it was woven entirely by hand, what does this tell you about the craftsperson who created it? Would you consider this person an artist? Why or why not?
2. We discussed visual movement in painting. In sculpture and in crafts, physical movement is also a possibility. How did this artist create the feeling of movement?
3. Consider the historical information of this work found in the credit line. What do you think might be some reasons for the artists' choice of these colors? How might a particular craft determine some of your creative choices?
4. Do you think this blanket was successful as applied art? Explain.

Unknown. Chilkat Blanket. c. 1900. Woven cedar bark, mountain goat wool, fur. (Detail.) American Museum of Natural History, New York, New York. Courtesy of Department of Library Services.

▲ **This shrine has long been admired for its beauty. If you were asked to design a shrine how might it be different from this one?**

Temple of Athena Nike. 427–424 B.C. Acropolis, Athens, Greece.

CHAPTER 14

Architecture

When you look around any city, you notice many kinds of buildings. Houses, schools, churches, and office buildings are just a few of the different types of buildings. Each of them serves a different purpose.

What do you think the building on the left was used for? Who do you think used it? It was built in the fifth century B.C. in Athens, Greece. In this chapter you will explore the different purposes of buildings. You will also discover that buildings of the past still influence structural designs of today.

OBJECTIVES

After completing this chapter, you will be able to:

- Define architecture and explain what architects do.
- Describe three main uses of architecture.
- Explain how architects use floor plans and elevation drawings.
- Design a clay model of a house, a floor plan for a shopping mall, and a clay relief of a mall entrance.

WORDS YOU WILL LEARN

amphitheaters	elevation
architect	facade
architecture	floor plan
basilicas	post and lintel

ARTISTS YOU WILL MEET

Louis Sullivan
Frank Lloyd Wright

The Art of Architecture

Have you ever made a house out of playing cards or designed a sand castle? Maybe you have built a fortress from craft sticks. All these activities borrow ideas from the field of art called architecture. **Architecture** is *the planning and creating of buildings.* An **architect** is *an artist who works in the field of architecture.*

Architecture is considered to be both a fine art and an applied art. Like painters and sculptors, architects use color, line, shape, form, space, and texture. Like craftspeople, architects make works that are functional.

In this lesson you will look at the many uses of architecture. In later lessons you will try out some of the methods architects use in their work.

THE BEGINNINGS OF ARCHITECTURE

The first architects were cave dwellers who left their caves to build shelters from tree branches. Sun-dried mud and clay were some other materials used by early architects.

None of these materials, of course, could stand up long to wind or rain. In time, the buildings crumbled. Architects were faced with the task of finding or making stronger building materials. The early Egyptians found the solution by using stone. The most famous of their buildings are the pyramids. These amazing structures were built as tombs for the most important person in

▲ **Figure 14–1** **This wonder of the world had only two rooms. What do you suppose those rooms might have been filled with? Explain your answer.**

Parthenon. Acropolis, Athens, Greece. Begun 447 B.C.

Egyptian society, the Pharaoh. The Pharaoh was not only a king but also, in the eyes of his subjects, a god.

USES OF ARCHITECTURE

Because people need shelter to protect them from the weather and to provide privacy, creating dwellings has been a main purpose of architecture since earliest times. Other purposes were to create structures for prayer, business, and recreation. These remain key concerns of architects today.

Structures for Prayer

Because religion was central in their culture, the single most important building made by early Greek architects was the temple. The building on page **236** is an example of a Greek temple.

The Greeks did not gather inside their temples to worship. The temples were built as houses for their gods. Only priests and a few helpers were allowed inside. Everyone else prayed in front of the temple. For this reason Greek temples did not have to be large, nor provide areas for seats. Instead, Greek architects concentrated on making the temples perfectly proportioned. Their success is evident in the most famous Greek temple, the Parthenon (Figure 14–1).

In Europe in the 1200s and 1300s larger churches were built. Architects also began exploring new ways of using line and balance. Figures 14–2 and 14–3 show two views of the same church. Notice how the architect created a feeling of lightness and openness whether one is viewing the church from the inside or the outside. Colored light pouring into the interiors through the stained glass windows added to the drama of this church.

Think of the churches you've seen in your neighborhood. Can you tell by their architectural style when they were built? In what ways are they different from churches of old? How are they similar?

▲ Figure 14–2   Does this building appear delicate and charming to you? Does it appear strong and solid? Explain.

Cathedral of Leon-Outside. 13th-14th centuries. Leon, Spain.

▲ Figure 14–3   Stained glass windows in churches like these were used to color the light inside. Does looking at the church from the inside communicate the same feelings as those in Figure 14–2? Why or why not?

Cathedral of Leon-Inside. 13th-14th centuries. Leon, Spain.

Structures for Business

The ancient Romans, like the Greeks before them, built temples. But Roman architects were also called upon to create many other kinds of buildings. Figure 14–4 shows a public arena used for sports contests and entertainment. *Huge meeting halls* called **basilicas** (buh-**sil**-ih-kuhs) were also built.

After the time of the Romans, other kinds of business buildings began appearing in cities. Banks were designed. Schools and government buildings were built.

In our own time, buildings used for business have taken a new direction — up. Strong metals such as steel have allowed architects to use space efficiently. The modern skyscraper can be found in major cities throughout the world. Buildings today are built on skeletons, or frames, of steel. One of the first buildings to use this technique is shown in Figure 14–5. It was designed by Louis Sullivan, a pioneer of modern architecture. How is this "skyscraper" different from the ones of today? How is it similar?

▲ Figure 14–5   Rows of brick were used to cover the steel skeleton in Sullivan's building. Can you think of some coverings used today?

Louis Sullivan. Wainwright Building. 1890–1891. St. Louis, Missouri.

▲ Figure 14–4   Over the centuries, conquering rulers carried off stones from the Colosseum to build new buildings. Many of the great palaces of the 1500s are made from these stones.

Colosseum. Rome. A.D. 72–80.

Structures for Recreation

In addition to temples and buildings for business, the Romans designed amphitheaters (**am**-fuh-thee-uht-uhrs) for sporting events. **Amphitheaters** are *circular or oval buildings with seats rising around an open space.* The famous open-air amphitheater shown in Figure 14–4 could seat 50,000 people. Structures like this were early models of our modern sports arenas.

Sports arenas, of course, are not the only kinds of buildings designed for recreation. Concert halls and theaters are two others. Museums are a third. Figure 14–6 shows a museum by twentieth-century architect Frank Lloyd Wright. The building has one large main windowless room. The art works are hung on walls along a ramp that spirals upward. Would you know at a glance that this building is a museum? Why, or why not?

THE CHALLENGE OF ARCHITECTURE

Like other applied artists, architects are faced with a double challenge. That challenge is creating works that are both useful and pleasing to the eye. Since architecture is so much a part of everyday life, the search for new solutions is never-ending. These solutions show up not only in new styles but also in new and exciting building materials.

Take a close look at buildings going up in your town or city. There you are likely to see how architects combine a knowledge of engineering with an understanding of design to create buildings that are *both* attractive and functional.

✔CHECK YOUR UNDERSTANDING

1. What is architecture?
2. What are three main purposes of architecture?
3. What is an amphitheater?
4. Describe the double challenge facing every architect.

STUDIO EXPERIENCE

The buildings around us can become so familiar we don't even notice them. This studio experience will help you appreciate local architecture as an art form.

Choose a building in your community you believe is interesting. Sketch the building as accurately as you can. In class, draw your building in the center of a sheet of 12 x 18 inch (30 x 46 cm) paper. In the space around your building, draw a new, imaginary setting. This should be an *ideal* setting that allows your building to look its best. Without telling the name of your building, see if your classmates recognize it. Can you identify theirs?

▲ **Figure 14–6   Not everyone liked Wright's design. Some said it looked like a giant cupcake. What do you think of it? Do you think it is an appropriate design for a museum?**

Frank Lloyd Wright. Solomon R. Guggenheim Museum. 1943–1959. Guggenheim Museum, New York, New York, 1988.

Building a Clay Model

To make a house of cards, you stand two cards on end and lay another across them. A similar approach was used by the architect of the temple in Figure 14–7. **Post and lintel** (**lint**-uhl) is *a building method in which a cross-beam is placed above two uprights*. The posts in this temple are the ridged columns. The lintels are the connected slabs of stone held up by the pillars. How many posts can you count in the picture? How many lintels?

WHAT YOU WILL LEARN

You will design and build a three-dimensional clay model for a vacation house. You will use the clay slab method you learned in Chapter 13 to cut and assemble a variety of square and rectangular shapes. Your house will have a porch built using the post and lintel method.

WHAT YOU WILL NEED

- Pencil and sheets of sketch paper
- Sheet of cloth 14 inches (36 cm) square
- 2 wood strip guides, each about 1/2 inch (13 mm) thick
- Clay
- Rolling pin and ruler
- Clay modeling tools and fork
- Container of water
- Slip

WHAT YOU WILL DO

1. Make pencil drawings to plan your house. Begin by drawing a floor plan. A **floor plan** is *a scale drawing of how a room or building would appear without a roof as if seen from above*. Floor plans show how the space inside a building is to be used. Don't forget to show the porch in your floor plan. Clearly label each room.

▲ **Figure 14–7** Which elements and principles of art do you think this architect was most concerned with?

Parthenon. Acropolis, Athens, Greece. Begun 447 B.C.

2. Make a second drawing. This time, draw the front of the house as it would appear from outside. Such *a drawing of an outside view of a building* is called an **elevation**. An elevation can show any outside view. This one is of the **facade** (fuh-**sahd**), *the front of a building*. Your elevation should show a second view of your porch using posts and lintels.

3. To achieve a slab of clay of uniform thickness, place the wood strip guides on the cloth 8 inches (20 cm) apart. Place

the clay between the wood strips. Flatten it with the heel of your hand. Resting the rolling pin on the wood strips, roll out the clay.

4. Using the ruler and a needle tool, lightly mark off a large rectangle. This is to be the floor. Using the measurements from the length and width of your large rectangle, mark off two pairs of rectangles. One pair is to be the front and back walls. The second pair is to be the side walls. If you wish to have a house with a sloping or gabled roof, cut the front and back slabs so they come to a point. You will also need slabs for the roof. Carefully mark off windows and doors. Cut along the marks you have made and remove the clay rectangles. Keep each slab damp until you are ready to use it.

5. Using the fork to score the ends of the walls and some slip, attach the back wall and a side wall. Make sure they form an *L*. Carefully attach the joined walls to the floor. Then add the second side wall and the front wall.

6. Attach the floor, or deck, of the porch to the front wall. Attach the posts to the deck. Carefully add crossbeams, between posts and to the front wall.

7. Measure and cut additional clay slabs to be used for the roof and the porch. Attach these securely with slip after scoring.

8. Add decorations and details to your house by cutting into slabs or adding other details.

9. Fire your house in a kiln. Consider color schemes and glaze to add color and texture.

EXAMINING YOUR WORK

- **Describe**   Display the floor plan with your model house and the elevation drawing you used in planning your house. Identify the different rooms on your floor plan. Tell how each is to be used. Point out the posts and lintels you used in designing the porch. Tell how the slabs were tightly joined before your model was fired.
- **Analyze**   Show how your model is made from a variety of square and rectangular shapes. What forms have you created?
- **Interpret**   Tell how a viewer would know that your model represents a vacation house. What word would you use to describe the feeling your house gives — comfortable, peaceful, unusual? List ways in which the family living in your house could use the porch.
- **Judge**   Tell whether your work succeeds as architecture. Explain your answer. If you were to do another, what would you do differently?

10. *Optional*: Your house may be glazed and fired again, or you may wish to paint your model with acrylic paint. One or two coats of polymer resin coating will give acrylic colors a great luster.

OTHER STUDIO IDEAS

- Design a garage for the vacation house. Decide how many cars will be kept in the garage. Make a clay model of the garage.
- Make a pencil drawing of a place of worship to be used today similar to the one in Figure 14–7. Use the post and lintel method. Decide what kinds of designs you will use to decorate your place of worship. Use cardboard and make a model based on your drawing.

Drawing Floor Plans

Today in many places bits of crumbled stone, brick, and adobe stand alone as reminders of past cultures. In its day, the Forum in Rome (Figure 14–8) was a busy public square and marketplace. Here people gathered to chat or do business. Visitors standing before these grand ruins today can almost hear the echoes of ancient voices and footsteps. It is a powerful reminder of the past.

The design idea behind the Forum—many shops clustered together—lives on. Today we call such groupings of stores shopping malls (Figure 14–9).

Imagine that your community needs a new shopping mall. You are one of many architects community leaders have asked to design plans for a unique new mall. Leaders want to be sure there will be space inside the mall for businesses and for large groups of people to move about freely. They also want a large parking area for mall visitors. Most important, they want people of the community to find the mall useful.

WHAT YOU WILL LEARN

You will design a floor plan for a one-story shopping mall. Your mall will have one department store, 10 smaller shops, and two restaurants. The department store should be emphasized as the most prominent place of business in the mall. Divide the space in your mall so that large and small shops are cre-

▲ 14–8   At first, the Forum was used strictly for business. Later, temples were built around it. Today, only a few ruins remain to tell of its former beauty.

Forum of Julius Caesar. Begun 46 B.C.

▲ Figure 14–9   How is this building different from the one in Figure 14–8? Which do you like better, the new or the old? Why?

Modern Shopping Mall. Fashion Island, Newport Beach, California.

ated. Your mall will also have a wide, roomy public walkway linking the different stores. Finally, it will have a large parking lot for mall visitors.

WHAT YOU WILL NEED

- Pencil, ruler, and eraser
- Sheets of sketch paper
- Sheets of white graph paper, 18 x 24 inch (46 x 61 cm)
- Transparent tape

WHAT YOU WILL DO

1. Using pencil, ruler, and sketch paper, create different possibilities for floor plans. (You may use malls you have visited for ideas. The final design, however, should be your own.) A large department store will be the focal point of the mall. Decide what kinds of businesses you will have among the 10 shops. Decide which businesses will be next to each other along the walkway. Decide whether either or both of the restaurants will serve fast food. Decide how much floor space each business will need. Provide a large parking lot. Use the foot as a unit of measurement. Develop a scale for your design, such as 1/4 inch equals 1 foot.
2. Carefully line up two sheets of the white graph paper so their long sides touch. Fasten them where they meet with transparent tape. Turn the paper over. Neatly transfer the final design of your floor plan to the large sheet. Use your ruler. Neatly label each store. Label the walkway and parking area.

EXAMINING YOUR WORK

- **Describe**   Tell which store in your mall received the most floor space. Explain why. Tell what other kinds of shops you placed in your mall.
- **Analyze**   Explain how you divided the space in your mall. Point out why some shops received more space than others. Explain how the department store is emphasized in your plan. Tell whether the walkways in your mall are wide and roomy. Tell whether there is enough parking space for times when the mall is busy.
- **Interpret**   Show what features you added to make your mall inviting to visitors. Tell whether the stores and restaurants will appeal to many different tastes. Tell whether visitors would find your mall pleasant to visit. Explain why.
- **Judge**   Tell whether you think your work succeeds as applied art. Explain your answer.

3. Show where the entrance to the mall will be. Add any details that will be used as decoration.
4. Display your floor plan alongside those of your classmates. How are the plans different?
5. *Optional*: Select one plan from the class and construct it out of cardboard as a group project.

OTHER STUDIO IDEAS

- Design a detailed floor plan for one of the stores in your mall. Decide whether the store will have wide or narrow aisles. Decide whether it will have counters or shelves. Draw your plan.

- ●● Draw two elevations for your mall — one from the front and the second from any angle you choose. Add details such as arched windows, floor tiles, skylights, and landscaping. Use colored pencils, watercolors, pen and ink, or crayons.

Clay Entrance Relief

As with people, the faces, or facades, of buildings tell something about their personalities. Look at Figures 14–10 and 14–11. Both are entranceways to churches. Which church would you describe as simple and quiet? Which would you describe as bold and proud? What details of line support your guess in each case? What other elements or principles play a part?

Imagine that you have been called upon to design a second mall. This time, you are to begin by designing a model of the mall entrance. The design you create should give the mall a definite personality.

WHAT YOU WILL LEARN

You will create a three-dimensional elevation of a mall entrance out of clay. Using the slab method, you will carve and model details to create a variety of light and dark values. A variety of different actual textures will be used. Your relief will give the mall a personality.

WHAT YOU WILL NEED

• Pencil and sheets of sketch paper
• Rolling pin and ruler
• Sheet of cloth, 14 inches (36 cm) square

▲ Figure 14–10   How would you describe the mood of this church? Why?

Valle de Bohi-Romanesque.

▲ Figure 14–11   Compare this church entrance with the one in Figure 14–10. How are they different? How are they the same?

Mission San Jose. 18th century. San Antonio, Texas.

- 2 wood strip guides, each about 1/2 inch (13 mm) thick
- Clay and modeling tools

WHAT YOU WILL DO

1. Make pencil sketches of different mall entrance designs. As you work, think about the personality you would like the mall to have. Is the mall going to have a fun-filled look or a classic, expensive look? Think about what features would help capture the mood you prefer. Select your best drawing.
2. Place the wood strip guides on the cloth about 6 inches (15 cm) apart. Flatten the clay between the guide sticks, and roll out the clay. Measure and cut out a 6 x 8 inch (15 x 20 cm) rectangle.
3. Arrange the rectangle so a long side is facing you. Working from your elevation drawing, carve and model details of your mall entrance. These details should stick out or be cut into the clay to create a variety of dark and light values. As you work, consider the effects of gradual and abrupt value changes created by carving or adding rounded and angular details. (See Figure 4–12.) Use a needle tool to show the brick or other surface textures. Carve out doors and any details above or to the sides. If you like, include the name of the mall.
4. Using the pencil, poke a small, shallow hole in the back of your relief. The hole should be at the center and about an inch from the top, made at an upward angle.
5. When your relief is dry, fire it. Hang your finished relief from the hole you made in the back on a nail or hook.

OTHER STUDIO IDEAS

- Create your dream home. Draw four views of your dream house (front, back, both sides). Design the outside view to include a porch, garage, trees, and/or bushes. Color your views with colored pencils.

EXAMINING YOUR WORK

- **Describe** Point out the doors and other details of your mall entrance. Show the places in your relief where you carved. Show the places where you modeled. Point out the different actual textures you added to your relief. Show where light and dark values are created.
- **Analyze** Explain how a variety of textures makes your mall more interesting. Explain why a variety of values was needed.
- **Interpret** Identify the personality of your mall. Explain what you did to express this personality in your design of the mall entrance.
- **Judge** Tell whether your work succeeds as applied art. Explain your answer.

▲ Figure 14–12 Student work. Clay entrance relief work in progress.

- •• Create a city block viewed from the front. Include shops, office buildings, museum, movie theater, and other buildings of your choice. Create exteriors that reflect the kind of activity that goes on inside each building.

CHAPTER 14 REVIEW

BUILDING VOCABULARY

Number a sheet of paper from 1 to 8. After each number, write the term from the box that best matches each description below.

amphitheaters	elevation
architect	facade
architecture	floor plan
basilicas	post and lintel

1. The field of art dealing with the planning and creating of buildings.
2. An artist who works at planning and creating buildings.
3. Huge meeting halls.
4. Circular or oval buildings with seats rising around an open space.
5. A building method in which a crossbeam is placed above two uprights.
6. A scale drawing of how a building would appear as if seen from above and there were no roof.
7. A drawing of an outside view of a building.
8. The front of a building.

REVIEWING ART FACTS

Number a sheet of paper from 9 to 18. Answer each question in a complete sentence.

9. Who were the first architects? What did they build? What media did they use?
10. What building material was used by the early Egyptians? What was an advantage of this material over ones used before it?
11. What are four main uses for architecture?
12. Why was it not important that Greek temples be large?
13. In what ways were churches of the 1200s and 1300s different from earlier temples?

14. What made it possible for architects to start building upward?
15. For what modern structures did early amphitheaters pave the way?
16. Name three kinds of buildings used for recreation.
17. What challenge faces every architect?
18. What kind of drawing reveals how the space inside a building is to be used?

THINKING ABOUT ART

On a sheet of paper, answer each question in a sentence or two.

1. **Compare and contrast.** What does architecture have in common with the other visual arts, such as painting and sculpture? In what ways is it unlike those arts?
2. **Analyze.** Why are both floor plans and elevations important in planning works of architecture?
3. **Extend.** From what you learned in this chapter, what other subjects besides art do you suppose architects study? Explain your answer.

MAKING ART CONNECTIONS

1. **Community Affairs.** A zoning law specifies what type building may be built in a certain part of a city. In teams, research whether there are laws that keep certain types of buildings away from schools. When research is complete, prepare reports to give to the class.
2. **Social Studies.** Research famous walls around the world. Tell about the way these walls affected the people who lived near them. Explore the structure of these walls.

LOOKING AT THE DETAILS

The detail shown below is from the Temple of Athena Nike on the Acropolis in Athens, Greece. Study the detail and answer the following questions.

1. The name of the temple means "Athena Victorious." Look at the figures on top of the building. What kind of victory did these people worship?
2. Does any part of this temple remind you of sculpture? If so, how and, what kind?
3. This temple was constructed without mortar or cement. Study the way the elements and principles of art are organized in this detail. Which ones do you think were most important to the Greeks? Why?
4. Consider the building's size. What kind of mood does this temple create?

Temple of Athena Nike.
427–424 B.C. (Detail.) Acropolis, Athens, Greece.

▲ **Where would you expect to find photographs like this? Does this photo tell a story?**

Margaret Bourke-White. *Mahatma Gandhi*. 1946. Photograph. George Eastman House, Rochester, New York.

CHAPTER 15

Photography, Film, and Video

Throughout this book you have learned about the many different ways that artists express themselves. Painters do this with brushes. Sculptors use clay, wood, or metal. Illustrators use pen or pencils.

Look at the photograph at the left. How is it like other works of art you have studied? How is it different? In this chapter you will learn about artists who use the camera to produce their art works.

OBJECTIVES

After completing this chapter, you will be able to:

- Tell what photography is and describe the history of photography.
- Define *motion picture* and tell how movies are made.
- Talk about the beginnings of video games.
- Make a photogram, a silent movie, and a video game.

WORDS YOU WILL LEARN

camera	negatives
cinematographer	photogram
daguerreotypes	photography
director	producer
microprocessors	video game
motion picture	wet plate

ARTISTS YOU WILL MEET

Margaret Bourke-White	Dorothea Lange
Mathew Brady	Harold Lloyd
J. L. M. Daguerre	Alfred Stieglitz
D. W. Griffith	William Henry Fox Talbot
Fritz Lang	Orson Welles

LESSON 1

The Art of Photography

What do all works of art have in common? All try to present an image in a way that makes it special. In recent times artists have discovered new ways of creating special images. In this lesson you will learn about one of those ways—photography. In later lessons you will learn about two others—the arts of film and video.

PHOTOGRAPHY

Today we take photographs for granted. They are all around us. Newspapers, magazines, and books are full of them. It is strange to think that photography was an expensive and difficult process just over 150 years ago. **Photography** is *the art of making images by exposing a chemically treated surface to light.* Photographs are made using *a dark box with a hole controlling how much light enters*, better known as a **camera**.

THE HISTORY OF PHOTOGRAPHY

The idea of capturing an image using light is a very old one. Attempts to do this date back to the time of Leonardo da Vinci (Figure 15–1). It was not until the 1800s, however, that the first true photographs were made. L. J. M. Daguerre (duh-gehr) was the French inventor of an early method of photography. These were called **daguerreotypes** (duh-**gehr**-uh-types), *silvery, mirrorlike images on a copper plate.* Figure 15–2 shows a hand–colored version, taken by an unknown photographer. Notice how worn and scratched the image is. Can you identify the subject of this photograph without reading the credit line?

Daguerreotypes took a long time to make. They were also very costly. The wet plate method, introduced in the 1850s, brought improvements in both these areas. **Wet plate** is

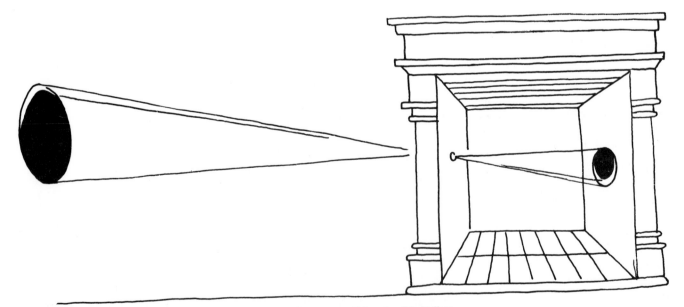

▲ **Figure 15–1** The word *obscura* means "dark" and *camera* means "chamber" in Italian. Can you think of other inventions, in which the idea for the invention was around a long time before the invention itself?

◄ **Figure 15–2 How would you describe the colors in this picture? Consider the technique. What might affect the color?**

Unknown/French. *Street Flutists.* c. 1852. Stereograph daguerreotype. 8.7 x 16.8 cm (3.4 x 6.6"). International Museum of Photography, George Eastman House, Rochester, New York.

a method of photography in which an image is created on glass that is coated with chemicals, then transferred to paper or cardboard, as in photography today. Also like photographs today, wet plate photographs used **negatives**, *reverse images of the object photographed.* The wet plate method was used to photograph impor-tant news events through the 1870s. Figure 15–3 was taken by Mathew Brady, a famous Civil War photographer. Figure 15–4 was taken by Dorothea Lange. She was a photo-journalist in the 1930s. What could pictures like these add to a news account that words could not?

▲ **Figure 15–3 In what ways are photographs like these more telling than a drawing would be?**

Mathew Brady. *Civil War.* c. 1865. Photograph. National Archives, Washington, D.C.

▲ **Figure 15–4** If this were a painting, would its impact be different from this photograph? **Why or why not?**

Dorothea Lange. *White Angel Breadline*. Photograph. Oakland Museum, San Francisco, California.

◀ **Figure 15–5** Stieglitz once waited in a New York blizzard for several hours to photograph a horse-drawn carriage. What does this tell you about him as a photographer?

Alfred Stieglitz. *The Steerage.* 1907. Photogravure. George Eastman House, Rochester, New York.

PHOTOGRAPHY AS ART

As picture taking methods improved, some photographers turned to photography for art's sake. You read in Chapter 7 about ways photographs affected painters of the late 1800s. The field of photography also produced some artists of its own. Alfred Stieglitz (**steeg**-luhts) was unusually gifted at capturing moments on film. Figure 15–5 shows a work Stieglitz always believed to be his masterpiece. This moment was captured on a ship taking immigrants from Europe to America. How would you describe the mood of the photograph?

✔ CHECK YOUR UNDERSTANDING

1. Define *photography*. Define *camera*.
2. When were the first real photographs made?
3. What were two methods for making photographs in the 1800s?
4. Name two similarities between the photographs taken in the 1800s and photographs taken today?

Making a Photogram

Look at Figure 15–6. This is a calotype (**kal**-uh-type), another early type of photograph. Like daguerreotypes, calotypes were made by transferring images onto materials affected by light.

You can get a glimpse of how these pioneering photographs were made by creating a **photogram**, *an image made on blueprint paper through the action of light and gas fumes.*

WHAT YOU WILL LEARN

You will create a shadow design on blueprint paper using found objects. Add interest to your design by considering each of the elements of art. You will use either formal or informal balance. Your design will show movement or rhythm. It should also express a mood or feeling. If you wish, mount your finished photogram on poster board for display. (See Figure 15–7.)

WHAT YOU WILL NEED

- Found objects, such as keys, coins, lace, pebbles, and small scraps of paper with unusual shapes.
- Sheet of white paper, 9 x 12 inch (23 x 30 cm)
- Blueprint paper, cut into 9 x 12 inch (23 x 30 cm) sheets and stored in a dark place
- Sheet of heavy cardboard
- Small sponge
- Ammonia (sudsy household type)
- Tray with 2 inch (5 cm) sides
- Piece of wire screen slightly larger than the tray
- Sheet of glass slightly larger than the tray
- White glue
- Sheet of poster board, 11 x 14 inch (28 x 36 cm)

▶ **Figure 15–6 Compare this image with Figure 15–2. Which one is the more realistic one? What differences can you name in the way the two images were captured?**

William Henry Fox Talbot. *The Ladder.* 1844. Calotype. George Eastman House, Rochester, New York.

WHAT YOU WILL DO

1. Experiment by arranging different found objects on the sheet of white paper. As you work, keep such art principles as balance and movement in mind. When you have created a design you find interesting, move on to the next step.
2. Place a sheet of blueprint paper on the sheet of cardboard. Carefully transfer your object arrangement to the blueprint paper. Cover the blueprint paper with construction paper.
3. Carefully carry your covered arrangement to a place where there is bright sunlight. Remove the construction paper. Wait about a minute or until the blueprint paper has changed color. Cover the blueprint paper with the construction paper once again. Move your arrangement to a darker part of the room.
4. Soak the sponge in ammonia, and place it inside the tray. Place the wire screen above the tray. Remove the found objects from the blueprint paper. Set the blueprint paper on top of the screen. Cover it with the sheet of glass. After 10 seconds, remove the glass.
5. Mount and display your photogram using white glue and poster board.

EXAMINING YOUR WORK

- **Describe** Identify the found objects you used in your photogram. Identify the elements of art used. Tell how you created the shadow design.
- **Analyze** Tell what kind of balance your design has. Explain how you created movement or rhythm in your design.
- **Interpret** Tell what mood your photogram expresses. Explain how you created this mood.
- **Judge** Tell whether you feel your work succeeds. Explain your answer.

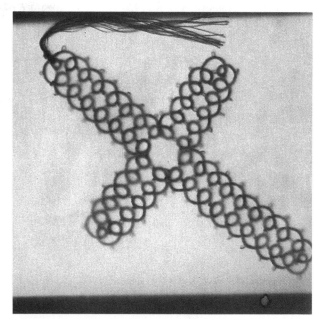

▲ **Figure 15–7 Student work. A photogram.**

OTHER STUDIO IDEAS

- Make a second photogram. This time use transparent objects, such as tissue paper scraps and bits of onion skin. You may tear the tissue paper and onion skin into non-objective shapes. Show movement, rhythm, and harmony in your unified work of art.

The Art of Film

"Lights. Camera. Action." These may not be words you would expect to hear spoken in an artist's studio. In some artists' studios, however, the words are spoken nearly every day. These are the kinds of studios where movies are made. The artist who speaks the words is known as the director.

In this lesson you will learn about the art of filmmaking.

THE BEGINNINGS OF FILM

After photographers learned to capture still images using light they began looking ahead to the next form of creative expression. By the end of the 1800s inventors had found a way to capture moving images using light. The **motion picture**, *photographs of the same subject taken a very short time apart and flashed onto a screen*, made the image appear to be moving (Figures 15–8 and 15–9).

MAKING FILMS

Every motion picture, or movie, is the combined effort of hundreds of people. The three most important of those people are the director, the producer, and the cinematographer.

The Director

The director is the single most important person in the making of a movie. The **director** is *the person in charge of shooting the film and guiding the actors*. He or she also helps with the script.

The director's main job is deciding how every scene should be photographed. To get just the right look, a director may shoot the same scene dozens of times.

▲ Figure 15–9   Compare this with Georgia O'Keeffe's cityscape on page 82. What similarities do you see?

Directed by Fritz Lang. Still from *Metropolis*. 1926. Museum of Modern Art. Film Stills Archive, New York, New York.

▲ Figure 15–8   This film was made by an American. The one in Figure 15–9 by a German. Do you think audiences in either country had trouble understanding the mood and setting of the foreign film? Why or why not?

Directed by D. W. Griffith. Still from *Intolerance*. 1916. Museum of Modern Art, Film Still Archive, New York, New York.

The Producer

The **producer** is *the person in charge of the business end of making a movie*. The producer is the person who finds the story and hires the director. He or she also figures out how much money it will cost to make the movie. Some producers take part in selecting actors and in writing the script.

The Cinematographer

The **cinematographer** (sin-uh-muh-**tahg**-ruh-fuhr) is *the person in charge of running the camera or cameras*. Like other artists, cinematographers are trained in using light and color.

Before filming, or shooting, the director and cinematographer will go over the script together. They will discuss different camera angles and techniques for shooting each scene.

THE ART OF FILM

The very first films made were silent. Since these films used no words, strong dramatic acting was required. They could be shown to audiences around the world. These films required strong and exaggerated acting.

The arrival of sound in the late 1920s opened up new doors to filmmakers. It also closed doors to actors whose voices did not sound right.

▲ **Figure 15–10** The man pictured here was the film's star and director. What problems do you think might exist for a person filling these two positions?

Directed by Orson Welles. Still from *Citizen Kane*. 1941. Museum of Modern Art, Film Stills Archive, New York, New York.

▲ **Figure 15–11** How can you tell this scene is not from real life? What is the mood of this scene? Explain

Directed by Tim Burton. Still from *Batman*. 1988. Courtesy of the Academy of Motion Pictures Arts & Sciences.

One of the most inventive motion pictures ever made was *Citizen Kane*. (See Figure 15-10.) Orson Welles' use of camera angles and editing were highly praised and are still imitated today. It, like many old classics, was made before color entered the motion picture industry.

The next advance in film, color, made possible the first colored film classics. These were movies such as *The Adventures of Robin Hood* and *The Wizard of Oz*.

The films of today, of course, use dazzling effects the earliest filmmakers probably never dreamed of. Computers and other high-tech equipment have allowed directors to shoot "the impossible." (See Figure 15–11.) One can only guess what astonishing screen images tomorrow's breakthroughs will bring.

✓ CHECK YOUR UNDERSTANDING

1. What are motion pictures? When was filmmaking invented?
2. What is a director? What are some of the director's tasks?
3. What is a producer? What are some of the producer's tasks?
4. What are two advances that have been made in filmmaking since the days of silent films?

Making a Silent Movie

Before the days of sound in movies, the filmmakers had their work cut out for them. They had to rely totally on action to tell the story (Figure 15–12). For those pioneering filmmakers, actions truly spoke louder than words.

WHAT YOU WILL LEARN

You will be part of a group that makes a silent movie. The group will be headed up by a producer and director. A cinematographer for the group will shoot the film using a home video camera. Music will be used to help the audience feel the mood and action. Captions will be used to help the audience understand the action. (See Figure 15–13.)

WHAT YOU WILL NEED

- Pencil
- Large notepad divided in half by a vertical pencil line
- Hand-held video camera with tripod
- Sheets of white poster board
- Black broad-line marker
- Audio tape recorder

WHAT YOU WILL DO

1. The class is to be divided into two groups. Each group is to choose from among its members a producer, a director, a cinematographer, and a three-member writing team. Every other group member is to be an actor.
2. The producer for each group is to meet with the writers. Together, the producer and writers are to agree on a story idea. The story, which is to be original, may be funny, serious, or suspenseful. The story should have parts for as many actors as there are actors in the group. As the writers create, they should tell what each character is doing at any given moment. The final version of the story should be written on the left half of the notepad.
3. While the writers work, the director and cinematographer should test the equipment. At the director's instructions, the cinematographer should take long shots and close-ups. The two should test out indoor shots using the camera's lighting attachment. They should test different uses for the tripod.

▶ **Figure 15–12 Comedians were especially popular during the silent film era. Do you find this scene funny? Explain your answer. How is movement shown in this picture?**

Directed by Harold Lloyd. Still from *Safety Last*. 1923. Museum of Modern Art, Film Stills Archive, New York, New York.

4. When the script is finished, the producer and director should read it. Together, they should decide which scenes need captions to help viewers understand the action. The producer should ask the writers to create these captions with poster board and marker. The producer and director should decide which actors are to play which parts. They should decide what kind of music best fits the mood of the story. The producer should search for and make tape recordings of particular pieces of music.

5. The director should read the script again, this time along with the cinematographer. The two should decide from which angle to shoot each scene or action. They should decide whether a scene calls for a close-up or a long shot. The director should make notes on the right side of the notepad. He or she should also note the points in the shooting where captions are needed.

6. The actors should rehearse the story. They will take their cues on where to stand and what to do from the director. The actors should try to show through their actions and expressions what is happening.

7. When the director feels the group is well prepared, shooting should begin. The finished film should be shown, with music, to the rest of the class.

- **Describe**   Describe what things the director did before and during shooting. Tell what decisions the director and producer made together. Tell what points the director and cinematographer discussed. Tell what decisions they reached. Tell whether the actors followed the director's instructions. Tell whether they showed what was happening through their actions and expressions.
- **Analyze**   Identify different ways the camera was used. Explain the results.
- **Interpret**   Tell what the story was about. Describe its mood. Explain how the captions helped tell the story and express the mood. Explain how the music added to the mood and emphasized the action.
- **Judge**   Tell whether you feel your work succeeds. Explain your answer.

▶ **Figure 15–13   Students shooting a silent film.**

OTHER STUDIO IDEAS

- Make a silent television commercial. You may use a real product, but the idea should be original. Use captions to help viewers understand the action.

- ●● Make a film with a sound track. Rather than have the actors speak, have a narrator tell what is happening. Use sound effects, such as rattling a sheet of lightweight metal to create thunder.

The Art of Video

In Lesson 3 you read that computers have opened up new worlds for filmmakers. Computers have also changed forever the face of home entertainment. How? By opening up the exciting and often magical world of video games.

In this lesson you will get a behind-the-scenes glimpse of that world.

VIDEO GAMES

Games have been around for as long as there have been humans. Video games have been around only since there have been computers. A **video game** is *an electronic form of entertainment run by a computer*. The computers that run, or drive, video games nowadays are small enough to fit on a fingertip. Such *tiny computers* are called **microprocessors** (my-kroh-**prahs**-es-uhrs). (See Figure 15–14.)

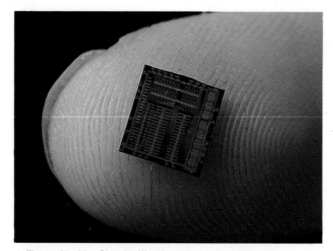

▲ Figure 15–14 Circuits like these are called chips. Do you know of any other electronic appliances that use chips?

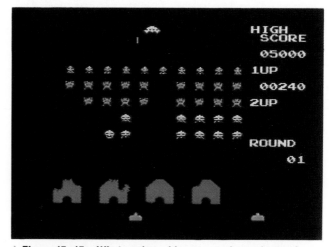

▲ Figure 15–15 What modern video games do you know of with a space theme?

Screen image from *Space Invaders*.

THE HISTORY OF VIDEO GAMES

Video games take their name from the fact that they use TV, or video screens. The first video game, *Pong*, came out in the early 1970s. The game was modeled on table tennis. It was made up totally of a moving green dot and a center-line "net." In 1979, a highly popular video game was produced called *Space Invaders* (Figure 15–15). This was the first of many video games with a space theme. In the early 1980s, *Pac-Man* gobbled up more video arcade quarters than any other game (Figure 15–16).

Today video games can be found dealing with just about every imaginable fantasy adventure or sport. Technical breakthroughs have led to the use of exciting colors and complicated sound effects.

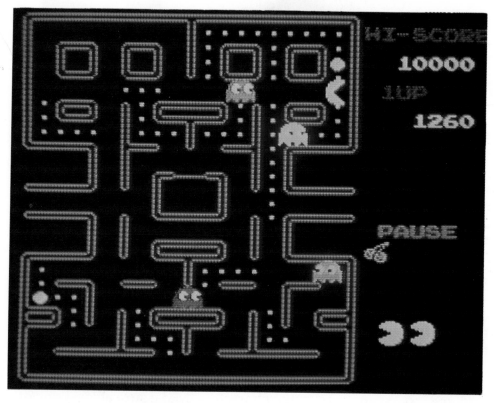

◀ **Figure 15–16** How are the art principles of balance, harmony and variety incorporated into this video game?

Screen image from *Pac Man*.

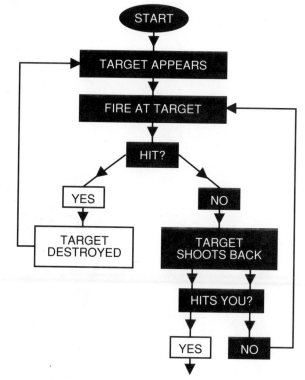

▲ **Figure 15–17** Flow chart.

VIDEO GAME DESIGN

Designers of video games draw with space-age tools, such as the light pen and electronic tablet.

Video game designers must do more, however, than just dream up dazzling images. They must also know how to do computer programming. This means creating a set of instructions a computer can follow. A program usually begins with a flow chart, an outline of steps the computer will take. Figure 15–17 shows part of a flow chart.

✔CHECK YOUR UNDERSTANDING

1. What is a video game? What is a microprocessor?
2. What was the first video game? When did it come out?
3. What tools do video game designers draw with?
4. What is computer programming? How is it tied to video game design?

LESSON 6

Designing a Video Game

Look at Figure 15–18. This shows a group from a very popular video game of the last few years. These characters star in a cartoon series and are featured in a comic book series. Do you know the name of this group? Do you know who the characters in this scene are?

WHAT YOU WILL LEARN

You will create characters and a story idea for a video adventure. You will write a description of the game that tells what part each character plays. The description will also reveal the goal of the player. You will create illustrations of the characters (Figure 15–19.) Line and color will be used to help show the mood of each character. These characters will be shown in action poses.

WHAT YOU WILL NEED

- Notepad
- Pencil
- Sheets of sketch paper
- Sheets of white paper, 12 x 18 inch (30 x 46 cm)
- Colored pencils

WHAT YOU WILL DO

1. Brainstorm with the class to come up with original ideas for adventures. On the notepad, write the setting of your adventure. Write the types and names of the characters. Make sure at least one of your characters is a villain or evil force. Give your game a title.

▶ **Figure 15–18** Are you familiar with the movie that was based on these characters? Are these characters visually appealing? Why or why not?

Teenage Mutant Ninja Turtles. New Line Cinema.

▲ Figure 15–19   Student work. An idea for an action video.

- **Describe**   Identify the different characters you created. Tell the part each one plays in your game. Reveal the setting of your game. Identify the goal of a player. Point to details of background that help emphasize a character's role.
- **Analyze**   Explain how the figures are drawn in action poses to show that they are moving. Show where you used line and color to help capture the mood of each character.
- **Interpret**   Explain what details of your game make it exciting. Describe how the dangers facing a player add to the excitement.
- **Judge**   Tell whether you feel your work succeeds. Explain your answer.

Sketch details of background that help emphasize the character's role in the game. Do separate studies of each character's face.

4. Using pencil, transfer the best of your action sketches to sheets of white paper. Lightly sketch details of the characters' faces from the studies you made. Using colored pencils, add detail and shading. Use line and color to capture the mood or personality of each character.

5. Present your finished illustrations to the class. Give a brief talk in which you explain the rules of the game.

2. On another page of the notepad, write notes about the action in your game. Identify the goal of the player. Tell what dangers or problems face the player. Describe different ways in which the player can score points.

3. On sketch paper, do gesture drawings of the characters in different action poses.

OTHER STUDIO IDEAS

- Using watercolors, do a painting of one of your characters. Imagine that this painting will appear on the package in which the game cartridge is sold.

●● Use a graphic software program such as MacPaint to draw one of your characters on a computer.

CHAPTER 15 REVIEW

BUILDING VOCABULARY

Number a sheet of paper from 1 to 12. After each number, write the term from the box that best matches each description.

camera	negatives
cinematographer	photogram
daguerreotypes	photography
director	producer
microprocessors	video game
motion picture	wet plate

1. The art of making images by exposing a chemically treated surface to light.
2. A dark box with a hole controlling how much light enters.
3. Silvery, mirrorlike images made on a copper plate.
4. A photography method in which an image is created on glass coated with chemicals.
5. Reverse images of an object photographed.
6. An image made on blueprint paper through the action of light and gas fumes.
7. Photographs of the same subject taken a very short time apart and flashed onto a screen.
8. The person in charge of shooting a film and guiding the actors.
9. The person in charge of the business end of making a movie.
10. The person in charge of running the camera in the filming of a movie.
11. An electronic form of entertainment run by a computer.
12. Tiny computers.

REVIEWING ART FACTS

Number a sheet of paper from 13 to 18. Answer each question in a complete sentence.

13. Who is L.J.M. Daguerre? What contribution did he make to photography?
14. In what two ways was the wet plate an improvement over earlier methods?
15. What is a calotype?
16. What is a cinematographer? What do they have in common with other artists?
17. Why were the first films made able to be shown to people around the world?
18. What part do flow charts play in the creation of video games?

THINKING ABOUT ART

On a sheet of paper, answer each question in a sentence or two.

1. **Compare and contrast.** In what ways are daguerreotypes and wet plate prints the same? In what ways are they different?
2. **Interpret.** Different shots of the same scene in a movie are called takes. In what way are takes similar to the studies done by painters and sculptors?

MAKING ART CONNECTIONS

1. **Social Studies.** Study the Brady photograph of the Civil War battlefield on page **253**. Notice the equipment and uniforms of the military personnel. Find news photos that document events from World War I or World War II. Report to the class how the dress and equipment have changed.
2. **Science.** Research the development of the materials used in photography and find out how the chemical process allows light to be captured on film.

CHAPTER 15 REVIEW

LOOKING AT THE DETAILS

The detail below was taken from Margaret Bourke-White's photograph *Mahatma Gandhi*. Study the detail and answer the following questions.

1. Margaret Bourke-White chose to photograph Gandhi without a shirt, wearing glasses and reading. Why is this important?
2. Mahatma Gandhi was India's leader of nonviolent rebellion for political independence. He encouraged weaving as an industry and for millions of Indians the spinning wheel was the symbol of their fight for independence. How can knowing your subject's historical background help you in taking his or her photograph? How does knowing more about Gandhi and his cause help you in understanding this photo?
3. Does this photograph tell you something about the photographer? Explain.
4. Would the mood of the photograph change if it were taken in color? Explain your answer.

Margaret Bourke-White. *Mahatma Gandhi*. 1946. Photograph. (Detail.) George Eastman House, Rochester, New York.

▲ Working on group murals is an excellent way to practice artistic skills, gain recognition, and at the same time, have fun.

HANDBOOK CONTENTS

1. Making Gesture Drawings

Gesture drawing is a way of showing movement in a sketch. Gesture drawings have no outlines or details. You are not expected to draw the figure. Instead, you are expected to draw the movement, or what the figure is doing. Follow these guidelines:

- Use the side of the drawing tool. Do not hold the medium as you would if you were writing.
- Find the lines of movement that show the direction in which the figure is bending. Draw the main line showing this movement.
- Use quickly drawn lines to build up the shape of the person.

2. Making Contour Drawings

Contour drawing is a way of capturing the feel of a subject. When doing a contour drawing, remember the following pointers:

- If you accidentally pick up your pen or pencil, don't stop working. Place your pen or pencil back where you stopped. Begin again from that point.
- If you have trouble keeping your eyes off the paper, ask a friend to hold a piece of paper between your eyes and your drawing paper. Another trick is to place your drawing paper inside a large paper bag as you work.
- Tape your paper to the table so it will not slide around. With a finger of your free hand, trace the outline of the object. Record the movement with your drawing hand.

- Contour lines show ridges and wrinkles in addition to outlines. Adding these lines gives roundness to the object.

3. Drawing with Oil Pastels

Oil pastels are sticks of pigment held together with an oily binder. The colors are brighter than wax crayon colors. If you press heavily you will make a brilliant-colored line. If you press lightly you will create a fuzzy line. You can fill in shapes with the brilliant colors. You can blend a variety of color combinations. For example, you can fill a shape with a soft layer of a hue and then color over the hue with a heavy layer of white to create a unique tint of that hue.

If you use oil pastels on colored paper, you can put a layer of white under the layer of hue to block the color of the paper.

4. Drawing Thin Lines with a Brush

Drawing thin lines with a brush can be learned with a little practice. Just follow these steps:

1. Dip your brush in the ink or paint. Wipe the brush slowly against the side, twirling it between your fingers until the bristles form a point.
2. Hold the brush at the beginning of the metal band near the tip. Hold the brush straight up and down.
3. Imagine that the brush is a pencil with a very sharp point. Pretend that pressing too hard will break the point. Now touch the paper lightly with the tip of the brush and draw a line. The line should be quite thin.

To make a thinner line still, lift up on the brush as you draw. After a while, you will be able to make lines in a variety of thicknesses.

5. Making a Grid for Enlarging

Sometimes the need arises to make a bigger version of a small drawing. An example is when you create a mural based on a small sketch. Follow these steps:

1. Using a ruler, draw evenly spaced lines across and up and down your original drawing (Figure T–1). Count

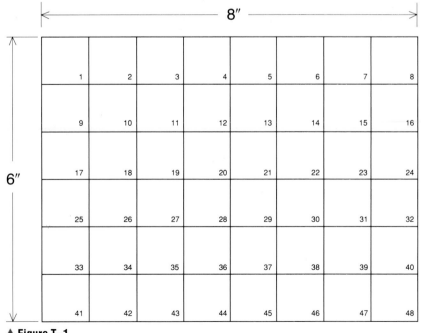

▲ **Figure T–1**

the number of squares you made from side to side. Count the number of squares running up and down.

2. Measure the width of the surface to which the drawing is to be transferred. Divide that figure by the number of side-to-side squares. The resulting number will be the horizontal measure of each square. You may work in inches or centimeters. Using a ruler or yardstick, mark off the squares. Draw in light rules.

3. Measure the height of the surface to which the drawing is to be transferred. Divide that figure by the number of up-and-down squares. The resulting number will be the vertical measure of each square. Mark off the squares. Draw in pencil lines.

4. Starting at the upper left, number each square on the original drawing. Give the

same number to each square on the large grid. Working a square at a time, transfer your image. (See Figure T–2.)

6. Using Shading Techniques

When using shading techniques, keep in mind the following:

- Lines or dots placed close together create dark values.
- Lines or dots placed far apart, on the other hand, create light values. To show a change from light to dark, start with lines or dots far apart and little by little bring them close together.
- Use care also to follow the shape of the object when adding lines. Straight lines are used to shade an object with a flat surface. Rounded lines are used to shade an object with a curved surface.

7. Using Sighting Techniques

Sighting is a technique that will help you draw objects in proportion.

1. Face the object you plan to draw. Hold a pencil straight up and down at arm's length. Your thumb should rest against the side of the pencil and be even with the tip.

2. Close one eye. With your other eye, focus on the object.

3. Slide your thumb down the pencil until the exposed part of the pencil matches the object's height. (See Figure T–3.)

▲ Figure T–3

4. Now, without moving your thumb or bending your arm, turn the pencil sideways.

5. Focus on the width of the object. If the height is greater, figure out how many "widths" will fit in one "height." If the width is greater, figure out how many "heights" will fit in one "width."

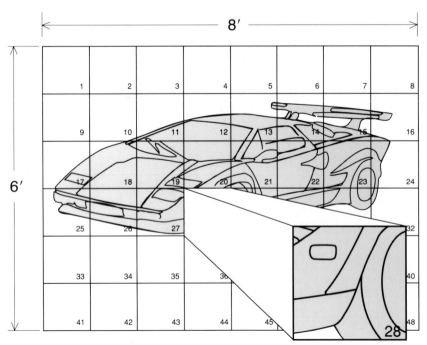

▲ Figure T–2

8. Using a Viewing Frame

Much in the way a camera is used to focus on one area of a scene, you can better zero in on an object you plan to draw by using a viewing frame (Figure T–4). To make a viewing frame do the following:

1. Cut a rectangular hole in a piece of paper about 2 inches (3 to 5 cm) in from the paper's edges.
2. Hold the paper at arm's length and look through the hole at your subject. Imagine that the hole represents your drawing paper.
3. Decide how much of the subject you want to have in your drawing.
4. By moving the frame up, down, sideways, nearer, or farther, you can change the focus of your drawing.

9. Using a Ruler

There are times when you need to draw a crisp, straight line. By using the following techniques, you will be able to do so.

1. Hold the ruler with one hand and the pencil with the other.
2. Place the ruler where you wish to draw a straight line.
3. Hold the ruler with your thumb and first two fingers. Be careful that your fingers do not stick out beyond the edge of the ruler.
4. Press heavily on the ruler so it will not slide while you're drawing.
5. Hold the pencil lightly against the ruler.
6. Pull the pencil quickly and lightly along the edge of the ruler. The object is to keep the ruler from moving while the pencil moves along its edge.

▲ **Figure T–4**

PAINTING TIPS

10. Cleaning a Paint Brush

Cleaning a paint brush properly helps it last a long time. *Always*:

1. Rinse the thick paint out of the brush under running water. Do not use hot water.
2. Gently paint the brush over a cake of mild soap, or dip it in a mild liquid detergent (Figure T–5).

▲ **Figure T–5**

3. Gently scrub the brush against the palm of your hand to work the soap into the brush. This removes paint you may not have realized was still in the brush.

4. Rinse the brush under running water while you continue to scrub your palm against it (Figure T–6).

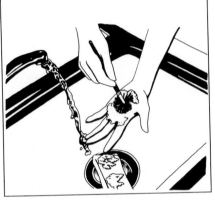

▲ **Figure T–6**

5. Repeat steps 2, 3, and 4 as needed.

When it is thoroughly rinsed and excess water has been squeezed from the brush, shape your brush into a point with your fingers (Figure T–7). Place the brush in a container with the bristles up so that it will keep its shape as it dries.

▲ **Figure T–7**

11. Making Natural Earth Pigments

Anywhere there is dirt, clay, or sand, there is natural pigment. To create your own pigments, gather as many different kinds of earth colors as you can. Grind these as finely as possible. (If you can, borrow a mortar and pestle.) (See Figure T–8.) Do not worry if the pigment is slightly gritty.

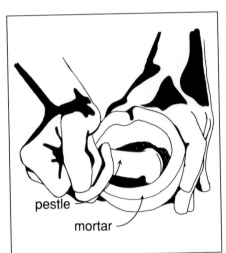

pestle

mortar

▲ **Figure T–8**

To make the binder, mix equal parts of white glue and water. Place a few spoonfuls of your powdered pigment into a small jar. Add a little of the binder. Experiment with different amounts of each.

When you work with natural pigments, remember always to wash the brushes before the paint in them has a chance to dry. The glue from the binder can ruin a brush. As you work, stir the paint every now and then. This will keep the grains of pigment from settling to the bottom of the jar.

Make a fresh batch each time you paint.

12. Mixing Paint to Change the Value of Color

You can better control the colors in your work when you mix your own paint. In mixing paints, treat opaque paints (for example, tempera) differently from transparent paints (for example, watercolors).

- *For light values of opaque paints.* Mix only a small amount of the hue to white. The color can always be made stronger by adding more of the hue.
- *For dark values of opaque paints.* Add a small amount of black to the hue. Never add the hue to black.
- *For light values of transparent paints.* Thin a shaded area with water (Figure T–9). This allows more of the white of the paper to show through.
- *For dark values of transparent paints.* Carefully add a small amount of black to the hue.

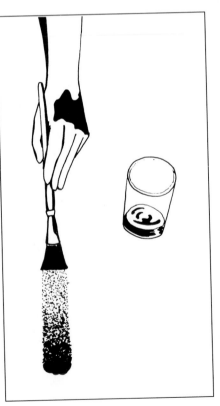

▲ **Figure T–9**

13. Working with Poster Paints (School Tempera)

When using poster paints (school tempera) remember the following:

• Poster paints run when wet. To keep this from happening, make sure one shape is dry before painting a wet color next to it.

14. Working with Watercolors

• If you apply wet paint to damp paper, you create lines and shapes with soft edges.

• If you apply wet paint to dry paper, you create lines and shapes with sharp, clear edges.

• If you dip a dry brush into damp paint and then brush across dry paper, you achieve a fuzzy effect.

• School watercolors come in semi-moist cakes. Before you use them, place a drop of water on each cake to let the paint soften. Watercolor paints are transparent. You can see the white paper through the paint. If you want a light value of a hue, dilute the paint with a large amount of water. If you want a bright hue, you must dissolve more pigment by swirling your brush around in the cake of paint until you have dissolved a great deal of paint. The paint you apply to the paper can be as bright as the paint in the cake.

15. Making a Stamp Printing

A stamp print is an easy way to make repetitive designs. The following are a few suggestions for making a stamp and printing with it. You may develop some other ideas after reading these hints. Remember, printing reverses your design, so if you use letters, be certain to cut or carve them backwards.

• Cut a simple design into the flat surface of an eraser with a knife that has a fine, precision blade.

• Cut a potato, carrot, or turnip in half. Use a paring knife to carve a design into the flat surface of the vegetable.

• Glue yarn to a bottle cap or a jar lid.

• Glue found objects to a piece of corrugated cardboard. Make a design with paper-clips, washers, nuts, leaves, feathers, or anything else you can find. Whatever object you use should have a fairly flat surface. Make a handle for the block with masking tape.

• Cut shapes out of a piece of inner tube material. Glue the shapes to a piece of heavy cardboard.

There are several ways to apply ink or paint to a stamp:

• Roll water-based printing ink on the stamp with a soft brayer.

• Roll water-based printing ink on a plate and press the stamp into the ink.

• Apply tempera paint or school acrylic to the stamp with a bristle brush.

16. Working with Clay

To make your work with clay go smoothly, always do the following:

1. Dip one or two fingers in water.
2. Spread the moisture from your fingers over your palms.

Never dip your hands in water. Too much moisture turns clay into mud.

17. Joining Clay

If you are creating a piece of sculpture that requires joining pieces, do the following:

1. Gather the materials you will need. These include clay, slip, (a creamy mixture of clay and water), a paint brush, a scoring tool, (perhaps a kitchen fork) and clay tools.
2. Rough up or scratch the two surfaces to be joined (Figure T–10).

▲ Figure T–10

3. Apply slip to one of the two surfaces using a paint brush or your fingers (Figure T–11).

▲ Figure T–11

4. Gently press the two surfaces together so the slip oozes out of the joining seam (Figure T–12).

▲ Figure T–12

5. Using clay tools and/or your fingers, smooth away the slip that has oozed out of the seam (Figure T–13). You may wish to smooth out the seam as well, or you may wish to leave it for decorative purposes.

▲ Figure T–13

18. Making a Clay Mold for a Plaster Relief

One of the easiest ways to make a plaster relief is with a clay mold. When making a clay mold, remember the following:

- Plaster poured into the mold will come out with the opposite image. Design details cut into the mold will appear raised on the relief. Details built up within the mold will appear indented in the relief.
- Do not make impressions in your mold that have *undercuts* (Figure T–14). Undercuts trap plaster, which will break off when the relief is removed. When cutting impressions, keep the deepest parts the narrowest.
- In carving a raised area in the mold, take care not to create a reverse undercut (Figure T–15).

If you want to change the mold simply smooth the area with your fingers.

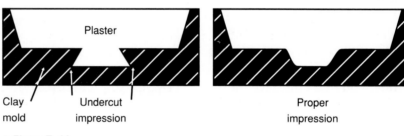

▲ Figure T–14

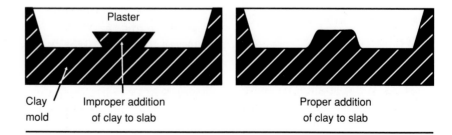

▲ Figure T–15

19. Mixing Plaster

Mixing plaster requires some technique and a certain amount of caution. It can also be a very simple matter when you are prepared. Always do the following:

- Use caution when working with dry plaster. Wear a dust mask or work in a well-ventilated room.
- Cover your work space to keep the dust from spreading.
- Always use a plastic bowl and a stick for mixing. Never use silverware you will later eat from.
- Always use plaster that is fine, like sifted flour. Plaster should never be grainy when dry.
- Always add the water to the bowl first. Sift in the plaster. Stir slowly.
- Never pour unused plaster down a drain. Allow it to dry in the bowl. To remove the dried plaster, twist the bowl. Crack the loose plaster into a lined trash can.

20. Working with Papier-Mâché

Papier-mâché (**pay**-puhr muh-**shay**) is a French term meaning "chewed paper." It is also the name of several sculpting methods using newspaper and liquid paste. These methods can be used to model tiny pieces of jewelry. They can also be used to create life-size creatures.

In creating papier-mâché sculptures, the paper-and-paste mixture is molded over a support. You will learn more about supports shortly. The molded newspaper dries to a hard finish. The following are three methods for working with papier-mâché:

- **Pulp Method.** Shred newspaper, paper towels, or tissue paper into tiny pieces. (Do not use glossy magazine paper; it will not soften.) Soak your paper in water overnight. Press the paper in a kitchen strainer to remove as much moisture as possible. Mix the mashed paper with commercially prepared papier-mâché paste or white glue. The mixture should have the consistency of soft clay. Add a few drops of oil of cloves to keep the mixture from spoiling. A spoonful of linseed oil makes the mixture smoother. (If needed, the mixture can be stored at this point in a plastic bag in the refrigerator.) Use the mixture to model small shapes. When your creations dry, they can be sanded. You will also be able to drill holes in them.
- **Strip Method.** Tear newspaper into strips. Either dip the strips in papier-mâché paste or rub paste on them. Apply the strips to your support (Figure T–16). If you do not want the strips to stick to your

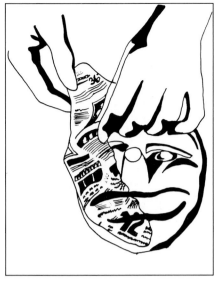

▲ **Figure T–16**

support, first cover it with plastic wrap. Use wide strips for large shapes. Use thin strips for smaller shapes. If you plan to remove your finished creation from the support, apply five or six layers. (Change directions with each layer so you can keep track of the number.) Otherwise, two or three layers should be enough. After applying the strips to your support, rub your fingers over the surface.

As a last layer, use torn paper towels. The brown paper towels that are found in schools produce an uncomplicated surface on which to paint. Make sure no rough edges are sticking up. Store any unused paste mixture in the refrigerator to keep it from spoiling.
- **Draping Method.** Spread papier-mâché paste on newspaper. Lay a second sheet on top of the first. Smooth the layers. Add another layer of paste and another sheet of paper. Repeat until you have four or five layers of paper. Use this method for making drapery on a figure. (See Figure T–17.) If you allow the lay-

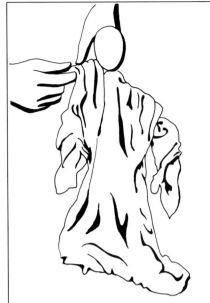

▲ **Figure T–17**

ers to dry for a day or two, they will become leathery. They can then be cut and molded as you like. Newspaper strips dipped in paste can be used to seal cracks.

Like papier-mâché, supports for papier-mâché creations can be made in several different ways. Dry newspaper may be wadded up and wrapped with string or tape (Figure T–18). Wire coat hangers may be padded with rags. For large figures, a wooden frame covered with chicken wire makes a good support.

▲ **Figure T–18**

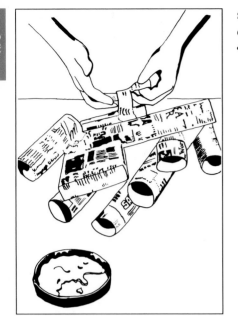

▲ **Figure T–19**

To create a base for your papier-mâché creations, tape together arrangements of found materials. Some materials you might combine are boxes, tubes, and bowls. (See Figure T–19.) Clay can also be modeled as a base. If clay is used, be sure there are no undercuts that would keep the papier-mâché from lifting off easily when dry. (For an explanation of undercuts, see Technique Tip **18**, *Handbook* page **276**.)

Always allow time for your papier-mâché creations to dry. The material needs extra drying time when thick layers are used or when the weather is damp. An electric fan blowing air on the material can shorten the drying time.

21. Making a Paper Sculpture

Another name for paper sculpture is origami. The process originated in Japan and means "folding paper." Paper sculpture begins with a flat piece of paper. The paper is then curved or bent to produce more than a flat

surface. Here are some ways to experiment with paper.

- **Scoring.** Place a square sheet of heavy construction paper, 12 x 12 inch (30 x 30 cm), on a flat surface. Position the ruler on the paper so that it is close to the center and parallel to the sides. Holding the ruler in place, run the point of a knife or a pair of scissors along one of the ruler's edges. Press down firmly but take care not to cut through the paper. Gently crease the paper along the line you made. Hold your paper with the crease facing upward.
- **Pleating.** Take a piece of paper and fold it one inch from the edge. Then fold the paper in the other direction. Continue folding back and forth.
- **Curling.** Hold one end of a long strip of paper with the thumb and forefinger of one hand. At a point right below where you are holding the strip, grip it lightly between the side of a pencil and the thumb of your other hand. In a quick motion, run the pencil along the strip. This will cause the strip to curl back on itself. Don't apply too much pressure, or the strip will tear. (See Figure T–20.)

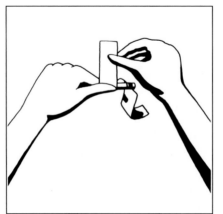

▲ **Figure T–20**

22. Measuring Rectangles

Do you find it hard to create perfectly formed rectangles? Here is a way of getting the job done:

1. Make a light pencil dot near the long edge of a sheet of paper. With a ruler, measure the exact distance between the dot and the edge. Make three more dots the same distance in from the edge. (See Figure T–21.)

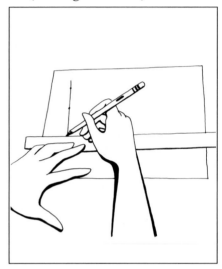

▲ **Figure T–21**

2. Line a ruler up along the dots. Make a light pencil line running the length of the paper.
3. Turn the paper so that a short side is facing you. Make four pencil dots equally distant from the short edge. Connect these with a light pencil rule. Stop when you reach the first line you drew. (See Figure T–22.)
4. Do the same for the remaining two sides. Erase any lines that may extend beyond the box you have made.
5. Trace over the lines with your ruler and pencil.

The box you have created will be a perfectly formed rectangle.

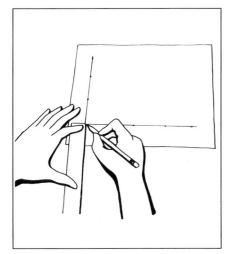

▲ Figure T–22

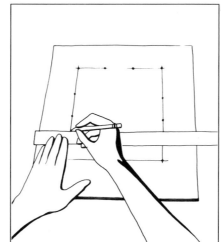

▲ Figure T–23

23. Making a Mat

You can add appeal to an art work by making a mat, using the following steps.

1. Gather the materials you will need. These include a metal rule, a pencil, mat board, cardboard backing, a sheet of heavy cardboard to protect your work surface, a mat knife with a sharp blade, and wide masking tape.
2. Wash your hands. Mat board should be kept very clean.
3. Measure the height and width of the work to be matted. Decide how large a border you want for your work. (A border of approximately 2½ inches on three sides with 3 inches on the bottom is aesthetically pleasing.) Your work will be behind the window you will cut.
4. Plan for the opening, or window, to be ¼ inch smaller on all sides than the size of your work. For example, if your work measures 9 by 12 inches, the mat window should measure 8½ inches (9 inches minus ¼ inch times two) by 11½ inches (12 inches minus ¼ inch times two). Using your metal rule and pencil, lightly draw your

window rectangle on the back of the board 2½ inches from the top and left edge of the mat. (See Figure T–23.) Add a 2½ inch border to the right of the window and a 3 inch border to the bottom, lightly drawing cutting guidelines.

Note: If you are working with metric measurements, the window should overlap your work by 0.5 cm (centimeters) on all sides. Therefore, if your work measures 24 by 30 cm, the mat window measures 23 cm (24 − [2 × 0.5]) by 29 cm (30 − [2 × 0.5]).

▲ Figure T–24

5. Place the sheet of heavy, protective cardboard on your work surface. Place the mat board, pencil marks up, over the cardboard. Holding the metal rule firmly in place, score the first line with your knife. Always place the metal rule so that your blade is away from the frame. (See Figure T–24.) In case you make an error you will cut into the window hole or the extra mat that is not used for the frame. Do not try to cut through the board with one stroke. By the third or fourth stroke, you should be able to cut through the board easily.
6. Working in the same fashion, score and cut through the board along all the window lines. Be careful not to go beyond the lines. Remove the window.
7. Cut a cardboard backing for your art work that is slightly smaller than the overall size of your mat. Using a piece of broad masking tape, hinge the back of the mat to the backing. (See Figure T–25.)

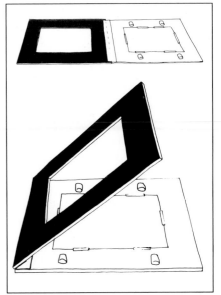

▲ Figure T–25

Position your art work between the backing and the mat and attach it with tape. Anchor the frame to the cardboard with a few pieces of rolled tape.

24. Mounting a Two-Dimensional Work

Mounting pictures that you make gives them a professional look. To mount a work, do the following:

1. Gather the materials you will need. These include a yardstick, a pencil, poster board, a sheet of heavy cardboard, a knife with a very sharp blade, a sheet of newspaper, and rubber cement.
2. Measure the height and width of the work to be mounted. Decide how large a border you want around the work. Plan your mount size using the work's measurements. To end up with a 3-inch (8 cm) border, for example, make your mount 6 inches (15 cm) wider and higher than your work. Record the measurements for your mount.
3. Using your yardstick and pencil, lightly draw your mount rectangle on the back of the poster board. Measure from the edges of the poster board. If you have a large paper cutter available, you may use it to cut your mount.
4. Place the sheet of heavy cardboard on your work surface. Place the poster board, pencil marks up, over the cardboard. Holding the yardstick firmly in place along one line, score the line with your knife. Do not try to cut through the board with one stroke. By the third try, you should be able to cut through the board.

▲ Figure T–26

5. Place the art work on the mount. Using the yardstick, center the work. Mark each corner with a dot. (See Figure T–26.)
6. Place the art work, face down, on a sheet of newspaper. Coat the back of the work with rubber cement. (*Safety Note:* Always use rubber cement in a room with plenty of ventilation.) *If your mount is to be permanent, skip to Step 8.*
7. Line up the corners of your work with the dots on the mounting board. Smooth the work into place. *Skip to Step 9.*
8. After coating the back of your art work, coat the poster board with rubber cement. Be careful not to add cement to the border area. Have a partner hold your art work in the air by the two top corners. Once the two glued surfaces meet, you will not be able to change the position of the work. Grasp the lower two corners. Carefully lower the work to the mounting board. Line up the two corners with the bottom dots. Little by little, lower the work into place (Figure T–27). Press it smooth.

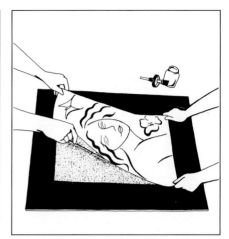

▲ Figure T–27

9. To remove any excess cement, create a small ball of nearly dry rubber cement. Use the ball of rubber cement to pick up excess cement.

25. Making Rubbings

Rubbings make interesting textures and designs. They may also be used with other media to create mixed media art. To make a rubbing, place a sheet of thin paper on top of the surface to be rubbed. Hold the paper in place with one hand. With the other hand, rub the paper with the flat side of an unwrapped crayon. Always rub away from the hand holding the paper. Never rub back and forth, since this may cause the paper to slip.

26. Scoring Paper

The secret to creating neat, sharp folds in cardboard or paper is a technique called scoring. Here is how it is done:

1. Line up a ruler along the line you want to fold.
2. Lightly run a sharp knife or scissors along the fold line. Press down firmly enough to leave a light crease. Take care not to cut all the way through the paper (Figure T–28).

▲ Figure T–28

3. Gently crease the paper along the line you made.

To score curved lines, use the same technique. Make sure your curves are wide enough to ensure a clean fold. Too tight a curve will cause the paper to wrinkle (Figure T–29).

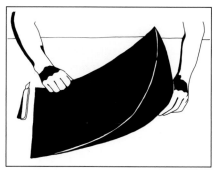

▲ Figure T–29

27. Making a Tissue Paper Collage

For your first experience with tissue, make a free design with the tissue colors. Start with the lightest colors of tissue first and save the darkest for last. It is difficult to change the color of dark tissue by overlapping it with other colors. If one area becomes too dark, you might cut out a piece of white paper, glue it over the dark area carefully, and apply new colors over the white area.

1. Apply a coat of adhesive to the area where you wish to place the tissue.

2. Place the tissue down carefully over the wet area (Figure T–30). Don't let your fingers get wet.

3. Then add another coat of adhesive over the tissue. If your brush picks up any color from the wet tissue, rinse your brush in water and let it dry before using it again.

4. Experiment by overlapping colors. Allow the tissue to wrinkle to create textures as you apply it. Be sure that all the loose edges of tissue are glued down.

28. Working with Glue

When applying glue, always start at the center of the surface you are coating and work outward.

- When gluing papers together don't use a lot of glue, just a dot will do. Use dots in the corners and along the edges. Press the two surfaces together. Keep dots at least ½ inch (1.3 cm) in from the edge of your paper.
- Handle a glued surface carefully with only your fingertips. Make sure your hands are clean before pressing the glued surface into place.
- *Note:* The glue should be as thin as possible. Thick or beaded glue will create ridges on your work.

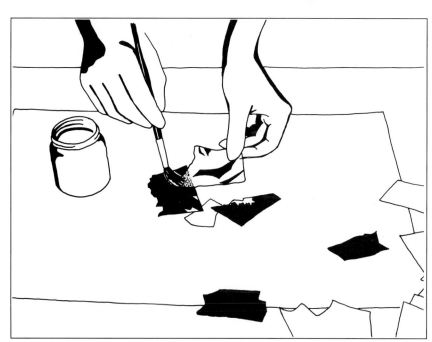

▲ Figure T–30

▲Artists, down through the ages, have helped us visualize what we learn about history. Art historians are responsible for much of what we know about the artists who have lived in the past.

Mary Cassatt

1845–1926
American Painter

At the Opera
  page **16**

Maternal Caress
  page **35**

The second half of the 1800s was an unparalleled age of discovery. People had learned to harness the power of steam to run locomotives. Streetcars powered by electricity rumbled down cobblestone streets.

For American-in-Paris Mary Cassatt (kuh-**sat**) the age was also one of discovery — bitter discovery. Cassatt had come to Paris to continue the study of painting she had begun in Philadelphia. What she soon discovered was that women had to work twice as hard as men to get noticed in the Paris art world.

Cassatt, however, refused to be beaten. Back home in Pittsburgh, she had overcome her parents' resistance, who were against her becoming an artist. She would not give in now.

One day a painting in a shop window caught her eye. It was by the great artist Edgar Degas (day-**gah**). She was unable to take her eyes off the work. "I used to go and flatten my nose against the window," she later said. "It changed my life."

It also gave direction to Cassatt's career. The soft lines and gentle colors of Degas's Impressionist paintings set the tone for her own works. Works by Cassatt, such as *Maternal Caress*, (page **35**), combine great skill and sensitivity. Much of her work includes women and children as subjects. Today she is widely held to be one of America's finest painters.

The early 1500s were a time of conquest. The Spanish conquistadors had already conquered major parts of North and South America.

The spirit of conquest was being felt in other parts of the world as well. In the world of German art, a bold new conqueror had emerged. His name was Albrecht Dürer (**ahl**-brekt **dure**-uhr).

Dürer was born in Nuremberg, Germany. He was the second oldest in a family of 18 children. When Albrecht was young, his parents assumed he would become a goldsmith, like his father. But the young Dürer showed unusual skill at drawing. At 15, he was sent to study with a local painter.

Like most young German artists of the day, Dürer learned Gothic style. But a trip he made to Italy while in his early twenties changed everything. There the period of artistic awakening known as the Renaissance was in full progress.

Dürer returned to Nuremberg with a fresh view of the world and the artist's place in it. He turned away from his Gothic style and went about the task of becoming a Renaissance artist. Working hard, he learned how to capture the beauty and balance he found in Italian painting. The ideals he taught himself show up in such works as his woodcut on page **158**.

Albrecht Dürer

1471–1528
German Painter, Printmaker

The Four Horsemen of the Apocalypse
  page **158**

Winslow Homer

1836–1910
American Painter

It is hard to think of any good coming out of a war. But for Winslow Homer, the American Civil War — or at least the scenes of the front lines he painted — were his passport to public recognition.

Homer was born in Boston. When he was six, his family moved to Cambridge, Massachusetts. At that time, Cambridge was mostly wilderness, and Homer learned to love the outdoors.

Like his love of nature, Homer's interest in art began early. By the time he was about 10, his talent for drawing was obvious to those around him. At 19, Homer went to work for a large Boston printing firm. There he designed covers for song sheets, a job he soon grew tired of.

For the next 17 years, Homer did magazine illustrations, mainly for *Harper's Weekly* in New York. It was for *Harper's* that he did his Civil War drawings and paintings.

After the war, Winslow traveled abroad. His work had become so much in demand that he paid for his trips with money earned by selling his paintings.

After 1883 he devoted his efforts almost totally to nature paintings. His home on the coast of Maine gave him a chance to study, and paint, the sea. Some of his best works, such as *The Fog Warning*, (page **316**), have the sea as their subject.

If you were going to fill a time capsule with symbols of life in mid-twentieth-century America, what would you include? One possibility might be a baseball. Another might be a photograph of a rock group.

Still another might be a painting by Edward Hopper. His works show the emptiness and loneliness that are as much a part of urban living as skyscrapers and traffic.

Hopper was born in Nyack, New York. He trained to be a graphic artist and worked for a time as an illustrator. Hopper did not gain recognition in painting until he was close to 40.

From 1901 to 1906 he studied with Robert Henri, who headed the Ashcan School. Critics provided this label to describe some artists of this period. They used a stark, realistic treatment in their city scenes, painting ashcans and all. Like other members of the group, Hopper used the city as a setting for his pictures. Unlike other members, he did not focus on the glitter and excitement. Rather, Hopper's works capture the impersonal, unfriendly feeling of the big city. People rarely are seen in his pictures. When they are, they are often seen as alone and lonely.

A notable feature of Hopper's work is his use of color to capture a quiet mood. Such a mood can be seen in the bleak but soothing landscape of his *Cottages at North Truro, Massachusetts* (page **42**).

Edward Hopper

1882–1967
American Painter

Wassily Kandinsky

1866–1944
Russian Painter

Improvisation #27
page 39

Several Circles
page 85

In the early 1900s two brothers named Wright proved that humans could harness the capability of flight. Their pioneering efforts at Kitty Hawk changed aviation history for all time.

Around the same time and a continent away, another person was changing history of a different sort. His name was Wassily Kandinsky (**vahs**-uh-lee kan-**din**-skee). The history he was changing for all time was art history.

Kandinsky was born in Russia in 1866. He studied law and worked as a lawyer through his twenties. In 1885 he visited an exhibit of French Impressionist paintings in Moscow. He was so impressed by the works that he found it hard to leave. In the months that followed, his thoughts drifted back to the paintings he had seen. Finally, he left his legal career and went to study painting in Munich, Germany.

In his early years as an artist, Kandinsky moved from one style to another. Then he spent some time experimenting with more original ideas. Around 1910 he completed an interesting watercolor. The work was bright and may have been based on some earlier landscape studies. What was most important about the work was that it had no recognizable subject. Non-objective art had been born! Today works such as *Improvisation #27* (page **39**) hang in the world's top art museums.

In 1889 the Eiffel Tower was built to celebrate the Paris Industrial Exposition. Around that same time, one of France's great artists began his career.

Henri Matisse (ahnh-**ree** mah-**tees**) had been born some 20 years earlier. Growing up in a small town in northern France, Matisse showed little interest in art. When he graduated from high school, his father sent him to Paris to study law.

When he was twenty-one years old, Matisse suffered an attack of appendicitis. He was forced to stay in bed for a long time. To ease his boredom, his mother bought him some paints. Suddenly Matisse felt as if a weight had been lifted. He had discovered an interest and a talent that changed his direction. He decided to become an artist.

While studying painting, Matisse began to experiment with different styles. By 1905 he had developed a style all his own. It made use of flat shapes and simple bold colors. An example of a work using this style is his painting *The Red Studio*, on page **128**.

While Matisse's paintings were revolutionary in his day, today they are hailed as masterpieces. They are seen as fulfillments of the goal Matisse had set for himself. That goal was to create "an art of purity and serenity without depressing subject matter."

Henri Matisse

1869–1954
French Painter

Woman in a Purple Coat
page 84

The Red Studio
page 128

Georgia O'Keeffe

1887–1986
American Painter

The 1920s marked the beginning of a new way of living in our country. The easygoing spirit of earlier times had been crushed by the arrival of the automobile. Americans suddenly found themselves rushing from one place to the next. Few had time to stop and think — to notice the beauty in the world around them.

One who did was the painter Georgia O'Keeffe. O'Keeffe had been raised on a small dairy farm in Wisconsin. Her strong interest in both nature and art had begun early. By the time she was 10, she knew she wanted to become a painter.

O'Keeffe's earliest training was in the styles of the great masters of Europe. Their subjects, however, held little interest for her. She wanted, instead, to paint the rocks, mountains, and wide open spaces around her. When she decided at age 29 to focus totally on nature, she burned her earlier work.

Among O'Keeffe's greatest achievements are the close-ups of flowers she began creating in the 1920s. One of these, *The White Calico Flower*, appears on page **212**. To catch the attention of people too busy to notice, she made the close-ups huge. Each fills its canvas with graceful curved surfaces and flowing lines. The beauty of every petal is seen again and again in the greater beauty of the whole flower.

The 1880s brought the world many wonderful inventions, such as the adding machine, the bicycle, and the car. It also brought the world a painter who would produce some of the greatest art in the history of the Western world. His name was Pablo Picasso.

Picasso was born in Malaga, Spain, in 1881. As a boy, he never stopped drawing. In fact, his mother claimed he could draw before he could talk. Everywhere young Picasso went, his pad and pencil went. He liked betting his friends he could draw anything — in one unbroken line — and he always won.

One day his father, a painter and teacher, came home to a surprise. His young son had finished a portrait. After examining the work, Pablo's father gave the boy all his art materials. So great was the boy's work that the father vowed never to paint again.

In his long and full life, Pablo Picasso passed through many different styles. For some time he created the fractured images that were the hallmark of the Cubist movement. He later returned to paintings of the human figure. The painting of *Seated Woman (after Cranach)* on page **170** shows his mastery of media and technique.

Pablo Picasso

1881–1973
Spanish Painter, Sculptor

Raphael (Sanzio)

1483–1520
Italian Painter

St. George and the Dragon
page **104**

The Small Cowper Madonna
page **132**

It was the eve of Columbus's voyage of discovery to the New World. It was also the eve of a discovery within the art world. A young boy in Columbus's native Italy showed a gift for art that was rare. The boy's name was Rafaello — or, in English, Raphael.

Raphael was born in a small town in central Italy. His first teacher was probably his father, who was a painter for a noble family. While still a child, Raphael studied with an artist named Perugino (pehr-uh-**jee**-noh). Perugino taught the youth how to use soft colors and simple circular forms. He taught him how to create gentle landscapes. Soon the student's work began to be mistaken for the teacher's. Young Raphael knew it was time to move on.

He went to Florence to study the works of the leading artists of the day. Among his teachers there were the two giants of art, Leonardo da Vinci and Michelangelo. From Leonardo, he learned how to use shading to create a sense of depth. From Michelangelo, he learned how to breathe life into his figures. Both these ideas are present in his masterpiece *St. George and the Dragon* (page **104**).

Raphael died when he was only 37. Yet the works he left behind rank him as one of the great artists of the Renaissance.

After the Brooklyn Bridge opened in 1883, bridge building would never be the same. After an exhibition of paintings in Paris a year later, art would never be the same. The exhibition contained works by a group who came to be known — at first, jokingly — as Impressionists. One of the group's leaders was a man named Renoir.

Pierre Auguste Renoir (pee-**air** oh-**goost** ren-**wahr**) was born in 1841. His artistic talents became apparent early. By 13, he was already making a living as an artist in a porcelain factory. His job was painting scenes on pieces of china. His earnings helped pay for his education at a famous Paris art school, the Ecole des Beaux-Arts.

It was at school that Renoir met two other young artists, Claude Monet (moh-**nay**) and Alfred Sisley. The three soon became friends. They also began experimenting together by making paintings outdoors in natural sunlight. Their goal was to give objects a shimmering, sunlit quality. At first, their works were scorned by critics. Today they are among the most admired in the history of art.

Unlike most of his fellow Impressionists, Renoir was interested in painting the human figure. His painting, *Girl with a Watering Can* (page **121**) highlights the best features of his own Impressionist style.

Pierre Auguste Renoir

1841–1919
French Painter

Girl with a Watering Can
page **121**

Regatta at Argenteuil
page **126**

Henri de Toulouse-Lautrec

1864–1901
French Printmaker, Painter

La Gitane
  page **36**

Jane Avril
  page **190**

The year 1864 was one of promising beginnings and promising endings. Union troops marched into Georgia, signaling a swift end to the Civil War. The birth of a baby boy in the town of Albi, France, promised new happiness for the Toulouse-Lautrec (tuh-**loose** low-**trek**) family.

Although no one knew it, baby Henri's arrival also held great promise for the art world. The Toulouse-Lautrecs were an old and wealthy French family. Henri's parents taught their child from an early age to appreciate art. By the age of 10, young Henri was making sketches. This was no surprise since his grandfather, father, and uncle were all draftsmen.

When he was 14, Henri broke both legs in two separate accidents. Although the limbs healed, they never grew properly. All his life he was self-conscious about his deformed legs and dwarf-like appearance.

This did not prevent Toulouse-Lautrec from becoming interested in the dazzling night life of Paris. He loved to sit in cafes and watch the colorful scene. He always carried a sketchpad and often would record what he saw.

Today the remarkable prints he created, many based on his sketches, are thought to be art treasures. One of these, of the performer *Jane Avril*, appears on page **190**.

By the late 1880s trains had become a popular form of transportation. A spirit of restlessness had gripped the Western world. Certainly one of the period's most important artists felt that restlessness. His name was Vincent van Gogh (van **goh**).

You may already know some of the facts of van Gogh's brief life. You have probably heard how he went mad and cut off his earlobe. You may know that he ended his own life at age 37. What you may not know is that this genius left the world 1600 remarkable art works.

Vincent van Gogh was born and raised in a small Dutch village. He spent much of his life contemplating his existence. He tried—and failed at—many different careers, including teaching and the ministry. At last he turned to art, which long had been a passion.

Van Gogh's first paintings were drab and dull. In 1886 he moved to Paris. There he was moved by several artistic forces. One was the color used in Impressionist paintings. Another was the style of Japanese woodcuts.

Van Gogh was not content simply to capture a scene. Instead, he needed to express his deep feelings about it. These feelings come through in short brush strokes of bright, intense color. An example of his unique style may be found in *Cypresses* (page **64**).

Vincent van Gogh

1853–1890
Dutch Painter

Cypresses
  page **64**

*Garden of the Rectory
at Nuenen*
  page **94**

Marie-Louise-Élisabeth Vigée-Lebrun

1755–1842
French Painter

Theresa, Countess Kinsky
page **131**

La Princesse Barbe Gallitzin
page **149**

When the French Revolution began in 1789, members of the ruling class fled. So did the woman who had painted many of them, Marie-Louise-Élisabeth Vigée-Lebrun (ay-**lee**-zah-bet vee-**zhay**-luh-**bruhn**).

Élisabeth Vigée-Lebrun's life story reads almost like a novel. She studied art in a convent. Before she was 20, she had painted many important French nobles. By age 25, she was working for Queen Marie-Antoinette. She did some 20 portraits of the queen.

The night the king and queen were arrested, Vigée-Lebrun escaped from Paris. The revolution had temporarily interrupted her career as a portrait painter. Luckily, she was able to continue her work in other capitals of Europe. Everywhere she went, there were requests for portraits. By the time she turned 35, she had earned over a million francs. This was a huge sum of money for an artist to have earned.

Vigée-Lebrun's portraits were very flattering to her subjects. She overlooked any flaws she saw. As in her portrait of *Theresa, Countess Kinsky* (page **131**), she gave all her subjects large eyes.

When Vigée-Lebrun died, a palette and brush were carved on her gravestone as she had asked. It was a fitting tribute to an artist who had completed over 800 paintings in her lifetime.

In the year 1917 the world was politically unsettled. Many of the major powers were at war. Russia was in the midst of a revolution. It was an odd time for an artist devoted to simple, quiet subjects to emerge. Such an artist is Andrew Wyeth.

Andrew Wyeth was the son of N. C. Wyeth, a successful illustrator of adventure stories. As a child, Andrew was sick much of the time. Since his father had little use for public schools anyway, Andrew was educated at home. As a boy, he was constantly drawing and painting with watercolors.

When Wyeth was 20, he had his first exhibit in New York. Every painting in the show was sold.

Several of Wyeth's paintings are based on Christina Olson, a family friend crippled by polio. One of these, *Christina's World* (page **115**), was made after Wyeth watched Christina bravely pull herself home using her arms. As Wyeth himself has explained, the work is more than a portrait. It is a glimpse of Christina's whole life and the things she experienced in it.

Wyeth creates his works by making many, many studies of a subject. For these, he uses both pencil and watercolor. He does his finished works using egg tempera.

Andrew Wyeth

1917–
American Painter

Christina's World
page **115**
(detail) page **179**

▲ There are many careers available in the field of commercial art. This group is discussing a display.

Advertising Artist

Every time you watch a TV commercial, you are experiencing the work of an advertising artist. The same goes for hearing radio commercials as well as reading magazine and newspaper ads. Advertising artists are people whose job is to help sell a product using art.

The field of advertising art dates back at least to ancient Egypt. A papyrus found in an ancient Egyptian tomb offers a reward for a runaway slave. In the Middle Ages, town criers often peppered their news announcements with advertisements for local businesses.

Nowadays advertising artists usually work as members of teams under the leadership of art directors. Some tasks of the ad artist might include designing illustrations and photographs for ads. Advertising artists are also often called upon to pick typefaces.

The success of advertising art is measured by how many people notice the advertisement and how well the product sells.

Animator

When the art of the motion picture was born, a number of fields were born with it. One of these was the field of animation. Animators are artists who create cartoons and cartoonlike figures for film and television.

Animators begin their work by picking a story to tell. They also choose the style of architecture and clothing that will fit the story. They then create the story in the form of storyboards. These are still drawings that show the action in the story. Storyboards are a series of panels that look similar to comic books but are larger. The animator will create about 60 sketches for each board. A short film will need three storyboards. A full-length film will require over 25 storyboards.

Once the storyboards have been created, the animators will create the major poses for each character. Other artists assist by filling in the many drawings that complete each movement.

Architect

Do you live in an apartment house or a private home? Whichever you live in, you are in a building designed by an architect. Architects are artists who design buildings of all kinds, including residences, office buildings, and museums.

The architect works with two major goals in mind. One is to make sure the building does what it was planned to do. The second goal is to make sure the building is pleasing to the eye. How a structure fits in with its surroundings is also a concern of the architect.

Architects must know a great deal about building materials. They must also understand how weather and other natural elements act on such materials. Architects are also trained in such matters as ventilation, heating and cooling, and plumbing.

Architects must have a strong background in mathematics and drafting. Most architects nowadays specialize in a particular type of building.

Art Adviser to Corporations

Up until a few years ago, the only art found in a company setting was purely decorative. A painting might be used to dress up a waiting area or conference room. Recently, there has been a growing interest among corporations in starting private art collections. With this interest, a new profession has been born — the corporate art adviser.

Art advisers to corporations have a number of duties and responsibilities. One duty is buying new art for the corporation collection. Another is advising the corporation head about tax laws having to do with art. A third duty is arranging traveling exhibitions and speaking to different groups about the collection.

Corporate art advisers often are hired as employees of the company. Sometimes they work on a free-lance basis and advise several companies at once.

Art Director for the Performing Arts

In order for a performance to run smoothly, a number of people must do their jobs well. In order for these people to do their jobs well, the show must have a strong director.

The art director oversees all the visual elements of the show and makes sure they fit together. Among the many people with whom the director works closely are scenery, costume, and lighting designers.

Art directors must have a background in art history as well as a knowledge of stagecraft. If a play is set in the past, the setting, furniture, and costumes all need to reflect that period.

Art Teacher

Many people with an interest in art and a desire to share their knowledge become art teachers.

A career in art teaching requires a college education. Part of that education is devoted to methods of teaching. Part is devoted to developing a broad background in art history, aesthetics, art criticism, and the use of art materials and techniques.

Good art teachers guide their students through a wide variety of art experiences. They give students the chance to create their own art and to react to the art of others. They also make sure their students learn about such important art subjects as aesthetics, art criticism, and art history.

Art Therapist

In recent years researchers have learned new ways of helping people with emotional problems. One of these ways is through art.

In the field called art therapy people trained as art therapists use art to open lines of communication with patients. Patients are invited to create images using different media. They are then encouraged to discuss the meanings of their creations. This process often serves to release feelings, allowing the therapists to better help the patients.

Art therapists find work in a number of different settings. Some work as members of teams in large hospitals. Others are employed by community health centers or clinics. Still others work in prisons. Some work in special schools for students with learning disabilities.

A career in art therapy requires professional training in psychology and art education.

City Planner

Have you ever wondered how big cities come to look the way they do? The two-word answer to this question is city planners.

City planners are people whose job is to supervise the care and improvement of a city. Every large American city has a planner.

A main task of city planners is to enforce zoning laws. These are laws controlling what part of a city may be used for what purposes. Thanks to city planners, garbage dumps are not located in residential communities.

A second task of the city planner is to look after the growth and development of the city. The planner works with the mayor and other city officials to create parks, harbors, and shopping malls.

City planners are trained as architects. Their knowledge of design helps them to plan a pleasing cityscape.

Exhibit and Display Designer

The next time you pass a display of clothing or other goods in a department store, look carefully. Somewhere within that display will be a hidden message: "Artist at Work."

Exhibit and display designers work in a number of retail and non-profit settings. Some are trade shows, department stores, showrooms, art galleries, and museums. Such designers plan presentations of collections, exhibits, and traveling shows of all kinds. They are responsible for such matters as deciding what items should be grouped together. They also take into account how displays should be lighted.

The display designer is an important part of the sales team. Displays attract customers. They can affect a customer's decision to buy. The way the display designer does his or her job can make all the difference between "sale" and "no-sale."

Fashion Designer

Some art is made to be worn. Creating art of this type is the work of the fashion designer. Fashion designers draw and plan clothing, hats, handbags, gloves, and jewelry.

Fashion designers must learn about different fabrics, colors, and their uses. Matters such as weight and texture are also important in the designing of clothing. A jacket designed for winter wear, for example, must not only be attractive, it must also be warm and comfortable.

Some fashion designers become involved in high-fashion design. These are the trend-setting fashions that are usually very expensive.

Fashion designers may work either as freelance artists or for clothing manufacturers.

Industrial Designer

What do toys, vacuum cleaners, and cars have in common? All are designed to work easily and have a pleasing look. These and countless other items you see and use each day are the work of industrial designers.

Industrial designers work for makers of products. These artists work closely with engineers who develop the products. Sometimes industrial designers are asked to work on things as simple as tamper-proof caps for medicines. At other times they are asked to work on projects as complicated as space vehicles. Before they begin work, industrial designers need to know how the product is to be used.

Because different brands of the same product are sold, industrial design sometimes crosses over into advertising. The appearance of a design becomes especially important in the case of very competitive products such as cars and entertainment systems, for example.

Interior Designer

Architects give us attractive, functional spaces in which to live, work, and play. Interior designers fill those spaces with attractive and useful furnishings and accessories.

The job of the interior designer is to plan the interior space. This includes choosing furniture, fabrics, floor coverings, lighting fixtures, and decorations. To do this job well, the designer must take into account the wants and needs of the users of the space. In planning a home, for example, the interior designer will learn as much as possible about the lifestyle of the family that lives there.

Interior designers help their clients envision their ideas through the use of floor plans, elevations, and sketches. Once a client has agreed to a plan, the designer makes arrangements for buying materials. He or she also oversees the work for builders, carpenters, painters, and other craftspeople.

Landscape Architect

In recent years the role of the landscape architect increasingly has been recognized as very important in making the business and industrial areas of our cities environmentally healthy and aesthetic. Landscape architects are people whose job is to design outdoor areas around buildings. They also create arrangements of shrubs and flowers for playgrounds, parks, and highways.

Landscape architects work closely with architects and city planners to improve the natural setting. Their goal is to make the setting both easy to maintain and beautiful to look at. Landscape architects work with a number of different materials and landforms. These include flowers, plants, trees, rivers, ponds, walks, benches, and signs.

Some landscape architects work independently. Others work for architectural firms, government agencies, or private companies.

Museum Curator

Like universities and libraries, museums have the job of preserving and passing on culture. The person in charge of seeing that the museum does its job is the museum curator (**kyoor**-ayt-uhr).

Curators are part guardian, part restorer, and part historian. The tasks of the curator are many. They include acquiring, caring for, displaying, and studying works of art. The curator makes sure works of art in the museum collection are arranged so the viewer can enjoy as well as learn from museum exhibits.

As holders of advanced college degrees, curators carry on research in their special areas of interest. They report their findings in books, lectures, and journals.

Print Motifs

Artists have always found nature to be a rich source for inspiration. Patterns created by repeated designs can be found in nature all around us. Interesting patterns left in the sand by an insect's tracks can inspire an artist's imagination.

Creating a pattern by repeating a motif can be easily accomplished by using a printing technique. Patterns on fabric, wallpaper, or wrapping paper are often printed. (See Figure S–1.)

WHAT YOU WILL LEARN

You will create a printed pattern to decorate wrapping paper for a special holiday. You will glue bits of styrofoam to a piece of wood to create a relief block for printing. Your wrapping paper will be decorated by a rhythmic pattern created by repeated printing.

WHAT YOU WILL NEED

- Scratch paper, pencil, and eraser
- Small piece of wood
- Styrofoam packing trays, or any pieces of reusable styrofoam
- Scissors or cutting knife, glue
- Butcher paper, 12 x 24 inch (30 x 61 cm)
- Printer's ink or tempera paint, brushes
- Newspaper

WHAT YOU WILL DO

1. Consider some of the holidays that are less advertised. You might research a special holiday celebrated in another country. Or you might decide to create wrapping paper that has a personal design for someone special. This person could be someone you know, someone famous or even an imagined character.

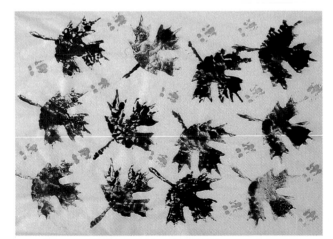

▲ Figure S–1   Wrapping paper decorated with a nature motif.

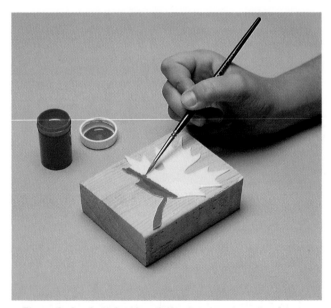

▲ Figure S–2   A student is painting tempera on a styrofoam stamp.

2. Using pencil and scratch paper sketch some designs that you might use. Remember you will be cutting out a piece of styrofoam to glue on a wood block. Use your pencil to draw the outline of a shape that can be cut out. Keep your design simple. Consider whether your design will have formal or informal balance. Remember even a small motif must have unity or a sense of wholeness to it.

3. Select your best sketch. Draw the shape on the styrofoam and cut it out. If you use more than one shape, carefully determine how they are to be arranged on the wood block. Remember the space between the shapes will be left white. Again think about the unity of your motif. When you are satisfied glue the shape down.

4. Place a pad of newspaper under the butcher paper for better defined prints. Carefully paint the styrofoam shape on your wood block with ink or tempera paint, as shown in Figure S–2, and begin printing. Be sure to add more paint each time you make a print.

EXAMINING YOUR WORK

- **Describe** Point out the shapes in your print. Point out which motifs in your pattern came out most clear. Tell what you did to achieve this clear print. Describe the theme of your wrapping paper.
- **Analyze** Tell whether you used formal or informal balance to create unity in your motif. Tell how you created rhythm with your motif.
- **Interpret** Tell what mood the theme of your motif suggests. Explain how adding different colors to your pattern enhanced the mood.
- **Judge** Tell whether you feel your work succeeds. Explain your answer.

5. You may decide to make prints using different colors. Let the paint dry on your block before adding a new color. Be sure to plan ahead of time when a new color will be added to your pattern.

OTHER STUDIO IDEAS

- Design a second block print. Create a pattern by printing the two motifs side by side. It will be important that this second wood block be a single shape.
- ●● Design a block print that will coordinate with the decor of either the living room of your home, or your bedroom. Choose a color and texture of cloth and color of paint or ink that harmonizes with the room in which it will be displayed. On a piece of cloth about 12 x 18 inches (30 x 46 cm) in size, print a motif using the technique you learned previously. The cloth may be used as a wall-hanging, a place mat, or table runner. It may also be sewn together with another piece of fabric the same size to make a slipcover for a pillow as in Figure S–3.

▲ **Figure S–3** Cloth can also be printed and used for table cloths, napkins, pillow covers, and curtains.

Action Painting

Look at the painting in Figure S–4. It was created by Jackson Pollock, who created his own technique to accomplish a style of painting, known as *action painting*. The colors in his paintings related to his feelings when he began the work. Notice how the lines appear to move or follow his feelings by being very quickly applied. Sometimes they are slowly dripped and drawn into his canvas. He did not use drawings or color sketches for his works but worked directly on the canvas.

▲ **Figure S–4** Jackson Pollock was known as an action painter. Can you see from this painting why he was called that?

Jackson Pollock. *Cathedral*. 1947. Enamel and aluminum paint on canvas. 181.6 x 89.1 cm (71½ x 35⅟₁₆"). Dallas Museum of Art, Dallas, Texas. Gift of Mr. and Mrs. Bernard J. Reis.

WHAT YOU WILL LEARN

You will create an action painting using tempera on a large sheet of white paper. Choose colors that reflect how you are feeling before you begin to work. Warm colors can be used for feelings of happiness, excitement, or anger. Cool colors can be used to reflect calm, peacefulness, sadness, or serenity.

WHAT YOU WILL NEED

- Sheet of white paper, 12 x 18 inch (30 x 46 cm)
- Tempera paints
- Brushes, varied sizes

WHAT YOU WILL DO

1. Select a color scheme that represents how you feel before you begin to paint. Remember the discussion in Chapter 4, Lesson 2, on the use of monochromatic, analogous, and complementary color schemes. You can create striking art work by combining colors in ways that use tints or shades of the same hue, (monochromatic). You may want to combine colors that share a hue, such as green, blue-green, and yellow-green, (analogous). Or you might choose a third way to combine colors using a complementary color scheme to achieve contrast colors that are opposite each other on the color wheel, for example, yellow and purple.
2. Put a layer or two of newspaper down on the floor and on your work area for protection. Tape the corners of your white paper to the newspaper. Tape the newspaper to the work surface to keep it from moving.

3. Load your brush with the paint. Hold the brush over your paper and let the paint drip from your brush. Let the paint drip to relate to your mood — fast or slow drips. Whether you have fast or slow drips depends on how full your brush is and on the consistency of the paint. A brush full of thin paint will result in fast drips. A brush that is not as full will have slower drips. Also, if the paint you use is thick the drips will be slower.

4. Observe that lines of color will probably dominate your work, but try to create shapes by accident. Be sure to create balance and harmony in your composition.

5. As you examine your art, also check to see if you are achieving balance and harmony. To check for balance look at your entire composition and see if any one area is too overpowering. However, keep in mind that balance need not be symmetrical. Next check for harmony. Make sure the various elements in your work (drip patterns, dark versus light, size of spatters) are blended in a pleasing way to create a harmonious whole.

6. Stop occasionally while you work to look at the parts from every side of the paper.

EXAMINING YOUR WORK

- **Describe**   Identify areas in the composition that were a result of fast and slow drips. Point to the way the colors were combined to form a color scheme.
- **Analyze**   Tell why you chose the colors you did. Are they warm or cool colors? Do you have fast or slow drips? Does a pattern show in your work? Is there any suggestion of subject in your painting?
- **Interpret**   Give your work a title. How do the colors make you feel? Do the drip patterns remind you of anything? Explain why you chose to use fast or slow drips.
- **Judge**   Tell whether you feel your work is successful. Explain your answer.

7. When you feel your art work is finished, make sure to give the painting enough time to dry in a flat position. If you must move the work to a drying area, carefully carry your painting (still attached to the newspaper) to a flat surface. Let the painting dry and then remove the tape and trim the edges to give a clean professional look to your painting.

8. Show your work to classmates and ask them to interpret your feelings.

OTHER STUDIO IDEAS

- To achieve another effect, you may want to dip strings into different hues of paint. Then holding the string at either end, keeping it taut, lay it down across the paper. Make several lines by redipping the string. Do one hue at a time, giving each a chance to dry before using the next color. By laying the strings across the paper in perpendicular patterns, you can make geometric designs.
- •• Marble art is another technique for a different effect. Choose three hues of paint and put each one in a different tin, filling the dish so there is a layer of paint covering the bottom. Put a marble in each tin.

Now fold some paper towels to use as you work. Place your art paper inside a shallow box lid. Take one of the marbles and put it in the lid on top of the paper. Tilt the lid so the marble rolls, causing paint tracks across the paper. Vary the track's shape and direction as you wish. When you are finished with that color put the marble in the extra dish, wipe your hands and start on your next color. Don't make too many tracks the first time because you still have two more marbles to go. Let your art work dry in the lid or on a flat surface.

Group Mural

Have you ever seen large pictures painted on walls of buildings? These pictures are called murals. Look at the mural in Figure S–5. What are the dimensions of the mural? Do you wonder how the artist was able to draw the mural on the wall and keep everything in proportion to one another?

To make murals, artists begin by making a small drawing on paper. They add details and color. Next they create an enlarging grid that is in proportion to the finished product. Using the grid as a guide, the picture is drawn on the wall. (See Technique Tip **5**, *Handbook* page **271**.)

WHAT YOU WILL LEARN

You will work with your classmates to create a wall mural. The mural will be planned for a specific wall in your school or community. Before you begin, get permission from your art teacher and school administrators and determine how the project will be financed. If that is not possible you can paint on butcher paper or plywood and display your art work temporarily in an appropriate area.

WHAT YOU WILL NEED

- Sketch paper, pencil, and eraser
- Ruler, tape measure, yardstick, or meterstick
- Chalk
- Acrylic paints and brushes
- Specific wall to be painted
- Drop cloth
- Safe ladder
- Cleaning materials, such as sponges, soaps, and buckets of water

WHAT YOU WILL DO

1. As a group brainstorm ideas that could be used for a mural. The subject for your mural could be based on native traditions, school or community events, or social statements. Discuss possibilities and as a group decide on a theme for the mural.
2. Develop thumbnail sketches based on the theme. Show these sketches to community officials, school administrators, teachers, and other students. Make adjustments to the plan as needed.

▶ **Figure S–5** **This is an example of a wall mural. Wall murals are popular all over the world. Why do you think this is so?**

Daniel Alonzo. *A Whale of a Mural*. 1983. Two city blocks long.

3. Identify the specific wall where the mural may be painted. Measure the length and width of the area that the final product will take. Determine the materials which make up the wall. Consult with your teacher to find out what pre-treatment is necessary and what medium should be used on the wall.

4. Assign one or two people to render the final composition, which includes ideas and sketches from the entire group. Render the final design in color. Show it to the entire group and make adjustments as needed.

5. Develop an enlargement grid, as shown in Figure S–6, for the drawing and identify a scale for the smaller drawing to the mural. For instance 1 inch = 1 foot (2.5 cm = 30 cm).

6. Place drop cloths on the floor and protect the surrounding area as needed. Divide the wall into squares and number the squares on the wall to match the squares on the paper. Begin to enlarge the plan one square at a time.

7. Continue working until mural is complete.

EXAMINING YOUR WORK

- **Describe** Explain what medium you used to produce the work.
- **Analyze** Identify how the work achieved unity.
- **Interpret** Describe how the mural is a good representation of your school or community.
- **Judge** Explain why this is a successful work of art.

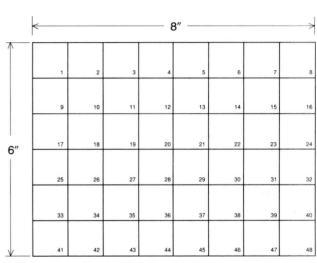

▲ **Figure S–6** An enlargement grid.

OTHER STUDIO IDEAS

- On newsprint or butcher paper paint a mural of an imaginary place — perhaps a city of the future, an Old Western town, or a medieval castle, and so forth. Work alone or with a partner. Display your finished work, explain what you wanted to do, and discuss whether you accomplished that aim.

- • You may want to do a "jigsaw" mural with a group of friends on newsprint. Make a drawing or choose a picture from a magazine. Draw a grid over it, then photocopy it. Cut the photocopy along the grid lines, and put the resulting squares in a container. Pass the container around so each person can choose a square to work from. Make the enlarged grid and begin work. Do not let the participants know what the completed mural should look like. The fun comes from trying to guess what it is as the work progresses. If the group is small, more than one square may be completed by each person.

Pop-up Cityscape

Art, as you have learned, may be judged using three different aesthetic views. One of these views holds that what matters most in a work is a realistic subject. A second view states that what is most important in art is form. A third view argues that content is what counts most. Look at the cityscapes in Figures S–7, S–8, and S–9. Which of these would be judged most successful by a critic of the first school, a critic of the second school, or a critic of the third school?

WHAT YOU WILL LEARN

You will create a three-dimensional pop-up cityscape. Your work will be guided by one of the three aesthetic views described previously. The cityscape will have three parts—a foreground, a middleground, and a background. You will use the principle of proportion to organize the element of space.

▲ **Figure S–7** **What aesthetic view do you think is best represented by this painting?**

Edward Hopper. *Drug Store.* 1927. Oil on canvas. 73.7 x 101.6 cm (29 x 40"). Museum of Fine Arts, Boston, Massachusetts. Bequest of John T. Spaulding.

◄ **Figure S–8   What kind of balance is represented in this painting?**

Stuart Davis. *Place Pasdeloup.* 1928. Oil. 92.1 x 73 cm (36¼ x 28¾"). Whitney Museum of American Art, New York, New York.

WHAT YOU WILL NEED

- Pencil and sketch paper
- Four pieces of illustration board: one 3 x 12 inches (8 x 30 cm), one 6 x 12 inches (15 x 30 cm), one 9 x 12 inches (23 x 30 cm), one 10 x 12 inches (25 x 30 cm)
- School tempera paints and several brushes
- Ruler, scissors, masking tape and white glue
- Two scrap pieces of illustration board, 3 x 2 inches (8 x 5 cm)
- Two strips of heavy construction paper, 7 x 2 inches (18 x 5 cm)

◄ **Figure S–9   What is the mood represented in this painting?**

El Greco. *View of Toledo.* Oil on canvas. 121.3 x 108.6 cm (47¾ x 42¾"). The Metropolitan Museum of Art, New York, New York. The H. O. Havemeyer Collection.

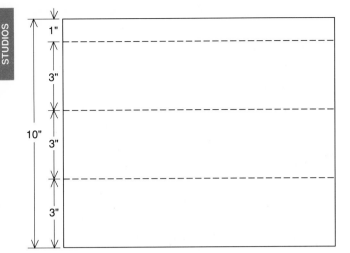

▲ Figure S–10   Light rules for lining up the foreground, middleground, and background of the cityscape.

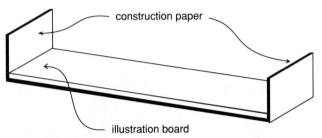

construction paper

illustration board

▲ Figure S–11   This is a connecting U-joint that supports the pop-up portions of the cityscape.

WHAT YOU WILL DO

1. Look once more at Figures S–7, S–8, and S–9. Decide which of the three paintings you want your cityscape to resemble most. Will it have a realistic subject, like Figure S–7? Will it focus on lines, textures, and shapes like Figure S–8? Will it capture a feeling, like the mood painting in Figure S–9?

2. Once you have chosen a style, make three sets of pencil sketches for your cityscape. One set should focus on the low buildings and shapes that will appear in the foreground. This set should have the most detail and color. A second should focus on the buildings and shapes of medium height that will appear in the middleground. A third should focus on the tall buildings and shapes that will appear in the background. Include details of design. The three sections of illustration board should be cut at the top edge to show the roofline of the buildings on each.

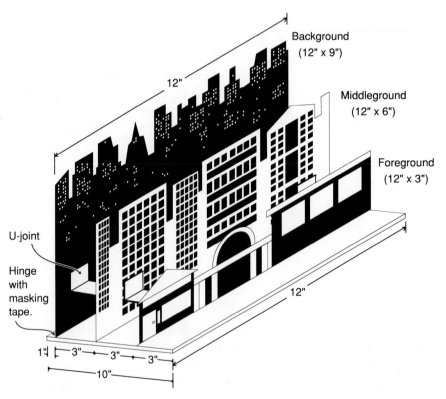

Background
(12" x 9")

Middleground
(12" x 6")

Foreground
(12" x 3")

U-joint

Hinge with masking tape.

► Figure S–12   Attaching the U-joint to the middleground of the cityscape.

3. Use the first three pieces of illustration board and transfer your best sketches to three of the sections of illustration board. Carefully paint the buildings and shapes in each section.

4. Turn the remaining piece of illustration board so the 12-inch (30-cm) side is facing you. Placing the ruler firmly against the near edge, make a pencil mark 3 inches (8 cm) from either end. Make two more pencil dots the same distance from the ends of the opposite side. Connect each pair of parallel dots with a light rule. (See Figure S–10.)

5. Line up the foreground panel (the smallest section) along one rule. Holding the foreground panel upright, attach it along its back to the base panel. Use strips of masking tape for this task. The tape should work as a hinge. Attach the middleground and background to the base in a similar fashion.

6. Center a scrap of illustration board on a strip of construction paper (Figure S–11). Join the two pieces with glue. When dry, bend the flaps up to form a letter U. Apply glue to one flap. Attach the flap to the back of the foreground panel. Be careful about keeping the U-joint as out of sight as possible. Apply glue to the other flap. Attach it to the front of the middleground panel. Repeat this task to join the middleground and background panels. (See Figure S–12.)

7. Display your work. Compare it with that of other students. (See Figure S–13.)

EXAMINING YOUR WORK

- **Describe**   Identify the aesthetic view that you chose. How did you express that aesthetic view in the design of your cityscape?
- **Analyze**   Tell which art elements and principles you used. Tell how you used the principle of proportion. Explain how you organized the element of space.
- **Interpret**   Does your work express a mood or feeling? Why did you choose to express this mood in your cityscape?
- **Judge**   Tell whether you feel your work succeeds. Explain your answer.

▲ **Figure S–13   A finished pop-up cityscape.**

OTHER STUDIO IDEAS

- Add to the three-dimensional feel of your cityscape. Create details out of illustration board, such as store awnings and window ledges. Paint these and glue them to your foreground panel.

- ● Create a second pop-up cityscape, this time adding a fourth, near-foreground, panel. This fourth panel should contain cutouts of people, dogs, cars, and so on. The style of these objects should blend with that of the other three panels.

LESSON 5

Applique Banner

One type of craftsperson uses needle, thread, and fabric to create works of art. The craftsperson who created the tropical birds in Figure S–14 stitched them onto a satin robe using multicolored silk threads. The artist used many different stitches but they are so fine that it is hard to see them in this reproduction.

WHAT YOU WILL LEARN

You will create a personal banner by sewing fibers and fabrics and small found objects onto a shaped piece of fabric. The banner must show objects or designs that are symbolic of you. Include your name or initials on the banner. To give the banner unity use harmony of color and rhythm through repetition

▶ **Figure S–14** This is one example of the art of stitchery. There are many different kinds of art that can be created this way.

of line and shape. Use variety in the size of the negative spaces between the shapes and in the textures of fabrics and stitches. See Figure S–15 for an example of a student banner.

WHAT YOU WILL NEED

- Sketch paper, pencil, and ruler
- Large sheet of newsprint
- Fabric scissors and straight pins
- Fabric for the banner
- Thick and thin sewing needles
- Small pieces of fabric
- A variety of fibers
- Small found objects
- *Optional:* A dowel rod or a wire coat hanger

▲ **Figure S–15   Student work. Banner in progress.**

WHAT YOU WILL DO

1. Plan the symbols you will include in your banner. List and draw them on your sketch paper. Remember to include your name or initials as one of the symbols. Collect a few small found objects that you might sew onto the banner such as a button from a special jacket, a ticket stub, an election button, a dried flower, a blue ribbon, or a stone from the river where you love to fish.
2. Practice some stitches on scrap fabric.
3. Plan the size and shape of your banner. Think about the space where you will hang it, and what you plan to include on it. If you plan to use a coat hanger, the banner can be no wider than the bottom rod of the coat hanger. Then design the way you will arrange the symbols on the shape of your banner. Remember to repeat lines and shapes to create a sense of rhythm. Vary the negative spaces. Make several rough sketches in your sketch book. Select your best design.
4. Make a pattern for the banner. Draw the shape on the newsprint paper. Use the ruler to measure and to make straight lines. Cut out the paper pattern. Pin it to your fabric, and cut the fabric to match the pattern.

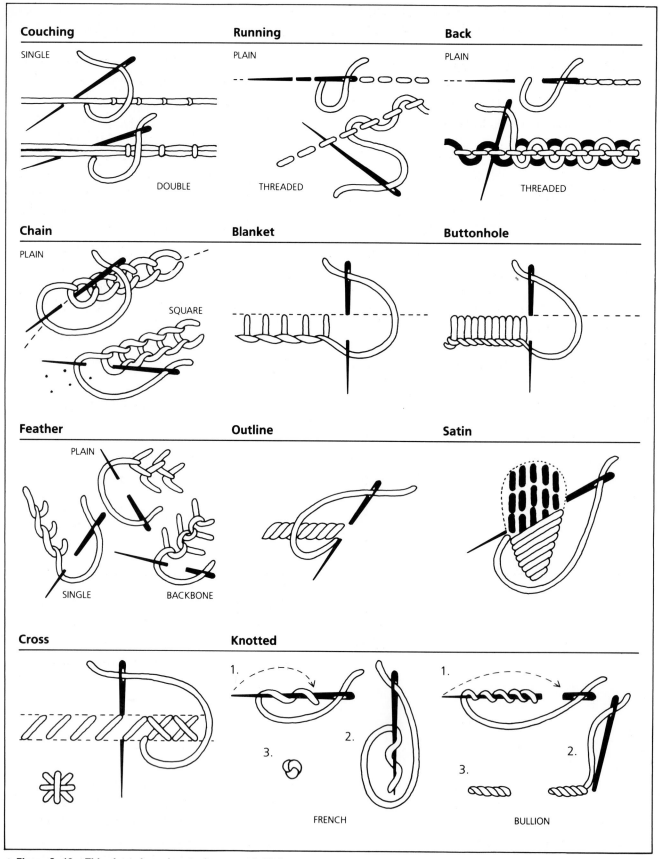

Couching

SINGLE

DOUBLE

Running

PLAIN

THREADED

Back

PLAIN

THREADED

Chain

PLAIN

SQUARE

Blanket

Buttonhole

Feather

PLAIN

SINGLE   BACKBONE

Outline

Satin

Cross

Knotted

1.

2.

3.

FRENCH

1.

2.

3.

BULLION

▲ **Figure S–16   This chart shows how to do some art stitches.**

5. Decide what harmonious color scheme you will use. Select fabrics and fibers to fit the color scheme.

6. Think about texture as you select fabrics and plan stitches. Decide which symbols will be made with fabric and sewn on to the banner, and which will be made with stitches. Draw on the scrap fabric with pencil and cut out the fabric pieces. Pin them in place, and sew them to the banner using the running stitch or the blanket stitch. Study the stitchery chart in Figure S–16. Draw the symbols to be made with stitches onto the banner and stitch them with a variety of fibers.

7. Turn the sides and bottom of your banner under ¼ inch and sew a hem. Sew the top over a thin dowel rod or the bottom rod of a wire coat hanger. Attach string to the rod so that you can hang it up or you may decorate the wire areas of the coat hanger.

8. Place your work on display with your classmates. Can you recognize any by the symbols alone? See Figure S-17 for ideas on different shapes for your banner.

EXAMINING YOUR WORK

- **Describe**   List the kinds of fabrics, fibers, and found objects you used in this project. List the symbols you included. List the stitches you used. Describe how you included your name or initials.
- **Analyze**   Describe the shape of your banner. What harmonizing color scheme did you use? Which lines and shapes did you repeat to create rhythm? Explain how you introduced variety into your design. Did you vary negative spaces? Did you vary textures?
- **Interpret**   Is your banner a symbol of you? Can your friends recognize the banner as your symbol?
- **Judge**   Are you satisfied with the quality of the banner? If not, what could you do to make it better?

▲ Figure S–17   Banners have many different uses. Can you name some of those uses?

OTHER STUDIO IDEAS

- Working in groups of three or four, using the above directions, make a large banner, (6 x 2 foot or 183 x 61 cm) to represent your school, community or state.

- ●● Working on a square felt piece make a stitchery design as a birthday present for a friend. Be sure to include symbols of that person in your design. Felt is easy to use because it doesn't require hemming. This allows you to make any style bottom edge you choose.

Wire Sculpture

Look at the wire sculpture in Figure S–18. Do you recognize the subject? What is she doing? Notice how the artist has used the principles of movement and rhythm to make the figure seem alive.

WHAT YOU WILL LEARN

You will construct a free-standing wire sculpture. The finished sculpture will be a three-dimensional objective form. It will be created entirely of wire lines. You can bend, curve, and twist the wire to make a variety of large and small shapes. Your figure should show movement. It should also suggest a feeling, such as happiness, sadness, or fright.

WHAT YOU WILL NEED

- Sketch paper, pencil, and eraser
- 14-gauge steel wire, 35 inch (89 cm) piece
- Pair of needlenose pliers
- *Optional:* styrofoam, or wood block for base, 6 x 6 inch (15 x 15 cm)

WHAT YOU WILL DO

1. Study the wire sculpture in Figure S–19. Decide what subject you will use for your true-to-life form. Think of the features and feelings that will be associated with your figure. Identify other objects that may be part of your sculptural form, such as a bike, kite, or balloon.
2. Make a pencil sketch of the form you see in your imagination. Use one continuous line to create this true-to-life form. Keep your form simple and concentrate on the line used. Continue to reshape and re-draw until you are happy with your sketch.

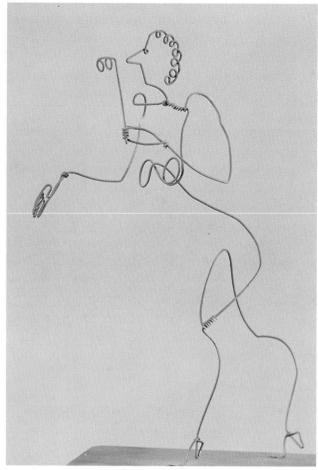

▲ **Figure S–18** Art often displays a sense of humor. Do you think this piece shows humor?

Alexander Calder. *The Hostess.* 1928. Wire construction. Museum of Modern Art, New York, New York.

3. Grasp your wire at one end. Choose the part of the subject in your sketch where your sculpture will begin. (You will not be cutting the wire; your sculpture will be made of one continuous wire line.) Bend, curve, and twist the wire until it resembles the part you chose. Then move on to the next part. Continue working on one part at a time.

4. As you work, use a mixture of large, curved twists and small, tight twists. This will give interest and variety to your sculpture.

5. If your sculpture can stand on its own, you won't need to mount it on a base unless you want to. But if your work needs mounting, attach it to a styrofoam or wood block, using wire bent into hooks, or small screws.

6. Display your finished sculpture with those of your classmates in a gallery in front of the class. (See Figure S–19.) Stroll through the gallery, comparing the different sculptures you and your classmates created. It is more important to catch the feeling of life, movement, and uniqueness than to be overly concerned with exact proportions and details.

EXAMINING YOUR WORK

- **Describe**   Point out the features in your work that identify the subject. Explain what features you added to create a true-to-life sculpture form.
- **Analyze**   Identify the variety of large and small shapes created in your wire line. Explain how your sculpture form shows movement.
- **Interpretation**   Explain how you made the sculpture express a mood.
- **Judge**   Explain why this is a successful work of art.

▲ Figure S–19   Student work. A wire sculpture.

OTHER STUDIO IDEAS

- Create a non-objective wire sculpture. Bend the wire in different directions to create movement and rhythm. Think about how you feel as you bend the wire. Create sharp angles, smooth curves, and straight passages to reflect your feelings. The sculpture can be constructed to stand freely or on a base.

- •• Create a relief wire sculpture by attaching the sculpture to a backing for a wall-hanging. Decide if you want the art work to be objective or non-objective. You may want to include washers, rings, bolts, and so forth to give your work extra interest and dimension.

Freestanding Mobile

Artists have always been fascinated with representing motion and movement. Look at Figure S–20. Alexander Calder represents motion by making objects or mobiles that actually sway in the wind. A mobile is made up of objects that are delicately hung and balanced by other objects. Unlike other sculpture pieces, you do not have to walk around them to see them completely.

Figure S–20 is a suspended mobile. The moving objects are suspended from sturdy wire and metal crosspieces that are part of the sculpture.

WHAT YOU WILL LEARN

You will create a freestanding mobile based on natural forms—animals, birds, fish, or plants. The forms will be made from paper and may appear to be realistic or abstract. You will use the principle of balance when constructing your mobile.

▲ **Figure S–20** Do you think mobiles would be successful as art if they were not designed to move?

Alexander Calder. *Untitled.* 1976. Aluminum and steel. 9.1 x 23.2 m (29'10½" x 76'). National Gallery of Art, Washington, D.C. Gift of the Collectors Committee.

WHAT YOU WILL NEED

- Cardboard from boxes, some pieces at least 16 inches (40 cm) long
- Pencil, ruler, and cutting knife
- Glue and string
- Construction paper
- 16-gauge wire, wire cutters, and round-nose pliers
- Paint and brushes

WHAT YOU WILL DO

1. Think of the natural forms—animals, birds, fish, or plants that can be used for your mobile. Decide if your forms will be realistic or abstract. Experiment with constructing the forms, using paper sculpture techniques. (See Technique Tip **21**, *Handbook* page **278**.)
2. Make the base for your freestanding sculpture. Study the diagram (Figure S–21) which shows how two pieces of cardboard can be joined together. Using a pencil and ruler draw the shape for the base. Measure one piece at least 16 inches (40 cm) tall. Make the other piece 3 or 4 inches (7.5 or 10 cm) tall and approximately 10 to 12 inches (25 to 30 cm) long to help make the base sturdy. Cut a slit about 2 inches (5 cm) long at the bottom of the large central piece. Cut a slit 2 inches (5 cm) long at the top of the bottom piece. Slip the cardboard slots together gently connecting the two pieces. Several smaller pieces of cardboard can be joined to the base to make it more interesting or to make it stand more solid. Continue joining them until the base stands alone and then glue the joint. Paint your base using colors that are appropriate to the theme of your mobile.
3. There are several ways that wire can be attached to the base. One way is to cut a small slot in the top of the cardboard and

then slide the wire down. This leaves both ends of the wire free for balancing objects on either side.

Another way is to poke about 3 or 4 inches (7.5 or 10 cm) of one end of the wire down between the cardboard layers. This leaves only one end free to hang objects.

4. Make your paper sculpture forms and decide how many you will suspend from your mobile. Consider proportion as you make the pieces and think of creative ways to balance the objects. Cut the pieces of wire to the desired lengths and use the round-nosed pliers to turn a small loop at the end. Use string to hang the paper sculptures from the wire loops.

5. Begin assembling your mobile with the lowest hanging pieces and continue working upward from there. After hanging two objects from either end of a piece of wire, locate its balance point by balancing the wire on your finger. Carefully form another loop in the wire to hang it from above.

6. When your work is complete display it in your classroom. (See Figure S–22.)

▲ Figure S–21   The base for the freestanding mobile.

At least 16"

EXAMINING YOUR WORK

- **Explain**   Identify the paper sculpture techniques that you used to create your paper forms. Describe how the base was constructed to give support to your mobile.
- **Analyze**   Tell how balance was achieved in the mobile. Explain whether your mobile creates visual movement.
- **Interpret**   Tell what natural form you had in mind while creating your mobile. Did you portray the form in an abstract or realistic view?
- **Judge**   Tell whether you feel your work succeeds. Explain your answer.

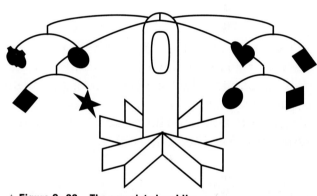

▲ Figure S–22   The completed mobile.

OTHER STUDIO IDEAS

- Make a mobile that is not freestanding, but is made to hang.
- •• Work with a partner. Each of you begin a cardboard base for a freestanding mobile. Find ways to connect your cardboard bases so that eventually you have one large base. Then, in cooperation with your partner, create one large mobile on the base.

STUDIO ═══════ L E S S O N **8** ═══════ STUDIO

A Picture That Tells a Story

Winslow Homer's painting in Figure S–23 shows a fisherman in a small boat surrounded by signs of danger. Can you identify these signs?

This work is a wonderful example of this artist's skill in arousing the viewer's curiosity. It suggests a great many questions and then allows the viewer to use his or her own imagination to answer these questions. For ex-ample, where is the fisherman looking? What does he see? What might he be thinking and feeling at this moment? Where must he go to reach safety?

In this lesson you will give your answer to one of the most important questions about this painting. You will decide the fate of the fisherman.

▲ **Figure S–23   Homer's paintings often tell stories. Can you see a story that might be told in this painting?**

Winslow Homer. *The Fog Warning*. 1885. Oil on canvas. 76.2 x 121.9 cm (30 x 48"). The Museum of Fine Arts, Boston, Massachusetts. Otis Norcross Fund.

WHAT YOU WILL LEARN

You will complete a painting in which you show what happens to the fisherman in Homer's picture. As in Homer's painting you will use large and small shapes to suggest deep space. You will also use real and imaginary lines to guide the viewer's eyes to the most important objects in your work.

WHAT YOU WILL NEED

- Pencil and sketch paper
- White paper, 9 x 12 inch
- Tempera paint
- Brushes
- Mixing tray

WHAT YOU WILL DO

1. Imagine that Homer completed another painting entitled *Fog Warning II*. In this work he showed what happened to the fisherman. Discuss with other members of your class what this second picture might look like.
2. On your own complete several sketches showing your version of *Fog Warning II*. Include all the facts and details needed by viewers to determine the fisherman's fate. Suggest space by using large shapes in the foreground and smaller shapes in the distance. Use real and imaginary lines to direct attention to the most important features in your work.

EXAMINING YOUR WORK

- **Describe** Identify the objects in your picture. Explain how these were suggested by Homer's painting.
- **Analyze** Show how you used large and small shapes to create an illusion of deep space. Point to real and imaginary lines and explain how these are used to guide the viewer to the important parts of your picture.
- **Interpret** Determine if others are able to use your picture to learn the fate of the fisherman. Can they identify a happy or a sad ending to the story?
- **Judge** State whether you think your painting is successful or unsuccessful. What aesthetic view would you suggest to viewers trying to judge your work?

3. Transfer your best sketch to the paper or illustration board. Paint your picture with colors that suggest a happy or sad ending to the story of the fisherman.

OTHER STUDIO IDEAS

- Paint another picture of this same subject. However, do not make this a realistic painting. Instead use colors, shapes, lines, and textures to create a *non-objective* work that suggests a happy or sad ending to the story. Then compare this painting with the first one. Which is most successful? Explain why.

●● Use watercolors on a large sheet of paper to paint a picture showing a storm at sea. Do not include figures or man-made objects. Select colors that suggest water, whitecaps, clouds, and fog. Apply these colors to show the power and fury of the storm. Try to reveal your *feelings* about the storm as you show what it looks like.

Pinhole Camera Photography

Look at Figure S–24. This is a photograph by American photographer Ansel Adams. As with other works of art, learning to make photographs like this takes skill and practice. It does not, however, take an expensive camera. A simple homemade pinhole camera (Figure S–25) will allow you to test your skills as a photographer. Pinhole cameras work by letting the photographed image enter a darkened box through a tiny hole. The image is captured on a piece of film attached to the inside lid of the box.

WHAT YOU WILL LEARN

You will build a pinhole camera using simple materials found around the house. You will make a photograph using your camera.

WHAT YOU WILL NEED

- Scissors or cutting knife
- Empty round oatmeal box with a lid
- Flat black spray paint
- Square of heavy-duty aluminum foil, 2 inch (5 cm)
- Needle or sharp pin
- Masking tape
- Square of cardboard, 1 inch (3 cm)
- Sheets of Kodak Plus-X film, 4 x 5 inches (10 x 13 cm)
- Sheet of white paper, 12 x 18 inches (30 x 46 cm)

SAFETY TIP

Use spray paint outdoors or in a well ventilated area. Be careful not to inhale the fumes from the paint.

► **Figure S–24** Photography is an art form that can be used in many different ways. What are some ways photography is used?

Photograph by Ansel Adams.

WHAT YOU WILL DO

1. Using the scissors or cutting knife, cut a ½-inch (13 mm) square hole in the bottom of the oatmeal box. The hole should be as close to the center as possible. Paint the inside of the box and the lid with spray paint. Set them aside to dry.

2. Hold the piece of aluminum foil against a hard, flat surface. Using the needle or pin, carefully poke a pin-size hole at the center. Make sure the hole is crisp and sharp. A ragged or too-large hole will produce a blurry image.

3. Place the foil inside the box. Line it up so the pinhole is centered over the hole at the bottom. Using masking tape, attach the foil to the bottom of the box. Place the cardboard square over the hole on the outside bottom of the box. Fasten the square along one side with tape, making a hinged flap. (See Figure S–25.)

4. In a darkroom, cut a piece of film to fit inside the lid of the box. Try to handle the film by the edges only because touching the film may cause blurs on the image. Tape the film in place. Place the lid on the box. Hold the cardboard flap closed until you are ready to shoot a picture.

5. Choose a subject that is outdoors in bright sunlight. Standing about 10 feet away from your subject, set the camera down on a flat unmoving surface. Prop the camera with cloth or crumpled paper towel, so it won't roll or move while you are taking your picture. Aim the bottom of the box at your subject. Lift the flap, and hold it open for about 15 seconds. Close the flap. Holding it in place, return to the darkroom to develop your photo.

EXAMINING YOUR WORK

- **Describe** Show that all inside surfaces of your camera are coated with paint. Tell whether you held the camera steady and kept the cardboard flap open for 15 seconds.
- **Analyze** Tell whether your photograph was blurry or clear. If blurry, explain why. If the photograph is too light or too dark, explain why.
- **Interpret** Explain how a viewer would recognize your work as a portrait. Give your photograph a title.
- **Judge** Tell whether you feel your work succeeds. Explain your answer.

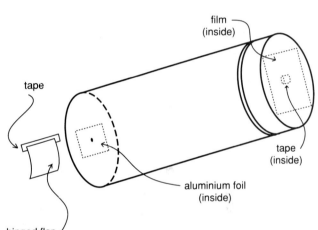

▲ **Figure S–25** This shows how a pin-hole camera is constructed.

OTHER STUDIO IDEAS

- Take a second photograph of a subject indoors. Experiment to find out how long the flap needs to be open for indoor light.

- •• Set up an indoor group portrait. Have your subjects strike an interesting pose. Take your photograph.

Artists and Their Works

ARTISTS AND THEIR WORKS

Glossary

Acrylic (uh-**kril**-ik)   A quick-drying water-based synthetic paint. (Ch. 10-1)

Additive   A sculpting method produced by adding to or combining materials. (Ch. 12-1)

Aesthetics (ess-**thet**-iks)   The philosophy or study of the nature and value of art. (Ch. 2-2)

Aesthetic views   Ideas, or schools of thought, on what to look for in works of art. (Ch. 2-2)

Amphitheaters (**am**-fuh-thee-uht-uhrs)   Circular or oval buildings with seats rising around an open space. (Ch. 14-1)

Analogous colors (uh-**nal**-uh-gus)   Colors that are side by side on the color wheel. (Ch. 4-2)

Analyzing   Noting how the principles are used to organize the elements of color, line, texture, shape, form, and space. (Ch. 6-3); Noting the style of a work. (Ch. 7-3)

Applied art   Art made to be functional, as well as visually pleasing. (Ch. 1-2), (Ch. 6-6)

Architect   An artist who works in the field of architecture. (Ch. 14-1)

Architecture   The planning and creating of buildings. (Ch. 14-1)

Art critic   A person who practices art criticism. (Ch. 6-1)

Art criticism   The process of studying, understanding, and judging art works, consisting of four stages: describing, analyzing, interpreting, and judging. (Ch. 6-1)

Art history   The study of art from past to present, consisting of four stages: describing, analyzing, interpreting, and judging. (Ch. 7-1)

Art movement   A group of artists with similar styles who have banded together. (Ch. 7-3)

Artists   People who use imagination and skill to communicate ideas in visual form. (Ch. 1-2)

Assembling   A sculpting method in which different kinds of materials are gathered and joined together. (Ch. 12-1)

Balance   A principle of art concerned with arranging the elements of art so that no one part of a work overpowers, or seems heavier than, any other part. (Ch. 5-1)

Basilicas (buh-**sil**-ih-kuhs)   Huge meeting halls. (Ch. 14-1)

Binder   A liquid to which the dry pigment is added. (Ch. 3-3), (Ch. 10-1)

Blending   A shading technique that involves adding dark values little by little by pressing harder on the drawing medium. (Ch. 8-1)

Brayer   A roller with a handle. (Ch. 9-1)

Camera   A dark box with a hole controlling how much light enters. (Ch. 15-1)

Carving   A sculpting method in which material is cut or chipped away. (Ch. 12-1)

Casting   A sculpting method in which melted material is poured into a mold. (Ch. 12-1)

Cinematographer (sin-uh-muh-**tahg**-ruh-fuhr)   The person in charge of running the movie camera or cameras. (Ch. 15-3)

Collage (kuh-**lahzh**)   Art arranged from cut or torn materials pasted to a surface. (Ch. 1-4), (Ch. 7-6)

Color wheel   An arrangement of colors in a circular format. (Ch. 4-2)

Complementary colors   Colors opposite each other on the color wheel. (Ch. 4-2)

Composition   How the principles are used to organize the elements. (Ch. 2-1)

Content   Message, idea, or feeling. (Ch. 2-1)

Contour drawing   Drawing an object as though your drawing tool is moving along all the edges and the ridges of the form. (Ch. 8-3)

Crafts   The different areas of applied art in which craftspeople work. (Ch. 13-1)

Craftsperson   Someone who has become an expert in an area of applied art. (Ch. 13-1)

Credit line   A listing of important facts about an art work. (Ch. 2-1)

Crosshatching   A shading technique using two or more lines that crisscross each other. (Ch. 8-1)

Daguerreotypes (duh-**gehr**-uh-types)   Silvery, mirrorlike images on a copper plate. (Ch. 15-1)

Describing   In art criticism, making a careful list of all the things you see in the work. (Ch. 6-1); In art history, telling who did a work, and when and where it was done. (Ch. 7-1)

Director   The person in charge of shooting the film and guiding the actors. (Ch. 15-3)

Edition   A group of identical prints all made from a single plate. (Ch. 3-2), (Ch. 9-1)

Editorial designers   Graphic artists who arrange words and illustrations and prepare the material for printing. (Ch. 11-1)

Elements of art   Basic visual symbols artists use to create works of visual art. The elements of art are line, shape, form, space, value, color, and texture. (Ch. 4-1)

Elevation   A drawing of an outside view of a building. (Ch. 14-2)

Emphasis   A principle of art that stresses one element of art or makes an area in a work of art stand out. (Ch. 5-3)

Encaustic (in-**kaw**-stik)   A painting medium in which pigment is mixed into melted wax. (Ch. 10-1)

Facade (fuh-**sahd**)   The front of a building. (Ch. 14-2)

Fauves (**fohvs**)   An art movement begun early in this century in France, in which the artists use wild, intense color combinations in their paintings. (Ch. 7-3)

Fibers   Any thin, threadlike materials. (Ch. 13-1)

Fine art   Art made purely to be experienced visually. (Ch. 1-2)

Fired   Hardened by heating in a kiln. (Ch. 13-1)

Floor plan   A scale drawing of how a room or building would appear without a roof as if seen from above. (Ch. 14-2)

Form   An object with three dimensions—height, width, and depth. (Ch. 4-5)

Freestanding   Surrounded on all sides by space. (Ch. 3-5), (Ch. 12-3)

Fresco (fres-koh)   A painting medium in which pigment is applied to a wall spread with wet plaster. (Ch. 10-1)

Gesture drawing   Drawing lines quickly and loosely to show movement in a subject. (Ch. 8-2)

Glassblowing   The craft of shaping melted glass by blowing air into it through a tube. (Ch. 13-1)

Glaze   A thin, transparent layer of paint. (Ch. 10-1)

Glazed   Coated with a mixture of powdered chemicals that melt during firing into a hard, glasslike finish. (Ch. 13-1)

Graphic artists   Artists that work in the field of art known as graphic design. (Ch. 11-1)

Graphic design   The field of art that uses pictures and words to instruct or to communicate a specific message. (Ch. 11-1)

Harmony   A principle of art concerned with blending the elements of art in a pleasing way. (Ch. 5-3)

Hatching   A shading technique that involves drawing a series of thin lines running parallel, or in the same direction. (Ch. 8-1)

High relief   Relief that stands out boldly from its background. (Ch. 12-2)

Hue   A color's name. (Ch. 4-2)

Illustrators   Graphic artists who create printed materials that explain or teach. (Ch. 11-1)

Impasto (im-pahs-toh)   Thick, buttery layers. (Ch. 10-1)

Intaglio (in-tal-yoh)   A printmaking method in which the image to be printed is cut or scratched into a surface. (Ch. 9-2)

Intensity   The brightness or dullness of a hue. (Ch. 4-2)

Interpreting   In art criticism, determining and explaining the meaning, mood, or idea of the work of art. (Ch. 6-4); In art history, noting how time and place affect an artist's style and subject matter. (Ch. 7-5)

Judging   In art criticism, making a decision about a work's success or lack of success and giving reasons to support that decision. (Ch. 6-6); In art history, deciding whether a work introduces a new style or if it is an outstanding example of a particular style. (Ch. 7-7)

Kiln   A special piece of equipment used to fire ceramics. (Ch. 13-1)

Layout   The arrangement of words and pictures on a page. (Ch. 11-1)

Line   The path of a dot through space. (Ch. 4-4)

Line quality   The unique character of any line. (Ch. 4-4)

Line variation   The thickness or thinness, lightness or darkness of a line. (Ch. 4-4)

Lithograph (lith-uh-graf)   A print made by lithography. (Ch. 9-2)

Lithography (lith-ahg-ruh-fee)   A printmaking method in which the image to be printed is drawn on limestone with a special greasy crayon. (Ch. 9-2)

Logo   A special image representing a business, group, or product. (Ch. 11-2)

Loom   A frame or machine that holds a set of threads that runs vertically. (Ch. 13-1)

Low relief   Relief that stands out in space only slightly. (Ch. 12-2)

Madonna   A work showing the mother of Christ. (Ch. 7-5)

Medium of art   A material such as paint, clay, or glass used to create a work of art. (Ch. 3-1)

Microprocessors (my-kroh-prahs-es-uhrs)   Tiny computers. (Ch. 15-5)

Mixed media   The use of more than one medium to create a work of art. (Ch. 3-1)

Modeling   A sculpting method in which a soft or workable material is built up and shaped. (Ch. 12-1)

Monochromatic colors (mahn-uh-kroh-mat-ik)   Different values of a single hue. (Ch. 4-2)

Monoprinting   A printmaking method in which the image to be printed is put on the plate with ink or paint and then transferred to paper or cloth by pressing or hand-rubbing. (Ch. 9-2)

Motif (moh-teef)   A unit that is repeated over and over in a pattern or visual rhythm. (Ch. 4-3)

Motion picture   Photographs of the same subject taken a very short time apart and flashed onto a screen. (Ch. 15-3)

Movement   A principle of art that leads the viewer to sense action in a work or a path that the viewer's eye follows throughout a work. (Ch. 5-5)

Negatives   Reverse images of the object photographed. (Ch. 15-1)

Non-objective   Having no recognizable subject matter. (Ch. 2-1)

Non-objective art   A work with no objects or subjects that can be readily identified. (Ch. 6-1)

Oil paint   Paint with an oil base. (Ch. 10-1)

Opaque (oh-pake)   Does not let light through. (Ch. 10-1)

Palette   Any tray or plate where paints are mixed before use. (Ch. 10-1)

Patrons of the arts   Sponsors, or supporters, of an artist or art-related places and events. (Ch. 1-3)

Perceiving   Looking at and thinking deeply about what you see. (Ch. 1-1)

Perception The ability to really see and think deeply about an object. (Ch. 8-1)

Photogram An image made on blueprint paper through the action of light and gas fumes. (Ch. 15-2)

Photography The art of making images by exposing a chemically treated surface to light. (Ch. 15-1)

Pigment A finely ground, colored powder that gives paint its color. (Ch. 3-3), (Ch. 10-1)

Point of view The angle from which the viewer sees the scene. (Ch. 1-1)

Post and lintel (lint-uhl) A building method in which a crossbeam is placed above two uprights. (Ch. 14-2)

Pottery The craft of making objects from clay. (Ch. 13-1)

Principles of art Guidelines that govern the way elements go together. (Ch. 5-1)

Print An image that is transferred from a prepared surface to paper or fabric. (Ch. 3-2)

Printing plate A surface onto or into which the image is placed. (Ch. 9-1)

Printmaking Transferring an inked image from a prepared surface to another surface. (Ch. 9-1)

Producer The person in charge of the business end of making a movie. (Ch. 15-3)

Proportion A principle of art concerned with the size relationships of one part to the whole and of one part to another. (Ch. 5-3)

Registration Careful matching up of plates in prints with more than one color. (Ch. 9-2)

Relief A type of sculpture in which forms and figures are projected from the front only. (Ch. 3-5), (Ch. 12-2)

Relief printing A printmaking method in which the image to be printed is raised from a background. (Ch. 9-2)

Renaissance (ren-uh-**sahns**) A French word meaning "rebirth." (Ch. 7-5)

Reproduction A photograph of a print. (Ch. 3-2)

Rhythm A principle of art concerned with repeating an element of art to create the illusion of movement. (Ch. 5-5)

Scoring Roughing or scratching clay with a clay tool (or fork). (Technique Tip **17** *Handbook,* page **275**)

Screen printing A printmaking technique in which the artist transfers the design to the screen through various processes. (Ch. 9-2)

Serigraph (**sir**-uh-graf) A screen print that has been handmade by an artist. (Ch. 9-2)

Shading The use of light and shadow to give a feeling of depth. (Ch. 8-1)

Shape An area clearly set off by one or more of the other five visual elements of art. (Ch. 4-5)

Slab A slice or sheet of clay. (Ch. 13-3)

Slip Clay that has so much added water that it is liquid and runny. It is used to fasten pieces of clay together. (Ch. 13-1)

Solvent A liquid that controls the thickness or thinness of the paint. (Ch. 3-3), (Ch. 10-1)

Space The distance or area between, around, above, below, and within things. (Ch. 4-5)

Stippling A shading technique achieved by using dots. (Ch. 8-1)

Style An artist's personal way of expressing ideas in a work. (Ch. 3-3), (Ch. 7-3)

Subject The image viewers can easily identify. (Ch. 2-1)

Subtractive A sculpting method produced by removing or taking away from the original material. (Ch. 12-1)

Super-realism A style of art devoted to extraordinarily realistic works. (Ch. 2-2)

Synthetic paints Manufactured paints with plastic binders. (Ch. 10-1)

Tempera (**tem**-puh-rah) A painting medium in which pigment mixed with egg yolk and water is applied with tiny brush strokes. (Ch. 10-1)

Texture How things feel, or look as though they might feel, if touched. (Ch. 4-7)

Three-dimensional Having height, width, and depth. (Ch. 3-5)

Transparent Clear. (Ch. 10-1)

Two-dimensional Having height and width but not depth. (Ch. 3-5)

Typefaces Styles of lettering for the printed material. (Ch. 11-1)

Unity The arrangement of elements and principles with media to create a feeling of completeness. (Ch. 5-7)

Value The lightness or darkness of a hue. (Ch. 4-2)

Variety A principle of art concerned with combining one or more elements of art to create interest. (Ch. 5-3)

Video game An electronic form of entertainment run by a computer. (Ch. 15-5)

Warp The lengthwise threads attached to the loom. (Ch. 13-4)

Watercolor A painting medium in which pigment is blended with gum arabic and water. (Ch. 10-1)

Weaving A craft in which fiber strands are interlocked to make cloth or objects. (Ch. 13-1)

Weft The crosswise threads pulled across the warp. (Ch. 13-4)

Wet plate A method of photography in which an image is created on glass that is coated with chemicals, then transferred to paper or cardboard. (Ch. 15-1)

Work of art Any object created or designed by an artist. (Ch. 2-1)

Index

Acknowledgements: The art work executed and submitted by the following students was exemplary. Because of book design constraints, all of the student work could not be included. The authors feel, however, that each student who contributed should be recognized.

Tory D. Almond, Camp Creek Middle School; Justine Altman, Crabapple Middle School; Grace Arbizo, Stanton High School; Brad Ash, Mandarin High School; Juan Atayde, Guillen School; Andre Leon Bailey, Colonial High School; Brett Barnes, Crabapple Middle School; Rob Bass, All Saints Episcopal School; Chad Bates, Burney-Harris-Lyons Middle School; Sonya Beard, Crabapple Middle School; Maria Betancourt, Guillen School; James M. Borwigi, Paxon, Middle School; Wright Branson, Haynes Bridge Middle School; Dennis Bright, Colonial High School; Whitney Brotherton, East Middle School; Lucius E. Burke, Jenkins County Elementary School; Sam Byrd, Burney-Harris-Lyons Middle School; Maurice Calloway, Burney-Harris-Lyons Middle School; Javier Calzadillas, Guillen School; Lamar Kinte Carter, East Middle School; Jason Charles, Magoffin Middle School; Lucy Cobb, Hilsman Middle School; Patrice Cone, Marvin Pittman Laboratory School; Becky Connors, Haynes Bridge Middle School; Josh Cooper, Sandy Springs Middle School; Leticia Corpos, Guillen School; Natasha Cox, All Saints Episcopal School; Forrest Davis, Paxon Middle School; Jason Davis, Paxon Middle School; Paul Davis, East Middle School; Elizabeth Dewey, Marvin Pittman Laboratory School; John Douglass, Jr., Colonial High School; Jessica Drewing, Stanton High School; Julie Drown, Crabapple Middle School; Lisa Duchemin, Tapp Middle School; Nancy Elliot, Hilsman Middle School; Joy Elliott, Hilsman Middle School; Yona N. Ellis, Burney-Harris-Lyons Middle School; Marshall English, Burney-Harris-Lyons Middle School; Melissa Epps, Floyd Middle School; Kim Farmer, Camp Creek Middle School; Christy Farr, Tapp Middle School; Thomas Feeney, Crabapple Middle School; Steven Fisher, Meher High School; Jamie Fraser, Sandy Springs Middle School; Danny Gallegos, Canyon Hills Middle School; Blanca Gandara, Guillen School; Phillip Gatlin, Colonial High School; J. R. Gay, Jenkins County Elementary School; Chris Gibbs, Bassett Middle School; Johnny Gomez, Bassett Middle School; Theodora Gongaware, Savannah Country Day School; Beth Gould, Haynes Bridge Middle School; Erin Graham, East Middle School; Marshall Graham, Hilsman Middle School; Rebekah Hagins, Marvin Pittman Laboratory School; Elsie T. Hall, The Savannah Country Day School; Jason Hall, Crabapple Middle School; Heather Halterman, Stanton High School; Theresa Hanson, Mandarin Middle School; Julie Harper, East Middle School; Billy Harrell, East Middle School; Cornelius Havgabook, Camp Creek Middle School; Elsie Hill, The Savannah Country Day School; Sara Hodgson, Burney-Harris-Lyons Middle School; Tamatha Hudson, Colonial High School; T. J. Hurt, All Saints Episcopal School; Amory Jeffries, Havenview Junior High School; Liza Jensen, Harris Middle School; Leslie Johnson, Treadwell Junior High School; Klay Keiser, Colonial High School; Stephanie Kimbell, Floyd Middle School; Patrick Klenke, Canyon Hills Middle School; Jon Lancaric, Canyon Hills Middle School; Christel Landers, Holcomb Bridge Middle School; Rory Lane, Burney-Harris-Lyons Middle School; Julie Leatherman, Stanton High School; Tommy Lerma, Magoffin Middle School; Tara Liebe, Sandy Springs; Lauren Littlewood, Holcomb Bridge Middle School; Christy Lord, Burney-Harris-Lyons Middle School; Marissa MacCaughelty, Marvin Pittman Laboratory School; Amy Malkey, Haynes Bridge Middle School; Jon Ed Mann, Camp Creek Middle School; Kaia Mapp, Camp Creek Middle School; Henry Martell, Bassett Middle Schoo; Ramon R. Martinez, Canyon Hills Middle School; Carlos Mascorro, Guillen School; Christian Mathis, Colonial High School; Ryan McDowell, Hilsman Middle School; Amy McEntee, East Middle School; Chase McGee, The Savannah Country Day School; Josh McGuire, Tapp Middle School; Justin Miller, Burney-Harris-Lyons Middle School; Torshike Miller, Camp Creek Middle School; Ronald Mitchell, Camp Creek Middle School; Oscar M. Mora, Guillen School; Elizabeth Morales, Guillen School; Gray Morgan, Colonial High School; Katherine Morgenstern, La Pietra School; Marie Mortenson, Meher High School; Riann Munn, Floyd Middle School; Gabriel Myers, Harold Wiggs Middle School; Matt Nall, All Saints Episcopal School; Scott Newman, Marvin Pittman Laboratory School; Michael Ngaujah, Camp Creek Middle School; Jason O'Brian, Mandarin Middle School; Charlie Occhipinti, Burney-Harris-Lyons Middle School; Dana D. Odom, Marvin Pittman Laboratory School; Omar Ontiveros, Bassett Middle School; Julie Parker, The Savannah Country Day School; Alejandro de la Pena, Bassett Middle School; Celena Perkins, Marvin Pittman Laboratory School; Jesus Pinales, Guillen School; Lindsay Podozil, Holcomb Bridge Middle School; Chamera Porter, Bassett Middle School; Maria Rameriz, Bassett Middle School; Juan L. Reyes, Guillen School; Amy Rhoads, Sandy Springs Middle School; Andrew Rippel, All Saints Episcopal School; Danny Roberts, Colonial High School; Ariel Robinson, Havenview Junior High; Joe Rodriguez, Guillen School; Brenda Ross, Burney-Harris-Lyons Middle School; Diego Rothenback, Canyon Hills Middle School; Katherine Sales, La Pietra School; Matt Samuelson, The Savannah Country Day School; Hayden Shore, The Savannah Country Day School; Rebekah Shower, Stanton High School; Chiquita Simmons, Havenview Junior High School; Scarlet Sims, Camp Creek Middle School; Adam F. Skibell, All Saints Episcopal School; Demelia Sloan, Camp Creek Middle School; Lori Slovisky, Crabapple Middle School; Jamie Smallwood, Marvin Pittman Laboratory School; Sok South, Treadwell Junior High; Charlie Stamphill, Crabapple Middle School; Adrian Staton, Crabapple Middle School; Brandi Stratton, Bassett Middle School; Michael Strickland, Paxon Middle School; Momoko Suzuki, La Pietra School; Antonio Taylor, Hilsman Middle School; Alice Thompson, Stanton High School; Kevin M. Thompson, Stanton High School; Lindsey Thompson, Burney-Harris-Lyons Middle School; Larry Townsend, Burney-Harris-Lyons Middle School; Anne Trainer, Colonial High School; Jami Vansant, Haynes Bridge Middle School; Teresa Villalobos, Guillen School; Telisia Wade, Hilsman Middle School; Amanda Walker, Haynes Bridge Middle School; Gerald Walker, Jenkins County Elementary School; Joanna Warchol, Marvin Pittman Laboratory School; Stephen Warneck, The Savannah Country Day School; Walter J. Warneck III, The Savannah Country Day School; Laura Lynn Weber, Glenrock High School; Jason Wheeler, East Middle School; Lakesha Whitaker, Treadwell Junior High School; Abigail White, Sandy Springs Middle School; Melanie Wiggins, Bassett Middle School; Latoya Wiley, Marvin Pittman Laboratory School; Andrew Williams, Jenkins County High School; Jana Williams, Jenkins County Elementary School; John Michael Williams, Colonial High School; Calvin Wilson, Havenview Junior High School; Makana Yasukawa, La Pietra School.